Images *of* Pastoral Care

For Donald Capps

Two are better than one,
because they have a good reward for their toil.
For if they fall, one will lift up the other.

Ecclesiastes 4:9–10a

Images *of* Pastoral Care

CLASSIC READINGS

ROBERT C. DYKSTRA, Editor

CHALICE ®
P R E S S

ST. LOUIS, MISSOURI

Biblical quotations, unless otherwise noted, are from the *New Revised Standard Version Bible*, copyright 1989, Division of Christian Education of the National Council of the Churches of Christ in the United States of America. Used by permission. All rights reserved.

Those quotations marked RSV are from the *Revised Standard Version of the Bible*, copyright 1952, [2nd edition, 1971] by the Division of Christian Education of the National Council of the Churches of Christ in the United States of America. Used by permission. All rights reserved.

Scripture quotations marked (TEV) are taken from the *Today's English Version*–Second Edition © 1992 by American Bible Society. Used by permission.

Scripture quotations marked (NEB) are from the *New English Bible*, copyright Oxford University Press and Cambridge University Press 1961, 1970. Reprinted by permission.

Excerpts from *The Jerusalem Bible*, copyright 1966 by Darton, Longman & Todd, Ltd., and Doubleday, a division of Bantam Doubleday Dell Publishing Group, Inc. Used by permission.

Scriptures marked KJV or AV are from the *Authorized King James Version*.

Cover art: "The Four Ages of Jesus" by Jyoti Sahi
Cover and interior design: Elizabeth Wright

Visit Chalice Press on the World Wide Web at
www.chalicepress.com

10   9   8   7   6   5   4   3   2   06   07   08   09   10   11

Library of Congress Cataloging–in–Publication Data

Images of pastoral care : classic readings / Robert C. Dykstra, editor.
   p. cm.
Includes bibliographical references (p.   ).
ISBN 13: 978-0-827216-24-2
ISBN 10: 0-827216-24-6 (pbk. : alk. paper)
1. Pastoral care. 2. Pastoral theology. I. Dykstra, Robert C., 1956-
BV4011.3.I63 2005
253–dc22

2005013221

Printed in the United States of America

Contents

Permissions

Chapter 1 contains excerpts from THE EXPLORATION OF THE INNER WORLD: A STUDY OF MENTAL DISORDER AND RELIGIOUS EXPERIENCE by Anton T. Boisen. Copyright 1936 by Willet, Clark, & Co. Reprinted by permission of HarperCollins Publishers Inc.

Chapter 2 reprinted from THE LIVING HUMAN DOCUMENT: RE-VISIONING PASTORAL COUNSELING IN A HERMENEUTICAL MODE by Charles V. Gerkin, copyright 1984. Reprinted by permission from Abingdon Press.

Chapter 3 contains excerpts reprinted by permission from THROUGH THE EYES OF WOMEN, edited by Jeanne Stevenson Moessner, copyright © 1996 Augsburg Fortress.

Chapter 4 contains excerpts from "The Christian Shepherd," by Seward Hiltner from *Pastoral Theology*, vol. 10, no. 92 (March 1959): 47–54. Copyright ©1959. Excerpt from this Kluwer Academic Publishers journal is reprinted with kind permission of Springer Science and Business Media.

Chapters 5 and 9 contain excerpts from *Rediscovering Pastoral Care* by Alastair V. Campbell. © 1981 Alastair V. Campbell. Used by permission of Westminster John Knox Press.

Chapter 6 contains excerpts reprinted by permission from WOMEN IN TRAVAIL AND TRANSITION by Maxine Glaz and Jeanne Stevenson Moessner, copyright © 1991 Augsburg Fortress.

Chapter 7 contains excerpts from THE WOUNDED HEALER by Henri J. M. Nouwen, copyright ©1972 by Henri J. M. Nouwen. Used by permission of Doubleday, a division of Random House, Inc.

Chapter 8 contains excerpts from *Pastoral Care in the Modern Hospital* by Heije Faber. © 1971 SCM Press. Used by permission of Westminster John Knox Press.

Chapter 10 contains excerpts reprinted by permission from REFRAMING: A New Method for Pastoral Care by Donald Capps, copyright © 1990 Augsburg Fortress.

Chapter 11 contains excerpts from "Intimate Strangers: The Role of the Hospital Chaplain in Situations of Sudden Traumatic Loss" by Robert C. Dykstra. Used with permission of *The Journal of Pastoral Care and Counseling*.

Chapter 12 contains excerpts from *Pastoral Counseling* by James E. Dittes. © 1999 James E. Dittes. Used by permission of Westminster John Knox Press.

Chapter 13 contains excerpts from *The Minister as Diagnostician* by Paul W. Pruyser. © 1976 The Westminster Press. Used by permission of Westminster John Knox Press.

Chapter 14 contains excerpts reprinted from THE MINISTER AS MORAL COUNSELOR by Gaylord Noyce, copyright 1989.Used with permission of Abingdon Press.

Chapter 15 contains excerpts from AFRICAN AMERICAN PASTORAL CARE by Edward P. Wimberly, copyright 1991. Used with permission of Abingdon Press.

Chapter 16 contains excerpts from "The Pastor as Agent of Hope," by Donald Capps. Used with permission of *Currents in Theology and Mission*.

Chapter 17 contains excerpts from "Minister as Midwife" by Karen R. Hanson. Used with permission of *The Journal of Pastoral Care and Counseling*.

Chapter 18 contains excerpts from CULTIVATING WHOLENESS: A Guide to Care and Counseling in Faith Communities by Margaret Zipse Kornfeld. Copyright © 1998 by the author. Reprinted by permission of the Continuum International Publishing Group.

Chapter 19 contains excerpts from chapter 8 of FEMINIST AND WOMANIST PASTORAL THEOLOGY, edited by Bonnie J. Miller-McClemore and Brita L. Gill-Austern, copyright 1999. Reprinted by permission of Abingdon Press.

The poem "What will you do, God, when I die?" on page 122 is by Rainer Maria Rilke, translated by Babette Deutch, from POEMS FROM THE BOOK OF HOURS copyright © 1941 by New Directions Publishing Corp. Reprinted by permission of New Directions Publishing Corp.

Acknowledgments

The idea for this book emerged from conversations in a special Society for Pastoral Theology working group of teachers in graduate programs in pastoral theology. I am grateful for the foresight of Chris Schlauch and Bonnie Miller-McLemore in convening this group, and for the wisdom and good cheer of those colleagues who joined in its discussions over the years. I am indebted as well to those pastoral theologians, past and present, who conceived and continue to sustain this remarkable discipline. Many of their works constitute the crux of this book. I also wish to thank Jon Berquist, former academic editor at Chalice Press, and Trent Butler, Sarah Tasic, and the whole Chalice Press staff for their generous support.

Donald Capps, Allan Cole, Molly Dykstra, Gregory Ellison, Brita Gill-Austern, Cedric Johnson, Bruno Linhares, Bonnie Miller-McLemore, Jeanne Stevenson Moessner, and Deirdre Greenwood White all deserve a special word of appreciation for their lively and encouraging comments on earlier drafts and for providing reassurance that this collection of metaphors is, for the moment, reasonably complete. Eleanor and Annie Dykstra offered daily infusions of laughter that lent perspective to the writing task.

I dedicate this book to my friend and colleague, Donald Capps. If, as Emerson once said, "the nonchalance of boys who are sure of a dinner…is the healthy attitude of human nature," then Don is a model of health. His unfettered intellect, childlike curiosity, wicked sense of humor, and unwavering loyalty to those in his care give reason to make one proud to be called a pastoral theologian.

Introduction

Contemporary pastoral theology serves as a key source for understanding the tasks of pastoral care and counseling today. It is therefore not without significance that the origins of pastoral theology in mainline Protestantism may be traced in large measure to the psychotic delusions of a particular Presbyterian minister some eight decades ago.

Unstable Origins

At the age of forty-four, Anton Boisen (1876–1965), the man eventually regarded as the father of the clinical pastoral education movement, but at that time a rudderless and unremarkable minister, began to obsess over thoughts in which his spiritual and vocational aspirations intermingled with what he described as a "precocious sexual sensitivity"[1] and an idealized, forever unrequited attraction to a woman named Alice Batchelder.

These obsessions, coupled with increasingly bizarre behavior, led Boisen's family to commit him, in 1920, to the Boston Psychopathic Hospital. There he was diagnosed with a severe and, his doctors believed, incurable schizophrenia characterized by violent hallucinations and delusions.[2] However, contrary to his doctors' expectations (and leading some scholars to speculate that he had been misdiagnosed[3]), Boisen became reoriented to reality after an initial three-week, and—shortly thereafter—a ten-week, period of delirium. Still, he chose to remain living in psychiatric hospitals—as both a chaplain and a patient—for a good portion of the remainder of his life, a man who would later be characterized by even devoted students and colleagues as distant, rigid, and humorless.[4]

In those initial months of hospitalization Boisen discovered what from that point on would become his singular calling. His own unsettling experiences convinced him that the emotional breakdowns psychiatric patients suffered

1

were often religious in origin. Therefore, he reasoned, they could not be effectively treated without taking religious and philosophical concerns into account.

On his release from the hospital Boisen immediately began searching out a way to bring more vital ministry into the clinical setting. He wanted to expose seminary students and ministers to the lives and struggles of psychiatric patients—those he called "living human documents." Such exposure, he believed, would enrich a seminary education based at that time almost exclusively on written texts. His efforts, described in Boisen's own words in chapter 1 of this book, led in 1925 to the formation of the clinical pastoral training movement, the forerunner of clinical pastoral education today.

The contemporary field of pastoral theology, as well as now familiar approaches to pastoral care and counseling, are thus indelibly marked with, even tainted by, insanity. Pastoral theology was born of madness and, one could argue, has yet to fully recover. A fragile, sometimes fragmented identity on the margins of church and society seems to be its peculiar portion and destiny.

In practical terms this means that pastoral theologians, along with the many ministers they influence, have rarely felt terribly certain of just who they are and of what exactly they are to do. This insecure professional identity understandably has been cause for consternation over the years. On the one hand, pastoral theologians must fend off charges of a lack of theological rigor or philosophical sophistication from critics within the church or seminary. On the other hand, they remain largely invisible to professionals whose cognate disciplines and practices—psychology, cultural theory, gender studies, among others—they have attempted to engage or emulate outside the church or seminary.

The present book can be read as a testimony to, but perhaps more significantly as a defiant embracing of, this insecure identity among pastoral theologians and their allies throughout the previous century. One finds here ongoing attempts by pastoral theologians to say, by means of a wide variety of imaginative metaphors, just how they have come to understand themselves and their colleagues in ministry and what in particular they hope their work will accomplish. In the chapters that follow, the reader will frequently find authors claiming the identity, or lack of identity, of marginalized and neglected persons. They wonder: *What is pastoral theology* like *? What is a ministry of care and counseling* like *?* They often answer by implying that pastoral theology and ministry are somehow *like* being outside the mainstream, off the beaten path, forgotten in the company of the downtrodden of their particular era and culture. They variously suggest that ministers are somehow *wounded, foolish, aesthetes,* or *strangers,* seldom at the center of the action and instead more likely to labor at its edges. Here, pastoral identity paradoxically seems to be found in a threatened *loss* of identity and pastoral theology's relevance in the perception that it *lacks* much relevance.

An Essential Insecurity

A number of the works gathered in these pages will be unfamiliar to a new generation of seminarians and clergy. Many of the essays, however, have left a lasting mark both on the discipline of pastoral theology and, more covertly, on the self-understanding and practices of care and counseling of countless contemporary ministers. Certainly many of them have been pivotal in my own formation over the years, having become almost indistinguishable from my personal self-understanding and approach as a minister, counselor, and pastoral theologian.

I return now to some of these works a number of years after first reading them, while others I have discovered for the first time in preparing this book. I have found myself reflecting on the considerable lengths to which pastoral theologians have gone and continue to go to say, by means of metaphors, just who they are or to what or whom their work compares. It is as though they are forever condemned to, while simultaneously embracing, a purposeful introspection and self-doubt.

It is hard to conceive of persons in other lines of work—construction workers, hair stylists, dentists, tennis pros, even systematic theologians or biblical scholars—bothering to concoct so steady a diet of metaphorical equivalents to their chosen fields. To my occasional envy as a pastoral theologian, those in other callings more often seem content to simply go about doing what they do. Why, then, does the vocational identity of the pastoral theologian or minister seem so much less secure? Why these incessant attempts to describe, understand, and justify our work by likening it to that of others—to shepherds, gardeners, physicians, or circus clowns? *Is this relentless pastoral self-scrutiny,* I began to wonder, *in part an unfortunate legacy of our inauspicious origins in that Boston psychiatric hospital so many decades ago? Are ministers somehow constitutionally endowed with madness?*

I have begun to conclude that ours probably is such a legacy, that we ministers probably are so endowed. As Donald Capps points out in chapter 10 in his discussion of the pastoral image of the wise fool, one problem inherent in professional ministry is that the minister "who claims to speak for God cannot know what he is talking about. God's prophet is also God's fool, because God's prophet cannot speak with any certainty"[5] on behalf of a mysterious, unfathomable God.

To be sure, ministers are not completely alone in this sort of predicament. Reflecting on the enigmas of her own line of work, British psychoanalyst Nina Coltart suggests that "[i]t is of the essence of our impossible profession that in a very singular way we do not know what we are doing."[6] Why? Because psychoanalysts seek to know the unconscious, that part of the self or soul that, by definition, is unknowable. How much more so the case, then, the madness of ministers in their attempts to know and speak on behalf of an unknowable, unspeakable God?

A certain insecurity is reflected as well in the kind of persons to whom pastoral theologians and caregivers have characteristically been drawn to attend, those not usually at the center of power in the social arena, but more likely far removed from view and otherwise forgotten. In chapter 3, for example, Bonnie J. Miller-McLemore critiques but also builds upon Boisen's metaphor of the living human document by inviting pastoral theologians to consider more attenuated voices on the edges of a complex "living human *web*" that joins persons across all barriers of cultural location and difference. Her plea on behalf of such persons, she points out, is entirely in keeping with the dynamic origins of the contemporary pastoral theology movement:

> Boisen, having suffered an emotional breakdown and finding himself inside a mental hospital, refused the marginalized, ostracized status of the mentally ill patient. He claimed the importance of what he learned about health, spirituality, and theology as learning that could occur from nowhere else than inside the experience of illness and suffering. This lesson—that we must hear the voices of the marginalized from within their own contexts—is one that pastoral theologians have known all along, even when Boisen claimed the validity of his own mental breakdown.[7]

Both the madness and the wisdom of pastoral theology and its resulting approaches to pastoral care and counseling derive from keen attention to life on the boundaries, making pastoral theology's own questionable origins, as well as its frequent identity confusion, less its burden than its calling and destiny.

Everyone Starts Afresh

James E. Dittes, reflecting on his recent retirement after nearly fifty years of teaching pastoral theology and the psychology of religion at Yale Divinity School—a ministry spanning most of the decades reflected in the evolving metaphors of this book—speaks of the haphazard way that, of necessity, he himself found his way into his subject matter. Dittes, whose image of the pastoral counselor as ascetic witness appears in chapter 12, eventually came to view the ambiguity and loneliness of his ill-defined field not as accidental but essential. For those in pastoral theology, he writes,

> [t]here is no knowledge being accumulated. The occasional attempt to manufacture an accumulation or tradition only proves the point. I came to realize that this is not a collective flaw [of] which we should all repent and correct. This is a merit and strength of those of us who work in some version of psychology and religion. This tentativeness, this everyone-needs-to-start-fresh custom, reflects the way things are.
>
> It's not just that there isn't accumulation and tradition. There can't be.[8]

There can be no accumulation of knowledge about God, nor about the depths of persons or the complexities of human communities, Dittes argues. These remain somehow always mysterious, beyond our grasp, elusive. Their truths are never benignly inherited, bestowed, or memorized from a textbook or catechism, but are instead hard-won and deeply personal. We therefore harbor suspicion toward those who claim to know with great certainty all that God desires for their lives, or just how others in their care should respond in the face of any particular struggle, tragedy, doubt, or despair.

Instead, Dittes affirms a necessarily unstable pastoral identity, less a birthright than an unspoken yearning or desire. To know with great certainty just who we are or what we are to do in relation to God or others is almost certainly to have gotten it wrong. There is no accumulation of knowledge. Everyone starts afresh.

Dittes's reflections on his chosen vocation resonate with earlier comments of the British psychoanalyst D. W. Winnicott regarding how students often experience their initial courses in psychology. In a lecture entitled "Yes, But How Do We Know It's True?" Winnicott describes two stages through which students typically pass in learning psychology:

> In the first stage they learn what is being taught about psychology just as they learn the other [subjects]. In the second stage, they begin to wonder—yes, but is it true, is it real, how do we know? In the second stage, the psychological teaching begins to separate out from the other as something that can't just be learned. It has to be felt as real, or else it is irritating and even maddening...Whereas most types of [learning] take you out of yourself, psychology, the psychology that matters, tends to throw you back into yourself...We can try to be objective and we can make every effort to learn about people without developing morbid introspection, but this requires effort, and you feel disturbed; this psychology is not going to behave itself properly as the other subjects in the curriculum do.[9]

So, too, pastoral theology, with its deep historic ties to the kind of psychology that "matters," typically refuses to behave, especially in terms of conclusively defining itself. The sheer accumulation of images and metaphors for pastoral care and counseling found in this book could, to a skeptic, seem maddening. *Why can't pastoral theologians or caregivers simply be who they are and do what they do?*

In my experience such a charge—and the frustration it represents—are familiar enough companions of most pastoral theologians themselves. The various contributors to this book intuitively seem to recognize that any remotely satisfying response necessarily entails indirection, analogy, even poetry. Anything short of this would mock the complexity of the human heart and mind and disregard the limitations of any individual perspective on the perplexities of the human condition. The authors' playful exercises of the imagination, like those of the artist or poet, instead attempt to join the mundane and the mysterious together in witness and service to persons whose cries from the heart, like those of the deranged Anton Boisen himself, have at times been neglected by professionals less disposed to vocational insecurity and introspection.

Collectively, the authors exhibit a kind of wisdom that, if Dittes is correct (and as this book's many metaphors appear to suggest), can never simply be accumulated but instead must be hard won and continually refashioned. The pastoral theologian's, indeed the Christian minister's, legacy of professional insecurity is not then so much lamentable as laudable, honorable, even essential to who we are and to what we are called to do. Our identity is somehow found in *not* usually knowing who we are, in *not* always knowing what we are doing. Our identity is sometimes found, as Jesus himself professed, in its occasional loss.

The Idea for this Book

The initial idea for this book emerged out of informal exchanges among colleagues over the course of several recent annual meetings of the Society for Pastoral Theology. A small group of faculty teaching at seminaries and divinity schools that offer doctoral programs in pastoral theology or related fields had begun to gather for an hour or so of conversation during those conferences with the modest agenda of exchanging ideas and learning more about our respective Ph.D. programs. We were seeking to answer questions concerning the specific emphases and requirements of the various programs, the kinds of professional positions to which each school's graduates typically gravitated, and the texts and topics we considered essential to a core graduate curriculum in the field.

Every institution represented around those tables used a distinctive nomenclature to designate the discipline. Claremont School of Theology offered a Ph.D. in theology and personality. At Garrett-Evangelical Theological Seminary it was a degree in pastoral theology, personality, and culture. Emory University graduates received a doctorate in person, community, and religious practice, while Vanderbilt students worked toward one in religion and personality. Boston University's program was in pastoral psychology, but Princeton Theological Seminary's was in pastoral theology.

These differing program names mirrored the sense of ambiguity that we ourselves as faculty confided to having experienced when expected to describe or justify our work to others, especially to those charged with assessing our academic standing or status. It became equally clear that a number of us struggled to determine what mix of texts and authors to include in core courses in the history and methodology of pastoral theology at a graduate level. Those texts that we did tend to use were as varied as our institutional designations for the discipline. We found disconcerting this collective inability to identify one or even a number of definitive texts that would lend our students confidence that they were indeed appropriating a coherent sense of the tasks, tools, or methods of pastoral theology.

Despite these common concerns, however, those involved in these conversations over the years clearly shared an undisguised devotion to what we could all somehow continue to name as pastoral theology. We were unwavering in the conviction that pastoral theology had something of critical value to offer. None of us expressed any qualms whatsoever about our mutual desire to see pastoral theology press forward in its service to church, academy, and society, however elusive the nature of its mission even to those entrusted with its oversight.

I typically found these conversations with colleagues to be oddly encouraging. Long after, they continued to lead me to reflect on that process whereby I had come to regard myself, with varying degrees of conviction, as a pastoral theologian. Central to this were certain of my own teachers—Donald Capps, Sandra Brown, James Lapsley, and John Florell, among them—who seemed to have attained some level of comfort in thinking of themselves as pastoral theologians. In their own ways they inspired me to enter challenging venues of ministry that would otherwise have seemed beyond my reach. Thus I found myself working in urban hospitals, psychiatric institutions, counseling centers, prisons, and, at times even more disorienting, in utterly ordinary suburban congregations and seminary classrooms.

Though my teachers, too, sometimes found it difficult to specify the nature of pastoral theology in explicit terms, there was no question, in my mind at least, that they were pastoral theologians *to me.* I saw them as caring, courageous iconoclasts. Their influence quite literally changed the trajectory of my life and contributed to a calling that, however difficult to name, captured my imagination and subsequently shaped a vision of what I hoped to be and do.

Those annual Society conversations led me as well to reflect on certain articles, chapters, and books that had been especially important to me over the years in forming my own pastoral and professional identity. Among them were a handful of philosophical works on hermeneutics, practical theological methodology, and the nature of interdisciplinary dialogue. More often they included many of the far more accessible, experience-near, even autobiographical works and metaphors for ministry that I have subsequently incorporated into this book.

The Image Is the Thing

I remembered how at crucial junctures in my ministry I was often guided, sometimes literally saved, by several of these works. I remember a conversation, for example, with a despondent woman in the immediate aftermath of an unsuccessful suicide attempt. In that instance my early, almost constitutional affinity for Henri Nouwen's image of the wounded healer (chapter 7), with its rich emphasis on empathy and depth in pastoral care, seemed to do more harm than good. The more empathic I tried to be with her, the more her despair seemed to increase. At such moments I found welcome respite and practical guidance in what were for me at that time the more alien images of the circus clown and wise fool of Heije Faber (chapter 8), Alastair Campbell (chapter 9), and Donald Capps (chapter 10), with their corresponding emphases on reframing, the intentional use of paradox and humor, and a productive focus on a problem's *surface* as much as its depth.

So, too, as a hospital chaplain facing tragic situations that accumulated over years of ministry to the point of taking a serious toll on my faith, I was able to gain needed perspective by conceiving of my work in terms of an image of the intimate stranger in the biblical witness and contemporary public life (chapter 11). In these and many other situations, then, the image was the thing. Having access to a variety of metaphors for ministry provided a modicum of courage and guidance at those not-infrequent moments when, as Capps and Coltart suggest, I could not possibly have known what I was doing. In gathering these images into one volume, I hope in turn to help ministers and seminary students not only to readily discern those dominant or "default" metaphors that typically orient their own pastoral styles, but also to discover an array of alternate metaphors for imagining their way into those inevitable circumstances in ministry in which a fresh vision and new approach are warranted.

Understanding Lions

Discussing John Wisdom's *Paradox and Discovery*, Charles M. Wood recounts how "Wisdom tells of a keeper at the Dublin zoo who had a record of unusual success at the difficult task of breeding lions. Asked the secret of his success, Mr. Flood replied, *Understanding lions.* Asked in what consists the understanding of lions, he replied, *Every lion is different.*"[10]

This expert zookeeper's impossible, paradoxical response–*How could one ever hope to understand "lions" as a species if every individual lion is different?*–captures the quandary of the pastoral theologian and, indeed, of every minister who seeks to become an agent of hope (Capps's metaphor in chapter 16) in complex situations of human tragedy and need. Since every person and every problematic situation is different, it stands to reason that in pastoral theology and ministry, as in breeding lions, one never finally arrives at some fixed body of knowledge for understanding or action. Still, despite essential differences among individuals and the many problems they face, the minister paradoxically can and sometimes eventually does come to the equivalent of the zookeeper's hard-won sense of understanding lions. What accrues, then, in the many images of care that follow is a generous sense of wisdom and hope for understanding persons, which derives in large measure from a growing appreciation for their inestimable differences.

William James once said that "one of the most philosophical remarks [he] ever heard was made by an uneducated carpenter who was doing some repairs at [James's] house." The carpenter told him, "There is very little difference between one man and another; but what little there is, *is very important.*"[11] The carpenter's observation is one that, a century later, even scientific research could be interpreted to confirm. Geneticists note, for example, that in terms of the chemical base pairs that comprise our DNA, human beings are 99.9 percent identical. Thus all individual human variations can be accounted for biochemically by a mere 0.1 percent of our genetic material. Still, what a difference that 0.1 percent makes![12] In reflecting on his carpenter's insight, James writes:

> The zone of individual differences, and of the social "twists" which by common confession they initiate, is the zone of formative processes, the dynamic belt of quivering uncertainty, the line where past and future meet. It is the theater of all we do not take for granted, the stage of the living drama of life; and however narrow its scope, it is roomy enough to lodge the whole range of human passions.[13]

This minute but infinitely fascinating zone of human differences and passions is, of necessity, what captivates the pastoral theologian's attention. This book's array of essays, metaphors, and images attests to the fact that pastoral theology, not infrequently in contrast to more firmly established or highly esteemed ecclesiastical disciplines, inhabits a messy, pluralistic, characteristically Protestant and thereby occasionally heterodox universe.

Valerie DeMarinis captures this sense of the unruliness of pastoral theology in telling of a conversation she happened to overhear between two professors of systematic theology:

> The topic was pastoral psychology in general, and the pastoral practitioner in particular. One said to the other, "They are just like scavengers. They have no real theory, just a hunting and pecking, a grabbing and applying. There is no order for them. And they can never explain what they do or why they do it, only that something works or not. It is all technique, and at best has some rationale to measure if it works. It is a very sad state of affairs."[14]

DeMarinis acknowledges that while she was initially troubled by the disparaging nature of this professor's depiction of her field, on further reflection she actually came to embrace his image. "Scavengers, though often thought of negatively, are in point of fact highly skilled at collecting, extracting, and cleansing," DeMarinis writes, thereby proving herself to be something of a capable scavenger in the process. "The responsible scavenger is one skilled at survival, one who knows how to search, salvage, purify, and transform the elements of the world into that which nurtures and sustains life."[15]

So, too, British psychoanalyst Adam Phillips claims a similar task and purpose for psychotherapy:

> If the aim of a system is to create an outside where you can put the things you don't want, then we have to look at what that system disposes of—its rubbish—to understand it, to get a picture of how it sees itself and wants to be seen. The proscribed vocabulary in anybody's theory is as telling as the recommended vocabulary.[16]

In this respect the pastoral theologian or caregiver, along with the psychoanalyst, must scavenge unapologetically, rummaging about resolutely in what others individually or collectively discard.

Long before DeMarinis chanced upon the conversation that revealed to her just how distasteful this sort of enterprise is to traditionally more fastidious systematicians, William James, in a plea for pluralism in philosophy, observed:

> It is curious how little countenance radical pluralism has ever had from philosophers. Whether materialistically or spiritualistically minded, philosophers have always aimed at cleaning up the litter with which the world apparently is filled. They have substituted economical and orderly conceptions for the first sensible tangible; and whether these were morally elevated or only intellectually neat, they were at any rate always aesthetically pure and definite, and aimed at ascribing to the world something clean and intellectual in the way of inner structure. As compared with all these rationalizing pictures, the pluralistic empiricism which I profess offers but a sorry appearance. It is a turbid, muddled, gothic sort of an affair, without a sweeping outline and with little pictorial nobility. Those of you who are accustomed to the classical constructions of reality may be excused if your first reaction upon it be absolute contempt–a shrug of the shoulders as if such ideas were unworthy of explicit refutation. But one must have lived some time with a system to appreciate its merits. Perhaps a little more familiarity may mitigate your first surprise at such a programme as I offer.[17]

If, as James asserts, philosophers tend to pursue "cleaning up the litter" of the universe by attributing to it some grand systematic structure, then pastoral theologians–with their modest parcel of diverse metaphors and images, a tolerance for the untidy, and a keen eye for the individual, the singular, the unprecedented–are those radical pluralists who, like James, engage in a more "turbid, muddled, gothic sort of an affair." If they attempt to unclutter the universe at all, they likely do so, as DeMarinis and Phillips suggest, at ground level as unassuming scavengers, that is, by confronting, even feeding on, but ultimately attempting to transform its refuse, its odds and ends.

More inclined to pluralism than to systematics, then, the authors whose works are gathered here would likely affirm the paradoxical truths both of the Dublin zookeeper and of James's carpenter. They would attest that while the difference between one individual, community, or system and another may be small, that difference is nonetheless *very important* for us to understand as we approach our own vocational variant on the difficult task of breeding lions, that is, as we consider our own attempts as pastoral theologians and caregivers to, in the words of DeMarinis, "search, salvage, purify, and transform the elements of the world into that which nurtures and sustains life."

A Seasoned Sensibility

In engaging this book's assortment of essays and images, the reader may well experience a sense, as I have in gathering them, of happening upon an embarrassment of riches. One finds here an at once ancient but surprisingly contemporary cache of practical wisdom for guiding acts of caring in Christian community. To be sure, these authors know their Bibles, church history, and theology; but they seem to know something more as well, holding however loosely to a kind of weathered, down-to-earth sensibility for tending to those who suffer or despair. Having traveled many paths into the darkness, they seem to have discovered there cathartic rays of light.

My hope is that this collective dose of images will serve to refresh and expand the repertoire of pastoral understanding and care and counseling approaches of already seasoned ministers and other caregivers. So, too, am I convinced that seminary students currently grappling with their own emerging sense of pastoral identity will find orientation and encouragement in the diverse array of images and styles of care reflected in these pages. To this end, I can envision the book being assigned in an introductory course in pastoral care and counseling, a unit of clinical pastoral education, or a field education or other setting of ministry.

In addition, those graduate students in pastoral theology whom my colleagues and I specifically had in mind when the idea for this collection first presented itself will discover here a unique entree into historical conversations and controversies in pastoral theology throughout the twentieth century. Usually subtle but occasionally overt clashes among pastoral theologians surface in these pages. They reflect differing understandings of the nature of the self and its healing, of the appropriate subjects and objects of pastoral and pastoral theological concern, and of the particular cognate disciplines perceived to be of most value to this field. Even as every lion, parishioner, or counselee is different; and even as every zoo, congregation, or social context is different; so, too, these essays collectively affirm that every zookeeper, caregiver, or pastoral theologian is different. One thus finds here competing philosophical, theological, and anthropological assumptions that reflect, or lead to, divergent clinical, congregational, and communal claims and strategies of care. The wounded healer who pursues the depths of what he conceives to be the singular core of another's fragile self may well experience as unsettling, for example, a wise fool's focus on superficial matters and her utter confidence in the sufferer's resilient multiplicity of selves. Yet it is certainly possible to conceive of philosophical and clinical common ground between the wounded healer and wise fool, along with the many other competing images for ministry here.[18] These various metaphors nonetheless reflect a kind of historical ebb and flow within recent pastoral theology. The image of the solicitous shepherd, which comes into ascendancy in the 1960s, gives way to the wounded healer in the 1970s, which in turn is displaced by the wise fool of the 1980s, while a host of alternative images arrive on the scene from the 1990s to the present.

Also evident to readers will be tensions among the authors and images regarding who or what is perceived to be the subject or object of pastoral concern. Is it an individual parishioner in need, as in Boisen's "living human document" as well as in Seward Hiltner's shepherd, Dittes's ascetic witness, Paul Pruyser's diagnostician, or Capps's agent of hope? Is it a larger congregation or community of persons, as in Miller-McLemore's "living human web," Gaylord Noyce's coach or moral counselor, Edward Wimberly's indigenous storyteller, or Margaret Kornfeld's gardener? Or is it at times the minister's or caregiver's own unique self and sorrows, apparent in Nouwen's wounded healer as well as in Jeanne Stevenson Moessner's self-differentiated Samaritan, or my own intimate stranger?

Though these positions are not always mutually exclusive, neither are they easily reconciled. They reflect differences both in the relative weight attributed to individuals, families, and the larger community as the source of problems and in the locus of intervention and the resources perceived to be essential for their amelioration.

Readers will also notice that the range of cognate disciplines engaged by pastoral theologians today has considerably expanded. Various schools of clinical psychology–particularly the psychoanalytic, analytic, and personal psychologies of Sigmund Freud, Carl Jung, Carl Rogers, and their disciples, and the functional psychology of William James–served prominently to inspire and undergird the contemporary pastoral theology movement in its early days of Boisen and Hiltner.

Recent pastoral theologians, however, are as likely to draw on systems theories, sociology or political science, or philosophical hermeneutics. They engage African American, feminist, or queer studies, as well as art history, literary theory, or even scientific brain research as much as or more than any individual or group psychology as their principal partners in dialogue and practice. This trend, too, can be readily traced through the historical progression of images and metaphors of the book. In this regard, then, the collection offers not only multiple ways to imagine one's own ministries of care, but also a unique narrative means by which to access the historical sweep of contemporary pastoral theology.

Pastoral Images as Evocative Art

The essays that follow may lead the reader to raise questions concerning the practical import of a metaphorical approach to pastoral theology and ministry. Presumably, it is not enough to say to a minister or seminarian, "If you see those in need of help, it is your job to help them." Such a response only begs further questions of what it means to help others in need and of what is unique about the kind of help a minister can offer. The essays and images of this book rarely attempt to answer these kinds of questions by providing detailed instruction for entering into particular situations of need. They function less as technical training guides or "how-to" manuals for basic counseling or crisis intervention skills than, as previously indicated, as works of art intent on inspiring ministry in more indirect and subtle ways. Like the evocative power of images in portraits, sculptures, films, or poetry, these pastoral images serve not so much to inform specific tasks of ministry, but to foster a richer sense of pastoral self-understanding, identity, and integrity.

There are a number of possible ways one can respond to an artistic image. One way is to view it with reverence and adoration, as one might contemplate an icon of the Virgin Mary or of Christ on the cross. Another is to see it as a "graven" image, as a sacrilege or threat, and seek to destroy it by any means possible. A third way is to engage, as art critics do, in a combination of appreciation and critical appraisal.

All these possible responses have their proponents, and the history of the church is replete with examples of all three. The third approach, however, seems to be one that both honors the tradition and enables its adherents to adapt to new realities. This is likely the most helpful way to consider the progression of pastoral images of this book, i.e., as ongoing attempts by contemporary pastoral theologians to honor their tradition while adapting to changing realities of church and culture. Thus in order to understand and assess the image of the living human web, for example, one would be served by knowing something of the living human document.

The reader may notice a tendency of authors in this collection to romanticize the particular image or model they are promoting, an inclination that may reflect a more widespread idealization of metaphors within pastoral theology in general. The authors understandably accentuate the positive features of the pastoral image they propose, less often highlighting its more questionable aspects or its limitations. A shepherd, after all, is not always known to be solicitous or courageous; a web is often a sticky nuisance; a coach is held accountable for the team's losses and for the behavior of players even off the field; a gardener can grow weary over decisions about which plants are worth trying to save. Individual essays therefore tend to function here more as exercises in art *appreciation*. Taken together, however, they also serve as a means of critical appraisal, as art *criticism*. The turn to each new metaphor in successive chapters may be seen in part as an implicit critique or recognition of the limitations of the old.

The Plan of the Book

The essays are grouped in three sections and, with few exceptions, appear chronologically within each part after a brief introduction of the whole. Part one introduces the early work of Boisen, in which he describes clinical patients as living human documents worthy of theological exploration. Two additional essays at once endorse and critique Boisen's original metaphor. This section also includes two other classical biblical metaphors of care. The good shepherd has shaped pastoral care for generations but comes to prominence in contemporary pastoral theology in the early work of Hiltner. The image of the good Samaritan is presented here with a contemporary twist from a feminist perspective in an influential essay by Jeanne Stevenson Moessner.

Part two introduces several additional images. Each image embraces internal contradiction or paradox to describe the bewildering nature of pastoral care and its impact especially on the minister's own life and faith. This section presents the images of wounded healer and wise fool (or circus clown) that have wielded significant influence in ministry for decades. It also includes more recent images of the intimate stranger and ascetic witness that, likewise, rely on paradox in attempting to capture the rich complexities of pastoral work.

Part three offers an array of additional images, a number of them emerging recently. These images suggest the growing emphasis within pastoral theology on broader social and spiritual concerns of congregations and communities, especially groups frequently marginalized. Such emphasis leads to a consideration of needs beyond those of individual parishioners who previously comprised the principal focus of pastoral care. Here the caregiver becomes a theological diagnostician, an athletic coach, an agent of hope, an indigenous storyteller, a midwife, a gardener, even an outlaw in the widening horizons of pastoral care.

Each of the essays has been drawn from its original source and, in most instances, substantially edited so as to concentrate specifically on its author's case for a particular image of care. This condensing makes for a single volume of a size capable of being read over the period of a week or two in an introductory course in pastoral care or a unit of clinical pastoral education. I trust that the images will linger and continue to spur reflection for a considerable time thereafter. While I have attempted to incorporate as many different images as possible and have consulted with a number of colleagues in pastoral theology in my effort to be comprehensive, no doubt I have overlooked some metaphors for ministry. I would welcome readers drawing my attention to these.

For the sake of fewer interruptions and a smoother read, I have chosen not to use ellipses to indicate those many points at which I have omitted words, phrases, sentences, paragraphs, or even entire or multiple pages of the original works. To break up the pages for easier reading, I have divided long paragraphs and added subheads not present in the original. I have tried to maintain the overall integrity of each author's contribution as well as a reasonable narrative flow. However, those readers interested in pursuing these works further for purposes of scholarly research would be served by consulting the original essays in their entirety. I have not attempted to alter the gender-exclusive language of the earlier essays, such usage itself an unfortunate aspect of a legacy that subsequent essays directly or obliquely address and redress.

Finally, though each of the chapters stands capably on its own, there is a certain method to my own madness in their collective ordering, since a number of them make reference to earlier works. For this reason it may be to the reader's slight advantage, especially in terms of gaining historical perspective on the discipline of pastoral theology, to encounter them as they are presented.

PART ONE

CLASSICAL
IMAGES *of* CARE

INTRODUCTION

The six essays of this section center on influential images of pastoral care championed by two pioneers of contemporary Protestant pastoral theology. The first three chapters focus and build on Anton Boisen's image of the living human document, the next three on Seward Hiltner's metaphor of the solicitous shepherd.

Anton T. Boisen

As noted in the Introduction, Boisen's convictions concerning the value of directly exposing clergy and seminary students to hospitalized patients, what has since become clinical pastoral education, came to him in mid-life as a patient himself emerging from a terrifying experience of mental illness. Boisen tells this story in chapter 1 of this book, derived from *his* first book, *The Exploration of the Inner World* (1936). The book was published some fifteen years after his initial hospitalization and was at one time prominent among texts in the psychology of religion.

Those today who take for granted the presence of chaplains and the routine access to patients afforded ministers in hospitals and other institutional settings may have difficulty imagining the world of the Boston psychiatric hospital that Boisen entered in 1920. He reports that it was unusual even for psychiatrists there to converse with the patients: "The doctors did not believe in talking with patients about their symptoms, which they assumed to be rooted in some as yet undiscovered organic difficulty. The longest time I ever got was fifteen minutes during which the very charming young doctor pointed out that one must not hold the reins too tight in dealing with the sex instinct. Nature, he said, must have its way. It was very clear that he had neither understanding nor interest in the religious aspects of my problem."[1]

During that time, however, Boisen became convinced that his own struggles and those of many of his fellow patients were indeed spiritual ones. He believed that their religious nature necessitated the presence and skilled intervention of ministers willing to explore the "little-known territory" of the patient's confusing inner world in order to "map [it] out."[2] "[My work] propose[s] to examine in the light of my own experience," he writes, "the experiences of other persons who have been forced off the beaten path of common sense and have traveled through the little-known wilderness of the inner life."[3]

Hence for him, every patient has the potential to become a "living human document" to the minister or seminary student. This "document" is as worthy of intensive study and as capable of revealing profound new religious insight as the Bible or any theological textbook or tome.[4] On Boisen's release from his first hospitalization, then, he put these convictions into action, beginning a fledgling revolution in education for ministry.

Charles V. Gerkin

In chapter 2, Charles V. Gerkin tells his experience as a young man taking a seminary class taught by one of Boisen's first students. Boisen himself came to one class session, "a strange man with his twisted face, penetrating eyes, and thumping cane."[5] The encounter left its mark, however, for in *The Living Human Document* (1984), Gerkin seeks to reclaim Boisen's metaphor for a new generation, considering it from the perspective of contemporary philosophical hermeneutics.

"Pastoral counselors are, more than anything else, listeners to and interpreters of stories."[6] The ways we speak of, or "story," our lives matter, Gerkin says. Individuals seek counseling when their usual ways of speaking, when the narrative flow and "plot" of their lives, become somehow confused, garbled, or otherwise insufficient to provide identity and meaning. Their stories— and their story—instead have come to seem unmanageable or destined for tragedy. They call for a fresh reading and infusion of hope from the counselor.

Gerkin, for many years a professor of pastoral theology at Emory University, points out that, as Boisen insisted, such an interpretation of another's life situation demands no less integrity, discipline, and nuance than one's study of meaningful written texts. He writes, "Just as the preacher should not look to proof texts to be twisted into the meaning sought for, so also the individual human text demand[s] a hearing on its own merit."[7] The difficulties of so careful a reading of another's life are compounded by the fact that counselors themselves bring to the encounter a particular set of stories and a life story of their own. These, too, come to bear, often unwittingly, on the narratives of the person seeking care. Gerkin thus argues for a certain humility amid this complexity, whereby counselors should not presume too much in terms of common language or understanding: "[T]o listen to stories with an effort to understand means to listen first as a stranger who does not yet fully know the language, the nuanced meanings of the other as his or her story is being told."[8]

Gerkin acknowledges that as a young seminarian, he found in the "language of psychotherapy" an exciting means by which to navigate this intricate intermingling of stories in counseling. Psychology was, for him, "both liberating from the stereotypical moralism of the Midwestern conventional piety on which I had been reared and concrete in its attention to the hidden dynamics of behavior…"[9] Over the years, however, he grew more cautious concerning psychology, yearning rather to reclaim theological language for pastoral tasks, until in 1984 he perceived:

> [T]he language world out of which the pastoral counselor shapes his or her perceptions and response to the other person becomes crucial. If that be a language world inhabited by the images of theology and faith, the counselee will be invited into a world shaped by those images. If that be, on the other hand, a language world shaped by the images of secularity, it is into that world that the counselor invites the one seeking help.[10]

It is thus to this task of reclamation that he commits himself in this work.

Bonnie J. Miller-McLemore

In chapter 3, Bonnie J. Miller-McLemore, a professor of pastoral theology and counseling at Vanderbilt University Divinity School, reinforces, a decade later, Gerkin's call for pastoral theology to move beyond its early emphases on psychology and the counseling of individuals. Desiring to refashion pastoral theology for an increasingly interconnected world at the turn of a new century, she stresses the delicate interweaving of multiple personal, social, and political strands that comprise every problematic situation and caring act. She seeks to supplant Boisen's living human *document* with her image of the living human *web*. Building on Catherine Keller and informed by other feminist and liberation theologies, Miller-McLemore presses for an arachnidian pastoral theology inspired by a spider's amazing ability to repair its broken web, "spinning oneness out of many and weaving the one back into the many."[11] Social and communal ties, she claims, have too long been neglected and torn.

As noted earlier, Boisen's gift was to insist that we, in Miller-McLemore's words, "hear the voices of the marginalized from within their own contexts."[12] She maintains, however, that from the start, pastoral theology has emphasized "hearing the voices" in this injunction at the expense of its "marginalized" and "their contexts." It has conceived of its task too narrowly, as empathic counseling with troubled individuals rather than as care that involves and implicates the wider community. The complexity of the living human web exposes the limitations of this preoccupation with empathy: "Sometimes a person must admit an inability to understand fully the lived reality of the oppressions suffered by another. There may be boundaries beyond which empathy itself cannot go."[13]

Like Gerkin, Miller-McLemore admits to some ambivalence concerning the diminishing influence of psychology, including feminist psychology, among pastoral theologians. This becomes especially significant given the pervasive, mostly unsupported, and usually unchallenged contempt for psychology often expressed by other theologians, who dismiss it out of hand for its presumed unchecked individualism.[14] Still, she concludes that psychology alone can no longer carry the day for pastoral theology. "In a word, never again will a clinical moment, whether of caring for a woman recovering from hysterectomy or attending to a woman's spiritual life, be understood on intrapsychic grounds alone. These moments are always and necessarily situated within the interlocking, continually evolving threads of which reality is woven and they can be understood in no other way. Psychology alone cannot understand this web."[15]

Seward Hiltner

Chapter 4 doubles back to the midpoint of the twentieth century, from which Seward Hiltner's metaphor of the solicitous shepherd anchors a second set of three essays in this section.[16] Hiltner was one of Boisen's first clinical students and came to prominence as an early theorist of the emerging new discipline of pastoral theology in seminary education.

Drawing from Jesus' parable in Luke 15 of the shepherd who left the ninety-nine sheep to seek the one that was lost, Hiltner conveys a fierce advocacy—what he calls a shepherding perspective—for individuals and small groups within Christian congregations. To be sure, he acknowledges that other equally essential and more communal perspectives frequently inform one's theology and practice of ministry, specifically perspectives of communicating the gospel and organizing the fellowship. But in those particular circumstances in which a shepherding perspective comes to bear, the needs of the one take precedence over those of the many.

Just what are such circumstances? Those, Hiltner says, that call especially for healing, or, if healing as such is impossible, for sustaining individuals in need.

He turns to the parable of the good Samaritan in Luke 10 to capture the essence of shepherding. Jesus' praise for the actions of the Samaritan implies, he argues, "that anything standing in the way of the best possible meeting of need for healing is an offense against God." The wounded man on the side of the road did not need a "verbal testimony" to faith. No, the sole "testimony called for was healing," the testimony of "oil, wine, bandages, and an inn" that, finally, only the Samaritan provided. Radically, the Samaritan's shepherding is in no way "ancillary to something else," but *itself* became "the one indispensable way of communicating the gospel."[17]

Hiltner's reading of the parable suggests something of his own early plea for a contextual theology of care. The parable insists, he says, that "the way in which one testifies to the gospel cannot be determined in advance by the preferences of the testifier. Testimony must be given according to the need and condition, on any particular occasion."[18]

Alastair V. Campbell

In chapter 5, Scottish ethicist Alastair V. Campbell acknowledges the pervasive influence, spanning decades in American pastoral theology, of Hiltner's understanding of shepherding as "tender and solicitous concern." Campbell sharply critiques this rendering of the metaphor, however, calling it a "mere cipher" of any actual shepherding depicted in the Bible. He sees it as having been derived instead from the client-centered psychotherapy of Carl Rogers prevalent in Hiltner's day.[19] Campbell himself advocates instead for a shepherd image that is more intense, self-sacrificing, and, in a word, *courageous*.

Hiltner's understanding of the shepherding perspective is too parochial, Campbell charges, excessively tethered to "a minister-dominated approach" to pastoral care and "insulated from theological critique by the nature of its purely practical starting point." Its "fatal flaw" is that it is, finally, "flat and uninteresting."[20] Campbell urges ministers and lay Christians alike rather to consider the fateful words, actions, and sufferings of Jesus as exemplary for courageous pastoral care.

Despite harsh words for Hiltner's model, Campbell's own approach ultimately shares much in common with it. Campbell echoes both Hiltner's expressed uneasiness with excessive dependence on therapeutic technique in complex situations of need and his consequent call for increasing humility in pastoral care. "[F]ar from giving us a simple paradigm for our caring concern," Campbell concludes, "the image of the shepherd seems merely to reveal our inadequacies."[21]

Moreover, Campbell, like Hiltner, also eventually opts for a certain pragmatism in assessing the relative outcome of pastoral interventions. One true test of shepherding, he suggests, is whether those who seek care find greater "rest and health" rather than "some narrowing, overburdening, or destruction of themselves." Another more sobering test asks whether the intervention has in some way proven costly and dangerous to the shepherd.[22]

Jeanne Stevenson Moessner

Finally, in chapter 6, Jeanne Stevenson Moessner, a professor of pastoral care at Perkins School of Theology in Dallas, Texas, offers a second critical, though some might say complementary, response to Hiltner's paradigm.[23] She affirms an early critique by Carroll A. Wise, a contemporary of Hiltner's, which was later reiterated by Campbell. The critique questioned Hiltner's subtle hierarchical privileging of shepherd over sheep. Despite this critique, however, Stevenson Moessner, too, like Hiltner, turns for guidance to the parable of the good Samaritan in Luke 10. Her revisionist interpretation shifts the focus from Hiltner's interest in what the Samaritan did at the side of the road to what he did after that, taking the wounded man to an inn and completing his own journey. These latter two actions of the Samaritan, she argues, lend essential support to a feminist model of pastoral care.

The parable begins, Stevenson Moessner reminds us, with Jesus' injunction to love God with all our heart, and with all our soul, and with all our strength, and with all our mind, and our neighbor as ourselves (Lk. 10:27). When a lawyer then challenges Jesus to define *neighbor*, he responds by telling the parable. Its traditional interpreters, including Hiltner, thus invariably and quite naturally concentrate on the way it depicts love of neighbor and, by extension, of God. But had not Jesus actually said, she asks, that we are to love our neighbors, thereby God, as *ourselves*? If one neglects this crucial third component in Jesus' injunction to love, that of self-love, the parable may do more harm than good, especially to women.

Why? Because through the ages, she argues, women have shouldered a disproportionate burden of responsibility for caring for others in need and have often come to think of themselves almost exclusively in terms of their caretaking roles and relationships. They grow uncertain of their own individual uniqueness, becoming diffuse and distracted over time. When the parable serves to further reinforce or intensify women's sense of urgency for the welfare of others, Jesus' teaching on the nature of love becomes twisted into an instrument of oppression. The self-love every bit as present—but usually overlooked—in the story of the good Samaritan is denied to women who need this very word.

As noted, Stevenson Moessner locates the parable's modeling of self-love in the symbol of the inn and in the Samaritan's completing his own journey. The Samaritan does not, in the end, assume sole responsibility for the needs of the wounded man. Instead, he relies on a wider network of care represented by the innkeeper and inn.

The inn, she counsels, may be a battered women's shelter, an Alcoholics Anonymous meeting, or a network of relationships with other healing professionals. The inn may also be a church, though she cautions that the church is widely perceived by women to have fostered rather than alleviated their burden. Beyond relying on the inn, the Samaritan demonstrates self-love, in conjunction with loving neighbor and loving God, by choosing in turn to complete his own journey.

"The Samaritan," Stevenson Moessner writes, "did not give everything away. In this enigmatic parable, he did not injure, hurt, or neglect the self. He loved himself, and he loved his neighbor."[24] In stopping to bind the injured man's wounds, in relying on the inn, and in completing his own journey, the Samaritan reflects not only the absolute value of another's life, but the infinite worth of his own. The parable implies, then, that loving neighbor and loving self together exemplify the pathway to loving God.

Worth Considering along the Way

It is worth noting here that Boisen's image of the living human document places a greater degree of emphasis on the person who is the object of pastoral concern than on the minister or caregiver. Hiltner's solicitous shepherd, on the other hand, while certainly not unconcerned with those in need of care, tends to draw one's attention to the person of the caregiver.

Looking back, the two models might have come to be seen as more fully compatible or mutually supportive had Hiltner, for example, focused on the minister as the "reader" of living human documents or, though anachronistic in his case, had Boisen considered the "sheep" who are the objects of solicitous shepherding. These two early images–of human document and solicitous shepherd–are not commensurate. If, however, the general thrust of the collection of images in this book can be taken as indication, the shepherding model's greater emphasis on the *giver* rather than the *receiver* of care appears to have become more definitive, purportedly at times to the consternation of Boisen, for the field of contemporary pastoral care.[25]

Again, both models still have their critics. Most of these, however, make their points only in relation to the particular approach that most concerns them, whether Boisen's or Hiltner's, not to both. Miller-McLemore critiques Boisen's human document but not Hiltner's shepherd. Campbell and Stevenson Moessner challenge Hiltner's shepherd but not Boisen's human document. This may or may not be a problem in terms of assessing the relative significance of their or the many other pastoral images in this book. My point is only to suggest that some images and models stress the giver or provider, while others the receiver, of pastoral concern, and that *this may lead the reader to want to ask what is being implied in each particular model about that aspect not explicitly emphasized.*

If recipients of pastoral care are "living human documents," what might this mean for the pastoral self-understanding and actual practices of "readers" of such documents? If the caregiver is a solicitous shepherd–making the recipients of such care "sheep"–what might the implications be? To raise questions of any given pastoral image or model concerning its relative weight of emphasis in this regard may be helpful as the reader approaches and begins to assess the essays that follow.

CHAPTER 1

The Living Human Document

ANTON T. BOISEN[1] (1936)

To be plunged as a patient into a hospital for the insane may be a tragedy, or it may be an opportunity. For me it has been an opportunity. It has introduced me to a new world of absorbing interest and profound significance; it has shown me that world throughout its entire range, from the bottommost depths of the nether regions to the heights of religious experience at its best; it has made me aware of certain relationships between two important fields of human experience which thus far have been held strictly apart; and it has given me a task in which I find the meaning and purpose of my life.

Sixteen years ago such possibilities were entirely undreamed of. Thus in the year 1920 I was riding on a train in the state of North Dakota when I noticed off to the south a large group of buildings standing in sharp relief against the horizon. I inquired of my neighbor in the seat what those buildings were. He informed me that I was looking at the State Insane Asylum. I thanked him and thought no more about it. It did not occur to me that I ought to be interested in those buildings or in the problem which they represented. And yet there were certain reasons why I ought to have been interested. During my course at Union Theological Seminary nine years before I had centered my attention upon the study of the psychology of religion with particular reference to the problem of mysticism. And at that very time I was in charge of a sociological survey of the state under the direction of the Interchurch World Movement, and as a part of my task I was investigating the situation as regards church hospitals. Probably I should have remained uninterested for some time longer, if, less than a year later, I had not found myself plunged as a patient within the confines of just such an institution.

The Disturbance

The disturbance came on very suddenly, and it was extremely severe. I had never been in better condition physically; the difficulty was rooted wholly in a severe inner struggle arising out of a precocious sexual sensitivity, dating from my fourth year. With the onset of adolescence the struggle became quite severe. It was cleared up on Easter morning in my twenty-second year through a spontaneous religious conversion experience which followed upon a period of black despair. An impulse, seemingly from without myself, bade me not to be afraid to tell. I was thus set free and given a new start in life. Two years later came a relapse into the land of bondage and then a desperate struggle to get free again. Following a decision to give up the teaching of languages, in which I was then engaged, and to enter upon the profession of forestry, there came a love affair which swept me off my feet. This love affair was on my part a desperate cry for salvation. It led to my decision to enter the Christian ministry. The woman I loved was a religious worker of the finest type. On her part it was a source of great embarrassment, but she gave me a helping hand at the critical moment and stood ready to undertake what for her was a task of mercy. But I failed to make the grade. Then followed nine years of wandering. This included several years in rural survey work, five years in the rural pastorate and two with the Y.M.C.A. overseas. On my return I had charge of a state survey for the Interchurch World Movement. All this time I was hoping to be reinstated with her. It was as though my life depended upon it. In 1920 such a reinstatement did occur. The disturbance followed shortly after, coming thus just at the time when the hopes of so many years seemed about to be realized.

I had had, when the Interchurch World Movement disbanded, an enticing opportunity to go on with the survey work. This I had turned down, having decided definitely to go back into the pastorate. I wanted to work out what I felt to be my religious message. The call to a church was slow in coming, and I went east. While waiting I decided to write out a statement of my religious experience, such as I had been required to do when I was a candidate for ordination. I became much absorbed in the task, so much so that I lay awake at night letting the ideas take shape of themselves, as I frequently do when I am writing. This time the ideas carried me away. First of all came the thought that I must give up the hope which meant everything to me. Following this there came surging in upon me with overpowering force a terrifying idea about a coming world catastrophe. Although I had never before given serious thought to such a subject, there came flashing into my mind, as though from a source without myself, the idea that this little planet of ours, which has existed for we know not how many millions of years, was about to undergo some sort of metamorphosis. It was like a seed or an egg. In it were stored up a quantity of food materials, represented by our natural resources. But now we were like a seed in the process of germinating or an egg that had just been fertilized. We were starting to grow. Just within the short space of a hundred years we had begun to draw upon our resources to such an extent that the timber and the gas and the oil were likely soon to be exhausted. In the wake of this idea followed others. I myself was more important than I had ever dreamed of being; I was also a zero quantity. Strange and mysterious forces of evil of which before I had not had the slightest suspicion were also revealed. I was terrified beyond measure and in my terror I talked. Of course my family was frightened, and I soon found myself in a psychopathic hospital. There followed three weeks of violent delirium which remain indelibly burned into my memory. There is probably no three-weeks period in all my life that I can recall more clearly. It seemed as if I were living thousands of years within that time. Then I came out of it much as one awakens out of a bad dream.

I remember distinctly one incident which helped me to find my way out. The idea which had first bowled me over was, as I have said, that of a coming world catastrophe. This same idea was dominant throughout as the premise on which my reasoning was based. I was therefore much impressed one night, as I lay awake out on the sleeping-porch, by the observation that the moon was centered in a cross of light. I took this as confirmation of my worst fears. Did not the cross stand for suffering? What else could it mean than this, that the moon–which, as so often happens in acute disturbances, I had personified–is in mourning over the coming doom? To be sure I called an attendant and inquired if he also saw the cross. He said that he did. I was greatly impressed and agitated. But some days later in the early watches of the morning as I lay awake looking at the moon, speculating about the terrible danger which that cross betokened, I made a discovery. Whenever I looked at the moon from a certain spot, the cross did not appear. I immediately investigated and found that from that particular spot I was looking at the moon through a hole in the wire screening! With this discovery the edifice I had reared upon the basis of the original premise began to fall. And only a few days later I was well again.

Concerning the severity of the disturbance I may say that the diagnosis was "catatonic dementia praecox" and that my people were told there was no hope of recovery. In consequence, when I did recover, I had difficulty in convincing them that I was well enough to leave, and my stay in the hospital was for this reason longer than it would otherwise have been. I may also say that during those three weeks I lost thirty pounds in weight, but three weeks after I had made the discovery in regard to the moon I had nearly gained it back and felt physically as fit as ever. And I was also fit mentally except for certain lurking fears which I stowed away in the back of my mind with a question mark after them.

The Search for Understanding

Very naturally I became interested during the days that followed in the attempt to find out just what had happened to me. I began by observing my fellow patients. I soon learned that there was a group of them that once each week took certain treatments. It seemed that they had a disease called "general paresis." There was one young man who had something the nurse called "post-encephalitis." She explained that this also had an organic basis. Then there were several old men on the ward, some of whom had hardening of the arteries in the brain. But aside from these my fellow patients seemed well enough physically. And some I met who had been inmates of the hospital for twenty-five, thirty, and even forty years, all the time apparently in good physical health. But they were on the whole a rather discouraged lot of men. I arrived at the conclusion that what had happened to me had happened also to them. Their inner world had come crashing down. They had perhaps been thinking intently on something until they had put themselves into an abnormal condition. I came also to the conclusion that the particular thing most of them had been concerned about was of the same general nature as that which caused some people to "hit the sawdust trail" at the meetings of evangelists like Billy Sunday. It came over me like a flash that if inner conflicts like that which Paul describes in the famous passage in the seventh chapter of Romans can have happy solutions, as the church has always believed, there must also be unhappy solutions which thus far the church has ignored. It came to me that what I was being faced with in the hospital was the unhappy solutions. Most of the patients whom I saw around me would then be in the hospital because of spiritual or religious difficulties.

Of course, I spent much time puzzling about my own case. I tried to get a chance to talk with the doctor about it. In this I met with little success. That particular hospital took the organicist point of view. The doctors did not believe in talking with patients about their symptoms, which they assumed to be rooted in some as yet undiscovered organic difficulty. The longest time I ever got was fifteen minutes during which the very charming young doctor pointed out that one must not hold the reins too tight in dealing with the sex instinct. Nature, he said, must have its way. It was very clear that he had neither understanding nor interest in the religious aspects of my problem.

A Second Disturbance

I was very happy to find that there were religious services on Sunday afternoons. But I soon discovered that the ministers from the neighboring village who conducted those services might know something about religion, but they certainly knew nothing about our problems. They did no visiting on the wards—which may not have been entirely their fault, as they probably received little encouragement to do so. All they did was to conduct a formal service on Sunday afternoons, and for lack of anything better they usually gave us the same sermons they had given their own congregations in the morning. There was one kindly old minister who gave us a series of sermons on missions—missions in China, missions in Africa, missions in Japan. Another preached on the text, "If thine eye offend thee, pluck it out." I was afraid that one or two of my fellow patients might be inclined to take that injunction literally.

For four and a half months I gave most of my attention to the attempt to understand my experience and also to convince my friends that I was as well as I had ever been. But the harder I tried the less they believed it. The result was to increase my own fears and my own sense of helplessness. There followed then another period of disturbance quite as severe as the first and ten weeks in duration instead of three. This also began suddenly and ended abruptly. On coming out of it, I changed my tactics and said nothing about release. Instead I looked around for something to do. I was struck by the number of patients in my ward who spent most of the day sitting still, looking off into the distance, and thinking apparently very gloomy thoughts. I suggested some games in which it might be possible to interest them. I ventured to suggest and write out a program for a play festival on the "Glorious Fourth" which was then about three weeks in the offing. I also looked around for a regular job and suggested several things I should enjoy doing, among them wood-working and photography. It so happened that they wanted someone to do photographic work, so they gave me the job. The doctors were really kind and responsive, and I [had found] something to do that I could enjoy. And I had an opportunity to study the hospital inside and out.

Exploring Some Little-known Territory

The question of what to do with myself after I left the hospital was, of course, a knotty problem. I myself had a very definite idea of what I wanted to do. I had not been three weeks out of the psychopathic ward before I was clear on that. The new-formed purpose was expressed as follows in a letter of February 14, 1921:

> This catastrophe has of course destroyed my hopes and my plans. I came back east in July with the intention of taking a pastorate. From that, I take it, I am now turned aside. My present purpose is to take as my problem the one with which I am now confronted, the service of these unfortunates with whom I am surrounded. I feel that many forms of insanity are religious rather than medical problems and that they cannot be successfully treated until they are so recognized. The problem seems to me one of great importance not only because of the large number who are now suffering from mental ailments but also because of its religious and psychological and philosophical aspects. I am very sure that if I can make to it any contribution whatsoever it will be worth the cost.

There were of course many difficulties to be overcome. The doctors did not favor it. My friends had to be convinced, and that was no easy task. Some even thought it was my duty to remain in the hospital as a patient for the rest of my life. Others assumed that something in the nature of simple manual work was all that would now be open to me. The following letter, written on August 14, 1921, will give an idea of the situation with which I was confronted at that time:

I am quite cheered by the fact that my cherished plan for the coming year meets with your approval...

I had a most welcome visit the other day from my old friend P. who has now an important church in M–. P. brought with him some good advice which he hatched out coming down on the train. He thought that some work which would keep me right down to concrete things would be the best way to regain or retain my sanity! I said to him: "Hang the sanity! You can't ever make life worth living if all you're doing is to try to keep from going insane. The object of life is to accomplish things worth while, to solve problems and to make contributions of some sort to this world in which we live. As I see it, a man ought to be willing to go through Hell if thereby he has even a chance of doing something which is really worth doing."

This reminds me of a little incident from my forestry days. One day during my sojourn in Washington in 1907, I walked into one of the rooms in the Forest Service Building and found there quite a little gathering. One of our old classmates at Yale had just returned from two years up in the north woods and was busily engaged in dishing out yarns about his experience in the wilds. One of the questions and its answer I'll never forget. "Say, Bill," asked one of the group, "have you ever been lost?" Bill straightened up, glared at him and replied with some heat: "Lost? Of course I've been. It's only the dubs who never go five miles from camp, who don't get lost sometimes." Now I do not mean to imply that those who do keep their poise and their sanity are able to do so only because they never venture off the beaten path. I only mean that for me to stick right to camp and wash dishes all the rest of my life for fear of getting lost again would take out of life all that makes it worth living for me. I am not afraid. I have always managed to find my way through; and I do think that in a very real sense I have been exploring some little-known territory which I should like now to have a chance to map out.

A New Start

In the end my plan went through. My mother gave her consent, conditioned upon the approval of Dr. Elwood Worcester. With him I had a series of helpful conferences which have left me with a high opinion of his insight and wisdom. In February, 1922, I enrolled for special work in the Andover Theological Seminary and in the graduate school of Harvard University. I was fortunate enough to be included in Dr. Macfie Campbell's seminar at the Boston Psychopathic Hospital. I found much help also in some work I took with Dr. Richard C. Cabot. The following year I continued my work with these men together also with Professor William McDougall. At the end of the second year I looked around for an opening. I wanted a chaplaincy in a hospital. I soon discovered that there were no such jobs. What is more, the hospital superintendents were not enthusiastic over the idea. I even tried to get a job as attendant with the stipulation that I might have access to the case records. But that stipulation barred me out.

The year 1923–24 was therefore spent at the Boston Psychopathic Hospital. I worked during the summer in the psychological department under Dr. F. L. Wells. In the fall I transferred to the social service department under Miss Susie Lyons. Here I found just the opportunity I was looking for to study cases from all angles. From the standpoint of one who had spent years in the making of sociological surveys, I made an interesting discovery. Before, as a mere inquirer, I had had to stop at the very points in which as a student of religion I was most interested. I did not dare in my survey work to inquire into the moral conditions or the inner experiences of people. I would not have gotten anywhere if I had. But now I was beginning with precisely those problems embodied in the cases of individuals in difficulty. And because my purpose was that of helping those individuals rather than that of mere inquiry the friends were ready to talk, and I received insights into the social situation otherwise impossible. In the course of this work at the Psychopathic Hospital I became interested in certain of the missions in the Negro section of Roxbury. Most of the last four months was spent in making a special study of their activities and influence.

The next year there came an opening at Worcester State Hospital. In Dr. William A. Bryan I found a superintendent who rejoices in making it possible for men with very different points of view to work together at the same problem. He did indeed have to put up with a good bit of chaffing from his fellow superintendents for such an unheard-of innovation as that of bringing a full-time chaplain into a mental hospital. This he met with the reply that he would be perfectly willing to bring in a horse doctor if he thought there was any chance of his being able to help the patients.

In the spring of 1925 through my friend, Professor Arthur E. Holt, who has done more than anyone else to help me in getting the new start, there came an opening as research associate in the Chicago Theological Seminary. I spent the fall quarter there. My first task was an experiment in a small mining community near La Salle. I sought to approach from my point of view the problems of some ordinary group of people such as the minister has to deal with. The time was too short to accomplish much in the way of results beyond the new insights into pastoral work and its possibilities which it gave me. The following fall quarter I had my first course at the seminary, and until the fall of 1930 I continued to spend three months of each year in Chicago.

Learning to Read Human Documents

In the summer of 1925 I was given the opportunity to try the experiment of bringing some theological students to the hospital. These students worked on the wards as ordinary attendants. My own experience had convinced me that there is no one upon whom the patient's welfare is more dependent than the nurse or attendant who is with him hour after hour during the day. I felt also that such work provided an unequaled opportunity to observe and understand the patient, and I was much concerned that theological students should have the opportunity to go to first-hand sources for their knowledge of human nature. I wanted them to learn to read human documents[2] as well as books, particularly those revealing documents which are opened up at the inner day of judgment. These students were allowed to have information in regard to the cases. They were permitted to attend the medical staff meetings, and for their benefit we held special conferences. There were four students the first summer. The plan was sufficiently successful to warrant another trial. Since then the number has increased rapidly. Whatever success my undertaking has had at Worcester and at Elgin as well has been due to the fine work of these students and the favorable impression they have left upon the hospital community.

During the last week in November, 1920, three weeks after I had made my little discovery in regard to the moon, I had written a long letter setting forth my explanation of what had happened to me. I had at this time done no reading whatever in psychiatric literature, and I did not even know that such a man as Freud existed. The conclusions were drawn entirely from my own experience and observations in the light of the work I had previously done in the psychology of religion. In the years that have followed the original hypothesis has been considerably modified and elaborated, but in its essence it remains unchanged as the working hypothesis which has determined all my subsequent work. The following paragraph from that letter may be taken as [my] thesis:

> As I look around me here and then try to analyze my own case, I see two main classes of insanity. In the one case there is some organic trouble, a defect in the brain tissue, some disorder in the nervous system, some disease of the blood. In the other there is no organic difficulty. The body is strong, and the brain in good working order. The difficulty is rather in the *disorganization of the patient's world.* Something has happened which has upset the foundations upon which his ordinary reasoning is based. Death or disappointment or sense of failure may have compelled a reconstruction of the patient's worldview from the bottom up, and the mind becomes dominated by the one idea which he has been trying to put in its proper place. That, I think, has been my trouble, and I think it is the trouble with many others also.

[My work] proposes to examine, in the light of my own experience, the experiences of other persons who have been forced off the beaten path of common sense and have traveled through the little-known wilderness of the inner life. I seek, so far as possible, to arrive at some comprehensive view of this inner world throughout its entire range, [examining] not only the unhappy solutions of inner conflicts but also the happy ones. This I do with the ever-deepening conviction that only as we study the one in the light of the other shall we be able to understand either one or to gain any insight into the laws of the spiritual life with which theology and psychiatry are equally concerned.

CHAPTER 2

Reclaiming the Living Human Document

CHARLES V. GERKIN[1] (1984)

Pastoral counselors are, more than anything else, listeners to and interpreters of stories. Persons seek out a pastoral counselor because they need someone to listen to their story. Most often the story is tangled; it involves themes, plot, and counterplots. The story itself is, of course, an interpretation of experience. To seek counseling usually means that the interpretation has become painful, the emotions evoked by the interpretation powerful and conflicted. The search is for a listener who is an expert at interpretation, one who can make sense out of what has threatened to become senseless, one whose interpretation of the story can reduce the pain and make the powerful feelings more manageable. To seek counseling sometimes means to seek an ally who will confirm one's own interpretation of experience as over against another interpretation insisted upon by another person whose interpretations carry weight with the seeker. For these and other complex reasons the one seeking counseling comes asking for a fresh interpretation of what has been experienced, a new "story" for his or her life.

The Stories of Counseling

The stories persons bring to the pastoral counselor are most often told in very ordinary language, the language of relationships to mother and father, sister and brother, children and neighbors, occasionally of relationship to God. The images and symbols that are used to tell the story come from the particular familial, cultural, and religious milieu of the person. The interpretive stories make use of (more accurately, are embedded in) a language world that the teller of the story takes for granted. That language world provides images, symbols, evaluative words, and word vessels for feelings that the storyteller uses to construct an interpretation of the raw stuff of experience. Indeed, for humans, it is impossible to separate experience from language.

If the pastoral counselor comes from the same language world as the teller of the story, he or she will likewise take these same meanings for granted. Anyone who has ever attempted to counsel with a person from a radically different cultural background than one's own will know quickly how dependent we are on taken-for-granted meanings and images.

But if the pastoral counselor is a good listener to stories, he or she will soon recognize that there are subtle differences in the way individuals within the same cultural milieu make use of language symbols and images. Private meanings that come from private interpretive experience permeate the telling of the story. So the pastoral counselor soon learns that he or she is living on the boundary, "looking over the fence," as it were, catching glimpses of the meanings, images, symbols, and mythic themes by which the other person is interpreting his or her experience. To listen to stories with an effort to understand means to listen first as a stranger who does not yet fully know the language, the nuanced meanings of the other as his or her story is being told. Needless to say, one of the first lessons of life on the boundary is that it is important to avoid, at all costs, the temptation to stereotype or take for granted.

The Pastoral Counselor as a Bearer of Stories

The pastoral counselor is not only a listener to stories; he or she is also a bearer of stories and a story. The pastoral counselor does not come empty-handed to the task of understanding the other's story and offering the possibility of a new interpretation. The pastoral counselor brings his or her own interpretation of life experience with its use of both commonly-held symbols, images, and themes from the cultural milieu of the counselor, and the private, nuanced meanings that have been shaped by the pastoral counselor's own life experience and its private interpretation. Not only that, the pastoral counselor brings to the task whatever he or she has collected from the images, concepts, theories, and methodologies of the disciplines that undergird pastoral counseling—theology, psychology, communications or systems theory, and the like. As a representative of the discipline of pastoral counseling, the counselor has stood and continues to stand on the boundaries that separate these language worlds, each of which offers its own interpretation of the human situation and condition. From all this experience of life on boundaries between language worlds, the pastoral counselor brings to his or her task a veritable storehouse of images, interpretive notions, and connections between meaning and the data of experience. The art of pastoral counseling is in large part the art of drawing upon that imagerial storehouse in the formation of a response to the heard story of the one seeking help. That process, when joined with the process of hearing accurately the story of the other as one having a language and integrity of its own, opens the way to a dialogical encounter from which a new and more hopeful interpretive story for the other's experience may emerge.

Pastoral counseling may thus be understood as a dialogical hermeneutical process involving the counselor and counselee in communication across the boundaries of language worlds. The dialogue takes place at many levels, some between the counselor and counselee, still more within the counselor as he or she sorts through the images, themes, and symbols of the various disciplines that have been appropriated in a search for those that seem apropos or make sense out of what is being heard. The interpretations that result must then be related to the one seeking help in ways that enable that person to restructure his or her own experience. A new set of images emerges that structures a new, less painful and more hopeful story. The old raw experience, now gathered into new image meaning vessels and integrated with new experience provided by the counseling relationship, takes on new meaning and a way ahead is opened.

The Story of My Pastoral Counseling Pilgrimage

Since the notion of pastoral counseling as hermeneutical dialogue may come as a strange and new one to the reader, it may be helpful for me to spell out in some detail the story of my pastoral counseling pilgrimage, which led toward the formulation and claiming of this image. Not all the details can be shared; that would be too lengthy and unnecessarily personal. The bare outline of the story will, however, be useful in giving the reader a sense of the process by which the concept came to have importance for me. Remember that, like all stories, this one involves and is itself an interpretation. My hope and expectation is that in sharing it I may make connection with the reader's story. It may in fact in certain ways be typical of the stories of members of my generation of pastoral counselors.

My father was a teller of stories. The stories he told were mostly of people he had known through his ministry as a circuit preacher beginning in the 1890s. He later served small town-and-country churches in the Midwest, moving frequently from place to place as the itinerant system to which he belonged required. His conversations with people, which as a small boy I often overheard, were much of the time made up of stories to which he listened and stories he told in response. I cannot rightly recall ever overhearing him engaging in a theological conversation with a member of his congregation, nor do I remember any such discussions with his fellow pastors, with whom he loved to converse at great length. But I remember stories, and most often stories with a point related to the follies and foibles of people, their good and bad morals, their successes and failures. His sermons were more overtly and directly theological, though they too were filled with anecdotes and moralistic stories. Thus I grew up hearing stories—stories about people.

The story about my ambivalent decision to follow my father into the ministry need not be told here except to note that it came late in college after earlier premedical studies that were academically relatively successful but personally dissatisfying. I remember a profound desire to work with people in relation to the real issues of living. That led me to an academic interest in psychology and sociology. My college academic work did not take me into religious studies at all, except for one very important directed study with a favorite professor who introduced me to William James and the other psychologists of religion of the late nineteenth and early twentieth centuries.

Seminary brought me into my first encounter with the serious study of theology, biblical studies, and church history. The content of the courses I found interesting, but, as with my earlier study of the hard sciences, somehow personally dissatisfying. Biblical studies, then preoccupied with the historical dating of materials and authentication of fragments, seemed removed from my vague, but definite, desire to be with people. Theological language seemed abstract and therefore unable to speak clearly to the problems of my own living as an adolescent becoming an adult and my beginning efforts at ministry. My psychological interests would not have found a home at the seminary (there was not yet a department of pastoral care!) except that I happened to take a course offered one term in the evening by Fred Keuther, then secretary of the Chicago group in the old Council for Clinical Training of Theological Students in the United States and Canada. Fred talked about people and their problems of living. He also talked about psychoanalysis and its new way of probing for the hidden causes of human problems. Keuther had been one of the first students of Anton Boisen, the founder of what was then called clinical pastoral training. Boisen came to one session of the class. I thought him a strange man with his twisted face, penetrating eyes, and thumping cane. But I was attracted to what he said about the study of "living human documents" and mental illness as a sickness of the soul analogous to fever in the body.

Boisen and the Study of the Living Human Document

Boisen is generally considered the founder of clinical pastoral education in America and thereby one of the progenitors of the twentieth-century pastoral counseling movement. His concern, however, was only secondarily with pastoral counseling as such. More basic was Boisen's concern that the objectifications of theological language not lose touch in the minds of pastors with the concrete data of human experience. His fear was that the language of theology was being learned by seminarians and pastors without that connection being made. Only the careful and systematic study of the lives of persons struggling with the issues of the spiritual life in the concreteness of their relationships could, in Boisen's view, restore that connection. For Boisen, this meant the study of "living human documents."

By his assigning of priority to the study of concrete religious experience, Boisen discloses his ties to the psychology of religion tradition shaped in the late nineteenth and early twentieth centuries by William James, Edwin Starbuck, James Leuba, G. Stanley Hall, and others. The pragmatism of that tradition is evident in the primacy Boisen gives to the question as to how religious experience functions to give shape to the encounters of individuals with problems of living. Boisen was, however, concerned with more than simply the study of religious experience. His research interest was accompanied by a passionate concern for the welfare of troubled souls. Though I do not recall ever hearing him use the term "pastoral counseling," clearly the pastoral activity that has come to be called by that name was not only of concern to him, but had for him profound religious meaning. In his later years he was, in fact, highly critical of the involvement of his followers in psychoanalysis and secular psychotherapy. For Boisen the cure of souls had to do fundamentally with the raw stuff of religious experience.

Parenthetically, a word about my own reaction to Boisen's critique of psychotherapy at the time I first heard it is worth noting. To a young seminarian then experiencing the excitement of the newly discovered language of psychotherapy as both liberating from the stereotypical moralism of the Midwestern conventional piety on which I had been reared and concrete in its attention to the hidden dynamics of behavior, Boisen's criticism seemed narrow and confining. Viewed from the vantage point of later historical developments and my own self pilgrimage as a pastoral counselor, his perspective makes more sense.

Anton Boisen's image of the human person as a "document" to be read and interpreted in a manner analogous to the interpretation of a historical text has, up to the present, simply been taken as an admonition to begin with the experience of persons in the development of ministry theory. That certainly was central to Boisen's intention. Boisen, however, meant more than that. He meant that the depth experience of persons in the struggles of their mental and spiritual life demanded the same respect as do the historic texts from which the foundations of our Judeo-Christian faith tradition are drawn. Each individual living human document has an integrity of his or her own that calls for understanding and interpretation, not categorization and stereotyping. Just as the preacher should not look to proof texts to be twisted into the meaning sought for, so also the individual human text demanded a hearing on its own merit. Furthermore, Boisen was wary of most of the attempts current at the time of his work to "explain" or assign specific organic or developmental causation to the phenomena exhibited by the troubled souls he studied. Rather he thought of them as persons whose inner world had become disorganized so that that world had lost its foundations. Boisen therefore wanted to take the language and the gestures of the troubled person with utmost seriousness as language and gesture that could be interpreted, understood, and given response as one would the language of a textual document. To the living human document he assigned the same authority and right to speak on its own terms as hermeneutical scholarship had learned to assign to the historical text, be that a New Testament text or any other written record of human experience left by a writer of another time and place. Boisen claimed that right for his own experience and his interpretation of it. The troubled person's own reporting of his or her inner world of experience was to be respected and heard as having an authenticity and right of its own, no matter how peculiar its language. What was needed was an interpreter and guide.

Pastoral Counseling as a Hermeneutical Task

As one who claims Anton Boisen as a spiritual ancestor, I have found myself in recent years more and more drawn to and intrigued by this central organizing image of Boisen's work as opening a possible avenue of reflection whereby some of the problems of the enterprise he helped spawn may today be considered. Does the image of the person who is the object of our pastoral care and counseling as a living human document open to us a possible way of approaching the task of restoring pastoral counseling to a sense of its mission and purpose defined theologically? Can that image and its implications help us rebuild the connections between what we as pastoral counselors do and say with persons in our ministering work and the language of the historic texts that have shaped our theological heritage?

It is common knowledge that pastoral counseling, as it has emerged in the late twentieth century, has built most of its operationally primary modes of reflection upon its work out of the images and concepts, the presuppositions and ontological assumptions of the psychological and behavioral sciences. So much has this been the case that the danger exists that the life-giving connection between historic Christian faith and pastoral counseling practice could be broken. Insofar as that becomes the case, the perceptual and conceptual world, the world of meaning in which the pastoral counselor does his or her work, becomes a world no longer inhabited by the representations of faith and salvation, sin and redemption. Rather one finds oneself looking for and seeing a world peopled by persons afflicted with neurotic symptoms, identity conflicts, and compensatory behavior—all good and useful word images, to be sure, but images largely sterilized of religious meaning.

Language constructs world. To have a world, to live in a world, means, for humans, to inhabit a time and place in which a certain language is connected with experience to give meaning to that experience. More than anything else, the capacity to make meaning marks the human as human. Whenever any event occurs in our lives, be that so small an event as stubbing one's toe on a crack in the sidewalk, or so "large" and significant an event as entering into a marriage or contracting a dread disease, it does not become an experience to us until language is attached to the event and it is given meaning. As a matter of fact, because we live in worlds constructed by language, the connection of language and event is an automatic process. Reflection may create new meanings, but the immediate connection of words to experience happens quite unselfconsciously.

To speak of a person as a living human document is to acknowledge this connection between life and language. It is to acknowledge that to understand what Boisen calls the inner world is dependent upon understanding the language by which that inner world of experience is connected to external events. To understand the inner world of another is therefore a task of interpretation—interpretation of a world of experience that is itself an interpretation of the myriad events and relationships that make up a life. Said another way, the task of understanding another in the depth of that other's inner world is a hermeneutical task. It is therefore subject to all the problems and possibilities that the interpretation of an ancient document, such as a New Testament Gospel or Epistle, involves. The difference is that this document is living and continues to disclose itself in new language and behavior that expresses its inner world.

Intersubjective Balance and Respect

The pastoral counselor as interpreter, like the reader of the New Testament, does not come empty-handed. He or she comes bearing a history and a language world. More accurately, he or she comes embedded in a personal and social history and immersed in one or more language worlds from which the images, symbols, and meanings are drawn with which to make an interpretation.

If one is to hear truly what the other person has to say in its own integrity, there must be a breaking through of the barrier that stands between the language world of the hearer and that of the speaker. Stated more fundamentally, to "know" another means to enter that person's world in such a way that a merging of experienced reality can take place. The ancient Old Testament image that associates knowing with intercourse between the sexes expresses the truth that an intimate merger or interpretation must take place if one is to truly know another. Theologically speaking, we encounter here the primordial sense of incarnation. To know another in the incarnational sense is to enter that other's world and to have the other enter our world. Hermeneutically speaking, this is possible only because of and to the extent that we are able to enter the other's language world, the world of the other's meanings. In the same way, if we are to be known by the other person, the other must in some degree enter our world, the language of meaning which we bring to the encounter. It is right at this point that the language world out of which the pastoral counselor shapes his or her perceptions and response to the other person becomes crucial. If that be a language world inhabited by the images of theology and faith, the counselee will be invited into a world shaped by those images. If that be, on the other hand, a language world shaped by the images of secularity, it is into that world that the counselor invites the one seeking help.

Traditionally in pastoral counseling theory this process has been spoken about in the language of empathy, rapport, and acceptance. To empathize with another is to put oneself in the other's place, to experience the actuality of life as the other experiences it. Anyone who has attempted to relate to another, particularly another who is troubled about his or her life experience, knows how difficult that is to do. Despite all our efforts, our own situation as an "other" to the one to whom we are relating enters into who we are in that situation.

Our own perceptual and interpretive capacities come quickly, automatically, into play. The question must indeed be asked as to whether it is possible for us in the fullest sense to abandon our own perceptual and interpretive world in order to empathize with, become one with, the world of another.

The studies that have been done concerning therapeutic outcome all tend to locate the factors that make for change in the therapeutic relationship. But precisely what is it in the therapeutic relationship that effects change? It is the richness, the delicate balance and respect experienced intersubjectively with both counselee and counselor open and vulnerable to the intrusion of the new that some fresh possibility for a changed way of being a person in relation to another and therefore to all others may be opened. The barest outline of an image of merging horizons of two or more persons, each a living human document now opened to interpretation and question by the other, begins to take form as the image of the context in which change is possible.

Making Sense of One's World

Boisen's major project [was] that of understanding the nature of suffering of the mentally ill and, most particularly, his own suffering. In [a] letter from the introduction to *The Exploration of the Inner World*, Boisen connects events in the troubled person's life with ideas concerning the nature of things.

> Something had happened which has upset the foundations upon which his ordinary reasoning is based. Death or disappointment or sense of failure may have compelled a reconstruction of the patient's worldview from the bottom up, and the mind becomes dominated by the one idea which he is trying to put in its proper place. That, I think, has been my trouble, and I think that is the trouble with many others also.[2]

Boisen places the problem of the troubled person at the point of linkage of events of experience and ideas concerning their meaning. One might say that he locates the problem at a point of blockage or distortion in the process of interpretation of what has occurred in the life of the person.

Here Boisen points to the existential problem and dilemma of life for the human as meaning maker. On the one hand, there is the flow of hard reality in the occurrence of events. From the time we are born we are affected by a whole range of aspects of reality and events over which we individually have little or no control. As finite creatures we are simply subject to these realities and events. They make up what Paul Tillich refers to as our destiny. There is something hard, unyielding, and forceful about that givenness of the human situation—a hard, unyielding force that takes multifarious shapes and forms in the uniqueness of the human situation for any individual.

In the midst of this givenness of our individual situation, each of us must, if we are to live with any integrity at all, somehow on the other hand retain a sense of our own agency, our own ability to do and be someone with power to act and choose. It is at this point that the human capacity to make meaning comes into play. We must exercise our need and capacity to make meaningful interpretations of who we are, what the world is, and what, given our situation, is most meaningful—what Tillich calls our ultimate concern.

When I think of the extent of this human need and capacity to make meaning out of any situation of givens, I always think of the child-beater's child. On more than one occasion I have had the painful opportunity to help such a young person try to make sense out of what has happened to him or her. Again and again I have seen the battered child struggle with the possibility, even certainty, that he or she must have deserved the beating, else it would not have happened. Such is the human insistence on retaining some sense of agency, of participation in whatever hard or unyielding force may be affecting our lives.

So the events and forces in our lives must be linked through language to meaning. Behind that human desire and insistence lies the threat of chaos and absurdity, the ultimate threat to our sense of being human agents. For Boisen, the problem of the deeply troubled person was just at this point. Ideas and meanings could not be fitted together with experience. A "reconstruction from the bottom up" must be undertaken.

The residues and sedimentations from a life of experience with both the givens of the person's existential situation and the givens formed by unconscious remnants of early and later childhood experience shape a certain forceful expectation that provides a certain "hard" contour to the horizon [of meaning] possible for that person. But the language of image, metaphor, and myth or narrative provides a softer, more malleable and permeable conscious and preconscious formulation of the person's horizon of understanding of that situation. The two levels of language are connected in complex ways, and it is the task of the helping person to attend to both levels of language. It is important to keep in mind that, for Freud, access to the deeper layers of unconscious experience with its force dynamics was only possible through what he termed its "representations."

The language of the living human document we bring to any human encounter, be that an encounter with the texts that form the basis of our religious and cultural tradition or with other human beings, is a two-sided language. It is the language of the deep forces that have shaped our lives and given them contour and existential specificity. And it is also the language of our meaningful interpretation of our experience and its underlying forces. This latter language draws upon and makes use of the images and symbols, the myths and metaphors that have been made available to us by the sociocultural milieu from which we come. But it also has about it a certain twist and movement, a disposition, that marks it as uniquely and privately our own.

Boisen was fundamentally correct in his placing of the crux of human spiritual suffering at the point of the connection between experience and idea, between the occurrence of events and a language of meaning for those events.

It is when that connection becomes blocked, distorted, or made impossible that the troubled person must seek a helper, an interpreter who may offer a new possibility of meaning.

Construed in this fashion, the role of the pastoral counselor as interpreter and guide in the reconstruction of a structure and language of meaning on the part of the troubled person or persons takes on a profoundly religious, if not theological, cast. At the center of any structure of meaning lie the questions of faith and ultimate purpose. The age-old function of religion has been that of binding together all of life into some unitary vision that is finally meaningful. It is the authority and role of the principal representative of that function that the pastoral counselor brings to the task of interpretive guidance.

CHAPTER 3

The Living Human Web

BONNIE J. MILLER-MCLEMORE[1] (1996)

Most pastoral theologians and educators would still assert that empathic listening skills and sensitive individual counsel are prerequisites for ministry. But significant changes are afoot: the focus on individual counseling and eductive listening has come under increasing criticism from a variety of angles; the prevalence of counseling courses [in seminaries] has waned; "pastoral theology" has replaced "pastoral psychology" as the overarching theme; and the notion of care has returned to center stage, with counseling regarded as an important but not comprehensive specialty. Ultimately, almost everyone acknowledges the limits of the therapeutic paradigm and talks about sharpening our understanding not just of theological paradigms but of the social context as well, through the study of sociology, ethics, culture, and public policy.

The focus on care narrowly defined as counseling has shifted to a focus on care understood as part of a wide cultural, social, and religious context. As pastoral theology curriculum in seminaries broadens, as the clinical identity of pastoral counseling solidifies, and as American health care reforms evolve, those in pastoral counseling training centers will have to address multiple questions about their appropriate ministerial, educational, and institutional place in relation to the congregation, the academy, and society. To be taken seriously by other mental health disciplines as well as by insurance companies and governmental structures, pastoral psychotherapy must develop its own evaluative criteria. To be taken seriously by churches and seminaries, it will have to affirm its connections and contributions to ministry and theological discourse. And to be taken seriously by people of color and by white women, it will have to include, even if only to a limited extent, social analysis of oppression, alienation, exploitation, diversity, and justice in its clinical assessment of individual pathology.

Feminism and the Context of Care

This final demand to attend to the wider cultural context, partially fostered by liberation perspectives, may be the most critical. At this point, let me delineate the ways in which a feminist perspective radically reorients perception and understanding. Black feminist bell hooks argues, and I agree, [that] feminists have frequently been careless in failing to clarify agreed-upon definitions of feminism. Without them—with an "anything goes" attitude that feminism can mean anything anyone wants—we lack a solid foundation on which to construct theory and engage in meaningful praxis. Beneath its many current forms and definitions, some of which are too focused on rights, personal autonomy, and social equality, feminism is, in a word, a radical political movement. Hooks writes,

> Feminism is a struggle to end sexist oppression. Its aim is not to benefit solely any specific group of women, any particular race or class of women. It does not privilege women over men. It has the power to transform in a meaningful way all our lives.[2]

To call feminism simply a movement to make men and women equal reduces and even confuses its full intent, especially when sexual equality in the midst of difference remains an elusive ideal and discounts the weight of other inequities. Feminism reclaims the lost and denigrated voices of women and strives to eradicate the underlying cultural biases, including imperialism, economic expansion, and others, that sustain sexism and other group oppression. A feminist perspective demands an analysis of structures and ideologies that rank people as inferior or superior according to various traits of human nature, whether gender, sexual orientation, color, age, physical ability, and so forth. Hence, to think about pastoral theology and care from this vantage point requires prophetic, transformative challenge to systems of power, authority, and domination that continue to violate, terrorize, and systematically destroy individuals and communities.

This emphasis on confronting systems of domination has been instrumental in creating the shift in pastoral theology from care narrowly defined as counseling to care understood as part of a wide cultural, social, and religious context. Many in pastoral theology have traditionally harkened back to Anton Boisen's powerful foundational metaphor for the existential subject of pastoral theology—"*the study of living human documents rather than books.*"[3] Today, the "living human *web*" suggests itself as a better term for the appropriate subject of investigation, interpretation, and transformation.

The Living Human Web

When I first pictured the "living human *web*" as a central theme of pastoral theology, I was thinking more of the three-dimensional net that a process-theology-oriented college professor etched on the flat classroom blackboard than the musty, sticky, annoying webs spun by insidious and numerous spiders in our old and not so clean house. Within the limits of chalk, blackboard, and his own imagination, John Spencer sought to illustrate the dense, multitudinous, contiguous nature of reality as he saw it over against the static interpretations of reality of much of Western philosophy and religion. As I tried to understand why I believed what I believed and to formulate fresh theological constructions of my own, this raw depiction made a great deal of sense to me. It still does.

While I did not consciously or intentionally make the connection, my use of the term "web" also results in part from feminist discourse. The most specific example that comes to mind is a book by Catherine Keller, *From a Broken Web: Separatism, Sexism, and Self*,[4] a theologian also significantly influenced by process theology from the work of John Cobb. *From a Broken Web* refutes thousands of years of misogyny embedded in Western myths, philosophy, religion, and psychology. Her thesis is that sexism and separatism—the view of the self as essentially separate from others—are intricately interlinked in this history. By sheer force of iconoclasm—juxtaposing hated images of women and images of monsters, serpents, spiders, dragons, Medusa, Tiamat, Tehom or the "deep" in Genesis (which Keller sees as the Hebrew equivalent to Tiamat), the "oceanic" in Freud—Keller reveals how repulsive, how frightening, the powers of interconnection and the wisdom of women have been made to appear. Distorted fears of enmeshment, entanglement, and loss surround the relationality represented by the female and the mother in Western history. The resulting animosity and fury toward women, monsters, serpents, spiders, dragons, Medusa, Tiamat, Tehom, and the "oceanic" has entailed the repression and banishment of connection itself.

By contrast, Keller asserts, the "self-structure of separation is a patriarchal artifice"; the "web is not originally a trap."[5] Using revised creation myths, object relations theory, process metaphysics, and feminist theology, she spins the new meanings of the connectivity of selfhood, religion, and all life. While aware of the limits of any one metaphor in a metaphysics of relationality, the image of the web "claims the status of an all-embracing image, a metaphor of metaphors, not out of any imperialism, but because, as a metaphor of interconnection itself, the web can link lightly in its nodes an open multiplicity of images."[6] What she calls "arachnean religion" involves the spider's genius of repairing the web that the separative self has broken, "spinning oneness out of many and weaving the one back into the many."[7]

Obviously, Keller's work is dense, highly technical, and not without its flaws; for my purposes, the important point is this: an alternative mythos resurrects the interconnectivity of selfhood. This mythos and the theology connected to it have funded a new approach in pastoral theology. More specifically, this means, for example, that public policy issues that determine the health of the human web are as important as issues of individual emotional well-being. Psychology serves a less exclusive, although still important, role, while other social sciences such as economics or political science become powerful tools of interpretation. In a word, never again will a clinical moment, whether of caring for a woman recovering from hysterectomy or attending to a woman's spiritual life, be understood on intrapsychic grounds alone. These moments are always and necessarily situated within the interlocking, continually evolving threads of which reality is woven, and they can be understood in no other way. Psychology alone cannot understand this web.

Retaining Psychological Analysis

The move away from psychology is not without its drawbacks. Maxine Glaz has provocatively observed that the newly critical perception of psychology in pastoral theology may be part of an "impetus to avoid issues of gender." Just when women in pastoral theology begin to find feminist psychology an incisive tool for reconstructing pastoral care and theology, the "people of a dominant perspective emphasize a new theme or status symbol."[8] Glaz is right: we have some cause for concern about this change as a covert attempt to disempower the new participants in the pastoral theology discussion.

Women in pastoral theology would do well to retain the power of psychological analysis. First, to move beyond psychology too quickly is to underestimate the power of men like Freud and psychological definitions of human nature and fulfillment as culture- and consciousness-shaping forces. Moreover, new resources, such as Jessica Benjamin's *Bonds of Love* or Luise Eichenbaum and Susie Orbach's *Understanding Women*–to name just a few– challenge conventional understandings of female desire in Freud and others. They provide fresh insight into intrapsychic need and interpersonal dynamics. Feminist psychology and therapy, joined by psychologies attuned to different ethnic groups, will continue to be vital tools. Indeed, women in pastoral theology need to correct the subtle biases of some theologians who dismiss too rashly all of modern psychology as individualistic and inept in social analysis. In truth, the use of recent psychology by pastoral theologians and by feminist theologians, as Keller herself reveals, will continue to reshape fundamentally the ways in which we think about selfhood, the needs of children, human development, religious behavior, and other phenomena. If those in theology understand mutuality better than they used to, feminist psychology is at least partially responsible.

Glaz's criticism points to the difficulty of bringing diverse voices into play. Criticism of the individualistic focus of pastoral care has come in part from feminist theology and black theology. Few books in pastoral theology have addressed cultural issues of gender, race, and class. Even the otherwise thorough, well-documented history of pastoral care by E. Brooks Holifield sees women, slaves, and "others" primarily as the objects of care, rarely as caregivers themselves, and never as the source of new ideas.[9] Some, like [Howard] Clinebell, have tried to revise their basic texts to add new sections on "transcultural" perspectives.[10] David Augsburger's *Pastoral Counseling Across Cultures*[11] has received wide acclamation.

However, such books represent—as the authors acknowledge—dominant perspectives. Augsburger's definition of an otherwise helpful idea, "interpathy," is a good illustration of the problem. He uses the term to encourage entering into a "second culture" with a respect for that culture "as equally as valid as one's own."[12] Many feminists and people of color have pointed out that the subordinates in a society already intimately know the foreign realities of at least two worlds, that of their own and that of the dominant group or groups. And they have often given the second culture undue credibility and deference. Augsburger's interpathy is absolutely necessary, but it is a trait more relevant for the dominant culture than for those in oppressed groups. They have been "embracing of what is truly other" for a long time.

Affirming the Second Culture

By contrast, the first step of those in the "second culture" is to affirm their own realities as worthy of equal respect. For many women, well trained in sensitivity to the needs of others and insensitive to their own suppressed desires, it is less a matter of bracketing and transcending one's own beliefs in order to feel as the other feels than of identifying for themselves what they feel and want at all. Significantly, even more than Caucasian women, African-American women, Asian women, and others must arbitrate between multiple, often hostile, cultures. For women, then, interpathy into the foreign beliefs of another culture necessarily implies envisioning distorted thoughts and feelings of repulsion, violence, fear, hatred—a problem Augsburger fails to note in his development of the concept (racism and sexism are conspicuous in their absence in the book's index).

With a few significant exceptions, women in pastoral ministry have come up through the ranks of higher education approximately one generation behind women in religion and theology such as Rosemary Radford Ruether and Elisabeth Schüssler Fiorenza. A few women, such as Peggy Way and Sue Cardwell, have significantly impacted the field, although this occurred less through publications than through their compelling personal styles of teaching, speaking, and counseling. One possible reason for the lag in the more active participation by women is the proximity of pastoral theology to the church and the conservative nature of congregational life. Despite the pastoral nature of much feminist theology and careful treatments of specific issues in pastoral care such as abuse or spirituality, there was no book by a single author on pastoral theology from a woman's or a feminist perspective until quite recently. With Valerie DeMarinis's *Critical Caring: A Feminist Model for Pastoral Psychology*,[13] the advent of a new era has commenced. Pivotal articles by Christie Neuger[14] and Carrie Doehring[15] suggest that further developments are only a matter of time.

These problems are partly less severe for black theology because of contributions from scholars with longer tenure in the academy such as Archie Smith[16] and Edward Wimberly.[17] Still, wider recognition and reliance upon their work has been slow in coming. And until the recent publication of *WomanistCare*,[18] the participation of African-American women has been almost entirely missing from the discussion. Furthermore, *WomanistCare* is not explicitly presented as a book in pastoral theology. Meanwhile, more general books in theology such as Emilie Townes's *A Troubling in My Soul*[19] are helpful resources and hopeful signs on the horizon for understanding care from a womanist perspective.

The Contributions of Women's Voices

What will it mean for the practice of pastoral care to bring new voices into play? *Women in Travail and Transition: A New Pastoral Care* offers an initial indication. Edited by Maxine Glaz and Jeanne Stevenson Moessner, the book includes the work of five authors in ministerial settings and four in the academy. It aims to nurture intellectual acuity in the midst of pastoral practice. Chapters on new pastoral understandings of women and new pastoral paradigms are the brackets for other chapters on work, family, and alternative family forms, women's body, sexual abuse, battered women and women's depression. Almost every man who has read this text in my courses testifies that it powerfully illumines women's lives. Women students want to send multiple copies to their ministerial colleagues, men and women alike. These students have heard a "cry," as one student expressed it, that they had never heard or understood before; they begin to hear in a different way.

Emma Justes states that if clergy "are unable to travel the route of hearing women's anger, of exploring with women the painful depths of experiences of incest and rape, or enabling women to break free from cultural stereotypes that define their existence," they should not be doing pastoral counseling with women.[20] This claim suggests limits to empathy that people in Carl Rogers's time never suspected. When those involved in pastoral care do not know how to recognize the realities of violence toward women, they foster further damage and violence. Particularly in situations of sexual abuse, for example, the problem in pastoral response is not too little empathy but too much indiscriminate empathy by an uninformed pastoral caregiver that surfaces long-repressed feelings that overwhelm rather than help the person in need.[21] All pastoral caregivers must sharpen their sensitivity to the stress that women experience as wage earners and homemakers,[22] the economic devaluation of women in the workplace and women's poverty,[23] health issues of concern to women, and the implications of female images of God for self-esteem.[24]

But these kinds of understandings are merely a beginning. The authors of *Women in Travail and Transition*, all white professional women in mainline faiths, invite "companion volumes written by nonwhite, ethnic, non-middle-class women within Western culture and by other women elsewhere throughout the world."[25] No Hispanic, Asian, African, or American Indian pastoral care and theology has been published, although Robert Wicks and Barry Estadt have recently edited a "brief volume" of the "*experience* and *impressions*" of pastoral counselors involved in ministry in ten different countries.[26] Few texts deal with the pastoral agenda for men that might include issues such as the fear, anger, and grief over role changes and vocational confusion or tensions between work and family. Protestant pastoral theology and related clinical associations have all but ignored rich traditions and histories of pastoral theology and spiritual direction in Roman Catholic, Jewish, evangelical, and other circles.

The New World of the Web

We cannot predict what difference other stories and traditions will make to general formulations of the field or in pastoral practice. When we admit that knowledge is seldom universal or uniform, and truth is contextual and tentative, we discover a host of methodological, pedagogical, and practical problems. If the field of pastoral theology can no longer claim unity in thought and mind, what commonalities of approach define the field as distinct and relevant? In many ways, teaching and ministry become harder, professors and clergy more vulnerable. We find that we do not yet have the right texts to assign in our classes or the right answers in the pastoral office. Pastoral theology's trademark of empathy for the living human document is confounded by the limitations of empathy in the midst of the living human web. Sometimes a person must admit an inability to understand fully the lived reality of the oppressions suffered by another. There may be boundaries beyond which empathy itself cannot go.

We do know that we can no longer ignore an author's or a parishioner's identity and cultural location. A "living human web" cannot simply be "read" and interpreted like a "document." Those within the web who have not yet spoken must speak for themselves. Gender, feminist, and black studies all verify the knowledge of the underprivileged, the outcast, the underclass, and the silenced. If knowledge depends upon power, then power must be given to the silenced. In part, the pastoral theology movement began with this claim: Boisen, having suffered an emotional breakdown and finding himself inside a mental hospital, refused the marginalized, ostracized status of the mentally ill patient. He claimed the importance of what he learned about health, spirituality, and theology as learning that could occur from nowhere else than inside the experience of illness and suffering. This lesson—that we must hear the voices of the marginalized from within their own contexts—is one that pastoral theologians have known all along, even when Boisen claimed the validity of his own mental breakdown.[27]

CHAPTER 4

The Solicitous Shepherd

Seward Hiltner[1] (1959)

As a focal concept concerning ways of bringing the gospel to the particular needs of men in their problems and their sin, I have chosen to return to the ancient metaphor of shepherding. When this function is being performed, he who performs it is a Christian Shepherd.

The terms that have been more common in the modern world–pastoral care, pastoral work, and pastoral counseling–are still of great importance, but the context from which they are drawn is a bit different from that of shepherding. I think of shepherding as a perspective. Any Christian shepherd, to some extent, has the shepherding perspective at all times. He is alert to the possible presence of particular need whenever or wherever it may emerge, but this will be his main or dominant way of viewing a situation only under some circumstances, not under all. Thus shepherding is always present as a readiness to emerge when called for by particular need, but it becomes the dominant factor in the situation only under particular circumstances.

Our whole inquiry is about Christian shepherding as one of the modes of outreach of the gospel to men in need. To be Christian, we must move from some such understanding of the faith as has already been suggested. To be relevant, we must study carefully and afresh the sense in which the roots and bases of shepherding are contained in the gospel itself. We need also to utilize any knowledge and wisdom we can get from any source–to the extent that it helps to clarify the meaning of the gospel, the nature of man's need, or the processes by which the riches of the gospel may be brought into revitalizing contact with that need.

The Testimony of Oil, Wine, Bandages, and an Inn

As we have understood it, shepherding from the biblical period to our day is unique to Christianity. Other high religions have spiritual directors of one kind or another who deal with people as individuals or in small groups. But dealing with people in terms of shepherding, the essence of which looks toward healing in a holistic sense, is unique to Christianity and Judaism, and even in Judaism its development since biblical days has been quite different from that in Christianity.

The essential meaning and significance of shepherding, as it is unique in Christianity, is seen pre-eminently in the familiar story of the good Samaritan. We recall that Jesus used this story in reply to the lawyer's question, "Who is my neighbor?"

> "A man was going down from Jerusalem to Jericho, and he fell among robbers, who stripped him and beat him, and departed, leaving him half dead. Now by chance a priest was going down that road; and when he saw him he passed by on the other side. So likewise a Levite, when he came to the place and saw him, passed by on the other side. But a Samaritan, as he journeyed, came to where he was; and when he saw him, he had compassion, and went to him and bound up his wounds, pouring on oil and wine; then he set him on his own beast and brought him to an inn, and took care of him. And the next day he took out two denarii and gave them to the innkeeper, saying, "Take care of him; and whatever more you spend, I will repay you when I come back." (Lk. 10:30–35, RSV).

Concluding his story Jesus asked the lawyer which of the three proved himself to be a neighbor. Even the lawyer had to reply, "The one who showed mercy on him."

This is, of course, a story with moral implications. One cannot profess one thing and do another. Every man is our neighbor. Good works are owed to every man in need. But the story says more than that. It implies that anything standing in the way of the best possible meeting of the need for healing is an offense against God. The priest and the Levite may well have been on their way to church. Nevertheless, Jesus' implied condemnation of them would not be lessened by any such possibilities. They were present. The testimony called for was healing. But they passed by on the other side. The unlikely Samaritan, on the other hand, despite the enmity between his people and the Jews, performed a healing service, as intelligently as possible under the circumstances. He manifested mercy and compassion in his attitude, and intelligence in his use of means.

Anything that should stand in the way of rendering the needed shepherding would be an offense against God, the story implies. Thus any gospel that is to be regarded as relevant to this situation must begin with shepherding. As we reflect on this, it becomes clear that we cannot grasp the deeper meaning of this parable without a consideration of timing. Perhaps the man going from Jerusalem to Jericho had made the trip a hundred times without incident. If the Samaritan had fallen in step with him on one of those occasions, he might well have presented verbal testimony to his faith. No oil or wine or bandages would have been required. But this time nothing else would do. What was needed was oil, wine, bandages, and an inn. This was the sole relevant testimony for this occasion. Whatever might be true in other places and at other times, the one way in which proper testimony might be given in this place at this time was by shepherding.

Shepherding as Autonomous

We may note further that the shepherding provided by the Samaritan on this occasion of need is not regarded in the parable as ancillary to something else. There is no suggestion that he got through this as an emergency in order that he might then move on to another order of function of more importance because it was "normal" in character. At this time, in the face of this need, shepherding was the thing. To put it in even sharper fashion, shepherding here was, for the time being, autonomous, requiring no justification from anything else.

The attitude revealed here, we are at once reminded, is like that of the shepherd devoting his energy and attention, at a particular time and place, to the one sheep that was lost, and temporarily diverting it from the ninety and nine who were not (Lk. 15:3–7; Mt. 18:12–13). When the timing and need are of this kind, no other justification is needed. There is no counting of statistics. There is no plea of emergency against normalcy. Instead, there is attention according to need.

To the best of my historical knowledge, the basic attitude revealed in these stories is unique to Christianity when the full dimensions are considered. Other religions, of course, recommend good works arising out of faith. But only in Christianity is the effort to shepherd and to heal, when needed, regarded as *itself* the one indispensable way of communicating the gospel on those occasions.

A Compound of Gospel and Need

To put the matter in more comprehensive terms, the way in which one testifies to the gospel cannot be determined in advance by the preferences of the testifier. Testimony must be given according to the need and condition, on any particular occasion.

One cannot say, "I have a single secure way of testifying to my faith on all occasions and do not have to take into account the relativities of human need." Instead, testimony to Christian faith is always a compound of the eternal gospel and specific need. Any attempt to wrap the gospel in a cellophane package, as if it could be given in the same way on all occasions, betrays what is required. The mode of testimony should be according to the need in the situation.

The great commission of Jesus to his apostles was "to preach and to heal," or "to preach and have authority to cast out demons" (Mk. 3:14–15, RSV).

Both aspects of the commission are ways of presenting the gospel to the needs of men. They are not categorically different types of activity, nor do they have basically different aims. They are different ways of bringing what is absolutely needed to the hearts and minds of men, taking into account different situations, occasions, times, and needs. We should misunderstand the commission if we felt one aspect of it depends upon and is subsidiary to the other. Both preaching and healing are ways of linking the eternal gospel with specific need. Both are ways of performing the life-giving function. Neither, alone, is to be confused with the function itself.

Shepherding and Healing

It is the gospel command to heal that gives us the basis for the shepherding task. Lack of clarity at this point has often distorted the understanding of shepherding in the past.

The good Samaritan principle calls for the mode of testimony to be relevant to the nature of the particular need. When the need is for healing, then shepherding is called for. When the need is of a different character, then something else should be done that is not to be confused with shepherding.

Suppose that, in the good Samaritan story, it turned out that the robber's victim was really a member of the secret police intending, as soon as he recovered, to infiltrate the Samaritan lines. Or suppose that the hundredth sheep, cared for so diligently by the shepherd when lost, should turn out to have a communicable disease against which the ninety and nine ought to be protected. In such situations other considerations than shepherding would become primary concerns, even though the need for healing would not be absent. We always hope that these various forms of interest will be united, and ideally they are. Curing the one sheep of his communicable disease is also the best protection for the ninety and nine. But we cannot assume that, in actual fact, these interests will always and automatically be in harmony.

Shepherding, therefore, does not describe the total function of the person we call a "pastor." He is also one who communicates the gospel and organizes the fellowship. Shepherding, communicating, and organizing—each of these provides a perspective from which all activities are examined. Each, under proper circumstances, becomes the principal concern. None should imperialize over the others. The ultimate goal of shepherding, like that of communicating and organizing, is to relate the gospel to the need and condition of men. Each is called on according to the nature of the need, not according to the subjective preferences of the one we call pastor.[2]

Rightly understood, all shepherding moves in the direction of healing even though circumstances may prevent actual healing or may prevent it at this time. This is to use the term "healing" in its general and comprehensive sense, involving the restoration of functional wholeness that has been impaired as to direction or timing. The aim of shepherding is to help the person (or the group smaller than the whole fellowship) to move as far in the direction of healing as circumstance permits.

Jesus Christ, said the early interpretations of our faith, is the great shepherd (Heb. 13:20). We who have been called to be brothers of and joint heirs with Christ are to be undershepherds one to another (Rom. 8:17). We are members one of another in the body of Christ (1 Cor. 12:12ff.; Rom. 12:4ff.). To be sure, we are imperfect and sinful members, but we are touched with his wholeness because we are organically interrelated in his body. To one another and to all men we are to act as shepherds, that is, as undershepherds, under the commission to preach and to heal (Jn. 10 and 21).

Love and Judgment

Despite the ambiguities that have often become attached to it, it is my conviction that the shepherding metaphor can be very powerful and useful to us. We do, however, need to purge it of possible wrong connotations. It grew out of a simple agrarian situation in which the shepherd took his flock by day out into the fields to graze, watched over them that they might not become lost or injured, protected them from enemies, and brought them at night to the safety of the fold. The Christian metaphor refers to the solicitous and tender and individualized care by the shepherd of the sheep. This is true whether the shepherd brought back a straying lamb with his crook or killed a wolf who threatened the flock. In the case of the straying lamb, the meaning of tender and solicitous concern in the shepherd does not prejudge the issue in favor of letting the lamb do anything he has a mind to do. If his straying in the interest of succulent morsels brings him too near a cliff, his recovery by the shepherd may appear to him to be judgment rather than love. If it is a person rather than a lamb, he will be consulted and not directed. Still, the experiencing of love or of judgment are both possible in shepherding.

When shepherding is so regarded, then it is clear that shepherding and healing, as defined above, are the same thing so far as aim is concerned. It is not that all shepherding can effect healing. Some shepherding has to be a matter of sustaining, of standing by, without power to bring about restoration, just as an injured sheep might die despite all the tender care of the shepherd or veterinary physician. But the aim is always healing.

Today we are so imbued with the great positive results that have emerged from modern scientific medicine, founded on differential diagnosis and treatment, that we tend to misunderstand the simple but profound conception of healing that is found in the New Testament. The New Testament intuitions are of a different order from that of differential diagnosis and treatment. We must separate them from such comparisons just as we do in connection with the physical worldview of people living at that period.

New Testament Intuitions

The basic intuitions about healing in the New Testament seem to center around two points, one of which may be put negatively and the other positively. The negative point appears in connection with the concept of demons. The New Testament intuition was this: That which is central and crucial about the person, or the total spirit, is always larger and deeper than the negativities that may adhere to him. Whatever demons may be, they are not all of him. We see this, for example, in Jesus' story of the Gadarene who, precisely because he could say that his name was Legion, was bigger and deeper than the thousand demons at work within him (Lk. 8:26ff.). Although we rightly reject a literal demonology, we note that the basic meaning of demons in relation to disease in the New Testament account was to distinguish the basic potential for oneness and integration and positive movement from the powerful and dynamic forces that threatened it and might even be, as with the Gadarene, for the time being in control.

Modern medicine and the related arts and sciences, in contrast to those of the previous century, are moving toward a similar idea. Categorical distinctions between healing of body and mind seem no longer possible. There is abundant evidence that, even in those persons who are most sick or most impaired, there is energy working in the direction of health that transcends all conscious calculation—even though it does not by any means always succeed. Fortunately, we no longer talk about demons, but we do know that a dominating mother or a detached father, no less than a tubercle bacillus, may act just as the ancients thought demons did.

The other conviction or intuition of the New Testament about healing is seen positively—that real healing is of the "spirit," when spirit is understood to mean very much the same thing that we mean today when we speak of a whole person. A person may become ill or impaired at any level, all the way from the cells of his body to his relationship to God. True healing embraces all levels. There may indeed be differences among them, but the differences are not absolute and categorical.[3]

Increasingly the scientific evidence seems to point toward the possibility, certainly now far from realized, of a general and comprehensive theory of healing that will have relevance for cells and for the whole human spirit. Some may be frightened by such a possibility, and indeed we ought to be frightened if what were envisaged were the reduction of the higher to the lower. If this were to be done by reducing "spirit" and "history" to "nature," then the Christian intuitions would stand against it. I am referring to a different kind of healing. We now see that there is more of what has been called spirit and history within nature than has previously been recognized. This implies the opposite of reductionism.

Christians stand for the unity of the human person, for man as a total spirit including body, for men as members one of another, and for men as both sinful and at the same time, made in the image of God. If man is to be healed, all aspects or organs or relationships must be touched; whence it follows that each of these levels or orders or perspectives must somehow affect the others even though it need not by any means wholly determine them. It follows that our attempts to shepherd and to heal never exist in some walled-off compartment labeled "religious."

The more possible it is to think of healing in the inclusive sense suggested above, the plainer it will become that shepherding and healing are of a piece. It is often asked whether healing and salvation are the same thing, since their etymological history is so similar. The answer given depends in large part upon the specific meanings ascribed to the words and the context in which the question is seen. As the terms are ordinarily used, they come from different contexts, and therefore, issues can only be clouded by any appearance of equating them. But it may be that someday we too shall be able to ask, "Which is easier to say, 'Your sins are forgiven you,' or to say, 'Rise and walk'?" (Lk. 5:23, RSV).

Basic Principles of Shepherding

[T]he place accorded to shepherding in Christianity is unique. It is not possible, however, simply to deduce all the operating principles from this fact. In order to advance our understanding, we need to examine actual shepherding situations. We shall do so in the light of our best theological understanding. We shall also look for any help we can get from such helping and healing arts and sciences as psychiatry, clinical psychology, and social work.

As actual shepherding situations have been studied in this way during recent years, it has become clear that some of the most basic things Christians have always believed about the process of shepherding are receiving strong reinforcement. Of all these convictions, the most important is that we cannot help a person in any real sense unless our interest in and concern for him are genuine. No matter how refined they may be, techniques alone, of any kind, will not be sufficient to help a person as a person. (They may of course help part of a person, or a person in some part of himself—as when a good bandaging job is done by someone we do not like.)

On the other hand, our modern studies have not confirmed all of our traditional notions of how to help or to shepherd. Some of our traditional practices have been found to be as wrong as was the medicine of an earlier day, when it tried to treat people by "bleeding" them. Thus we need to be careful and discriminating, so that our basic convictions are not wrongly associated with poor methods by which shepherding is to be carried out.

CHAPTER 5

The Courageous Shepherd

Alastair V. Campbell[1] (1981)

> Love is the greatest of all risks
> to give myself to you
> do I dare...do I dare
> leap into the cool, swirling, living waters
> of loving fidelity?
>
> Jean Vanier, *Tears of Silence*[2]

In order to revitalize the imagery of pastoral care we must restore to it a much neglected quality—courage. Those who have entered into the darkness of another's pain, loss, or bewilderment and who have done so without the defenses of a detached professionalism will know the feeling of wanting to escape, of wishing they had not become involved. Caring is costly, unsettling, even distasteful at times. The valley of deep shadows in another person's life frightens us too, and we lack the courage and constancy to enter it. One of the most vivid aspects of the biblical image of shepherding (from which the term "pastoral" derives) is such courage, courage to the point of risking one's own life. Thus young David, anxious to convince Saul that he is capable of fighting Goliath, uses as a testimonial his experiences as a shepherd boy:

> "Your Majesty," David said, "I take care of my father's sheep. Any time a lion or bear carries off a lamb, I go after it, attack it, and rescue the lamb. And if the lion or bear turns on me, I grab it by the throat

and beat it to death…The LORD has saved me from lions and bears;
he will save me from this Philistine" (1 Sam. 17:34–37, TEV).

It is this element of courage based on trust in God which seems most obviously neglected in modern accounts of pastoral relationships. But there are also other features of the shepherd's character–tenderness, skill in leadership, concern from wholesomeness–making up a rich picture of what it means to care. In order to recover these elements it is necessary to summarize the usage of the image in the Old and New Testaments, and then consider its relevance for a contemporary understanding of pastoral care.

Biblical Images of Shepherding

Shepherding in the climatic conditions of Palestine was (and is) a demanding and, at times, hazardous occupation. During the long dry season it was necessary to move the flocks over considerable distances in search of good pastures; suitable resting places and watering places had to be found; and danger lurked in the shadows of valleys in the form of robbers and wild beasts–as David's description so graphically demonstrates. The shepherd was with his flock day and night, often in remote places far from home, and he had to be skilled in keeping the flock together, in finding wanderers and stragglers, in recognizing the ailments of his sheep and knowing how to cure them, and in ensuring the safety of the vulnerable members of the flock.

We can see at once that there is a mixture of tenderness and toughness in the character of the shepherd. His unsettled and dangerous life makes him a slightly ambiguous figure–more perhaps like the cowboy of the "Wild West" than the modern shepherd in a settled farming community. The shepherd, like the cowboy, may be a hired man in a dangerous job, who cannot always be relied upon (Jn. 10:11ff.), especially since he wanders from place to place. Thus in Rabbinic writings shepherds are viewed with considerable suspicion. They are accused of handling stolen goods and trespassing on other people's pastureland, and (in common with publicans and tax gatherers) are not permitted to hold judicial office or give evidence in court.[3]

Tenderness, Skill, and Self-sacrifice

In the Old Testament, however, the disreputable aspect of the image is rarely if ever present. The positive attributes of the good shepherd are given prominence and used to express the loving leadership of God and of his promised Messiah. The shepherd leads, guides, nurtures, heals, seeks out the lost, brings the scattered flock back together, and protects it from harm. The image occurs most frequently in the Psalms and in the exilic prophecies of Jeremiah, Ezekiel, and Deutero-Isaiah.[4] Perhaps it is nowhere more vivid as an image of tenderness and hope than in Isaiah 40:

> He will feed his flock like a shepherd,
>   he will gather the lambs in his arms,

> he will carry them in his bosom,
> > and gently lead those that are with young. (Isa. 40:11, RSV)

The skill of the shepherd and his concern for wholesomeness are portrayed in Ezekiel 34:

> "I will look for those that are lost, bring back those that wander off, bandage those that are hurt, and heal those that are sick."
> (Ezek. 34:16, TEV)

The same healing skills are described in the familiar opening verses of Psalm 23:

> He lets me rest in fields of green grass
> > and leads me to quiet pools of fresh water.
> He gives me new strength.
> He guides me in the right paths,
> > as he has promised. (Ps. 23:2–3, TEV)

The idea that the shepherd's care for the sheep can even lead to his own death finds expression in Zechariah's accounts of the messianic shepherd whose death leads to a purification of the people (Zech. 11:4; 12:10; 13:7–9):

> They will look for the one whom they stabbed to death, and they will mourn for him like those who mourn for an only child. (Zech. 12:10, TEV)

Care of the Despised

In the New Testament we find the shepherd motif throughout the accounts of Jesus' birth, ministry, death, resurrection, and final triumph. In the Lucan nativity story, it is shepherds who are called to witness the Messiah's birth. They are sent by the angels to an animal stall, whose location they clearly already know, perhaps because they used it for their own flocks. The choice of shepherds–that rough and perhaps untrustworthy group–as the first witnesses of Jesus' birth accords well with Luke's stress on the humility of the nativity:

> He has brought down mighty
> > kings from their thrones,
> and lifted up the lowly. (Lk. 1:52, TEV)

Jesus uses the shepherd image in his teaching to express God's strenuous and often surprising concern for those who have gone astray (Mt. 18:12–14 and par.). It is perhaps significant that in Luke's version of the parable of the lost sheep the context is the accusation by the scribes and Pharisees that Jesus eats with outcasts (Lk. 15:4–7). In response, Jesus uses the care and concern of the distrusted shepherd as a paradigm for God's love, as elsewhere (Lk. 10:30–37) he uses the loving actions of the despised Samaritan. The death of Jesus–that final act of caring love–is referred to in terms which recall the messianic Shepherd of the Old Testament prophecies. In John 10, Jesus claims the title Good Shepherd, because (unlike the hireling) Jesus is willing to die for the sheep. In the Synoptic Gospels (Mk. 14:27f. and par.), Jesus quotes Zechariah's prophecy of the smitten shepherd in order to speak of his death, the sheeplike panic of his disciples, and his shepherding of them (Eastern fashion) by leading the way to Galilee after his resurrection. The same imagery of sacrifice and leadership is used in Revelation to describe the triumph of the Christian martyrs who are led to safety by him who is both sacrificial lamb and shepherd:

> The Lamb, who is in the center of the throne, will be their shepherd,
> and he will guide them to springs of life-giving water. (Rev. 7:17, TEV)

In similar terms the benediction at the end of Hebrews accords Jesus the title Great Shepherd, because of his sacrificial death (Heb. 13:20), just as earlier (2:10) he is called the "trail blazer" (*archegon*) to salvation.

Self-sacrificing Pastoral Leadership

In this widespread use of the shepherd image in the Bible we see an interesting picture emerging. The shepherd is undoubtedly a leader—a strong and courageous figure at the head of the flock. But this leadership has a very special quality. Concern is entirely focused on those entrusted for care, even to the point of life's surrender. Thus leadership is expressed in great compassion, sensitivity to need, and a knowledge of what is life-sustaining and wholesome. It is an image linked to the feel of strong supporting arms, to the taste of cool refreshing water, and to the sensation of receiving truly strengthening nourishment. It is a leadership of real physical involvement, basic and simple, leadership even when one's own blood is spilled and one's own body broken.

In view of its leadership associations it is perhaps not surprising that shepherd or "pastor" became a term to describe the leader of a Christian congregation. But in fact its use in this way is relatively unusual in the New Testament.[5] Most of the references consist of the use of the verb "to shepherd" (*poimainein*), to describe the duties of the elders (*presbuteroi*) or overseers (*episcopoi*) of the new Christian congregations. A good example can be found in 1 Peter:

> I appeal to you to be shepherds of the flock [*poimanate* to *poimnion*] that God gave you and to take care of it willingly, as God wants you to, and not unwillingly. Do your work, not for mere pay, but from a real desire to serve. Do not try to rule over those who have been put in your care, but be examples to the flock. (1 Pet. 5:1b–3, TEV; cf. Paul's words to the elders at Ephesus: Acts 20:28)

The *title* "Pastor" (*poimen*) is used only once in the New Testament to describe a church official (Eph. 4:11). The context is a list of gifts given by God to "build up the body of Christ" and here "pastors and teachers" are regarded as having a separate function from "apostles, prophets and evangelists." One can see how such a "pastoral" function became necessary as the young churches settled into an established life following the initial evangelization which established them. The task of pastor-teachers was one of ensuring continuity of life and doctrine, as years and generations passed. They were there to remind people of the meaning and practical implications of the gospel which led them into the Christian community in the first place.

It is unfortunate, however, that this pastoral teaching office (often combined with the office of leader of worship) quickly tended to absorb within itself the whole meaning of "pastoral." It becomes assumed that *this* leadership is the *only* leadership referred to when we speak of pastoral care. Nothing could be farther from the truth. The primary reference of the shepherd image is to Jesus' self-sacrificial love, which seeks a response from *every* one of his followers. Leaders and teachers of congregations have no special prerogatives in this central meaning of shepherding. We must learn to speak of the *pastorhood of all believers* and to explore the idea that *each* person has a call to lead in that special way characteristic of the Good Shepherd.

In exploring this use of shepherding I shall first examine a modern account of pastoral care given in the writings of the American pastoral theologian Seward Hiltner. A critique of this account will lead me to suggest some richer uses of the shepherding imagery to describe our call to be loving leaders.

A Modern Use of "Shepherding"

A Critique of Hiltner

The importance of Seward Hiltner for contemporary developments in pastoral care and pastoral counseling theory can hardly be overestimated. His books, notably *Pastoral Counseling, Preface to Pastoral Theology,* and *The Christian Shepherd,* have set the terms of reference for discussion of pastoral issues for the past two decades in the United States and have widely influenced writers in other countries. His work marks the beginning of a new academic rigor in pastoral theology, one which takes theory in the "secular" sciences seriously. But perhaps Hiltner's most important contribution has been to free the term "pastoral" from its association with the title "Pastor," which itself has become simply a synonym for "minister" or "leader of a congregation." It is evident from nineteenth-century textbooks on "pastoral theology" that, because of this association, "pastoral" had come to mean little more than "what the minister does," whether this was teaching, preaching or visiting the sick.[6] Other textbooks identified a specific area of ministerial work–"poiemics"–which was to take its place alongside homiletics, catechetics, etc.[7] In place of such functional and role-related definitions Hiltner argued that we must understand "pastoral" to be a *perspective* from which all activities of church and ministry may be viewed, a perspective based on "the shepherd's attitude of tender and solicitous concern." In certain activities of church and ministry this perspective may be the dominant one; in others it may give place to other concerns (for example, the need to communicate the gospel or to organize the fellowship), but it should never be wholly absent, since the shepherding attitude is an essential aspect of Christian faith.

The reorientation which Hiltner offers is a useful one in restoring some of the unique qualities of shepherding, but it also has some serious flaws. In the first place, Hiltner appears to remain trapped in an uncritical view of the nature of the church and the purpose of its ministry. His writings still assume a minister-dominated approach to pastoral care,[8] and the pastoral theology which he constructs on the basis of reflection on current "operations" of the church is insulated from theological critique by the nature of its purely practical starting point.[9] Another, and (for our purposes) fatal flaw in Hiltner's account of "the shepherding perspective" is that it is remarkably flat and uninteresting. We look in vain for the drama and vividness of the biblical imagery in his descriptions of pastoral care, pastoral counseling, and pastoral theology. Instead we find a fondness for the terminology of nondirective or client-centered counseling. Thus, in *The Christian Shepherd* he describes the "basic principles of shepherding" as concern, acceptance, clarification, judgment, humility, and self-understanding.[10] No doubt these are admirable qualities, but their connection with the shepherd image seems tangential at best. Moreover the biblical references given in the various explanations of the origins of the shepherd motif are remarkably selective. The parables of the lost sheep and of the good Samaritan are used to illustrate the meaning of care and concern,[11] but the Old Testament themes of consolation and hope are not mentioned, nor is the powerfully sacrificial element in the New Testament image. Jesus as the Great Shepherd of the Hebrews benediction is mentioned in one sentence, but nothing is said of the messianic hopes with which the New Testament writers viewed Jesus as shepherd. We are forced to conclude that in Hiltner the image is little more than a cipher which gives a religious appearance to statements about care derived from quite other sources, notably the faith-statements of Rogerian counseling theory. A consequence of this is that Hiltner's use of the concept of shepherding offers little or no illumination into how we can be shepherds to one another on that dangerous route which results from following Jesus. The encouragement to be nondirective counselors is a less than adequate account of the risks entailed!

A Call for Courage

Unhelped by Hiltner's "tender and solicitous concern" we are forced to return to a tougher aspect of "the shepherding perspective"–courage. Yet this at once seems to create a problem. The "tough man" image has been exploited to such an extent in fiction, films, and television programs that we tend to equate courage with violence and physical strength. In speaking of courage in pastoral care, how can we escape from the idea that some people are "natural leaders" and somehow superior to others in so being? The corrective must come from the constant reminders in the Old and New Testaments that God reveals to disciples what true shepherding is and saves them from the exploitation and neglect of false shepherds and untrustworthy hirelings. Thus it is in the steadfast love of God incarnate in Jesus that we see the shepherd's courage, not in the power and strength of earthly leaders. The courage of Jesus has a quality to it that is both strong and gentle. Above all, it is courage *for others*, not a courage for his own defense or aggrandizement. We shall look briefly at some aspects of this courage as they were shown in his life.

1. There is courage in the words of Jesus.

On many occasions Jesus is put to the test by his opponents: Should we render tribute to Caesar? By what authority do you do this? Who has sinned, this man or his parents? Is it lawful to heal on the Sabbath? Which is the greatest commandment? Why do you eat with tax gatherers and sinners? Are you the Messiah, the King of the Jews? The answers of Jesus are both calm and fearless. They spring from an inner strength which comes from his oneness with his Father and his certainty that no law and no earthly power can prevail against love.

2. There is courage in the actions of Jesus.

He touches lepers and speaks to the possessed. He confronts an angry crowd, preventing a stoning by his intervention. He eats with quislings and the socially outcast and joyfully accepts the tears and kisses of a prostitute. He rides into Jerusalem in a public procession, knowing that his enemies are watching his every move. He boldly enters the temple courts and drives out the moneymakers. He casts aside all dignity, humbly washing the feet of his friends. He shares bread with the man who will betray him and enters the garden to receive the kiss which leads to arrest, punishment, and death.

3. There is courage in the sufferings of Jesus.

He willingly shares the burden of the poor, the homeless, and the sick. He rejects the comforts of family and possessions, finding mother and brothers in those who will hear him. He accepts the friendship of those who misunderstand, neglect, and deny him. He overcomes the temptations of supernatural power, and in his agony in Gethsemane finds a way to bend his fear and sorrow to God's will. He endures taunts, flogging, and a slow death in dereliction, because he knows it is the way that love requires. In his dying moments he seeks only forgiveness for his executioners and the fulfillment of God's will.

Such is the courage of the Good Shepherd who lays down his life for the sheep. It is the courage of integrity, of an inner wholeness, of a oneness with God and with humankind, and of a constant, invincible love. In such a context our own attempts to care for others seem hopelessly weak and inadequate. There is a clear limit to the suffering most of us would be willing to endure for the sake of others, especially those with whom we have no ties of family or of close affection. We also lack courage in action and in words, mainly because there is no sure center to our being. We lean desperately on the good will and praise of others or on the reassurance of possessions and of social standing, because we have no trust in our own worth without these external validations. Since we lack an inner wholeness, we do not have the grace to speak to others with both tenderness and strength. It matters too much to us whether the other is pleased and too little whether we speak the truth as best we see it. We cannot be shepherds so long as comfort is our main concern and so long as the roads through the wilderness are too lonely and too dangerous for us.

The Eschatological Aspect of Care

Thus, far from giving us a simple paradigm for our caring concern, the image of the shepherd seems merely to reveal our inadequacies. If it is the sacrificial love of Jesus that the pastoral relationship demands of us, we know before we begin that the goal is unattainable. Yet perhaps it is no bad thing that the central image in pastoral care, when properly appreciated, has this humbling effect. It must surely finally dispose of all self-confident "management models" for pastoral care. There is no way of organizing our lives and the lives of others to *ensure* that the lost are found, that the weak are protected, that pastures are truly wholesome, that there is pure, clear water. Perhaps in a literal sense we can organize for physical needs (though the starvation and violence throughout the world show little promise of that), but the green pastures and still waters of total human well-being are still harder to find, and for each person the way is unique. If pastoral care begins to depend on some technique which can be easily taught and implemented, then we can be sure that it has become something else—a method of psychological adjustment to society perhaps, or a way of increasing church membership, or a system of spiritual consolation against the harsh realities of the world.

How then can we understand our task as "loving leaders," as undershepherds of the Great Shepherd? The answer lies in holding on to the eschatological element in all our attempts to describe pastoral care. The way of Jesus leads across stony ground, through dark valleys, to the living water. The peace and fulfillment given in Jesus is *both* in our midst *and* yet to come. To suggest that personal well-being and the wholeness of life on earth are easily within our grasp is to obscure with a facile optimism the judgment and hope in the message of Jesus; but to dismiss as futile all human efforts to love and care and to lead others to wholesomeness is to deny with a false pessimism the incarnate nature of God's love. Somewhere in the tension between these two extremes there lies the possibility for pastoral care. This possibility will come to different people at different moments. Sometimes it will be right for me to lead, sometimes gratefully to accept the leadership of another. No single human being possesses the competence, the strength, or the vision to lay claim to the role of the Good Shepherd. But when it is our place to lead the way for others, there are two signs that our shepherding is true leadership. The first is that those who follow our lead find rest and health, not some narrowing, overburdening, or destruction of themselves. (Much shepherding in the name of religion has such unwholesome results.)[12] The second sign is that true leadership is costly and dangerous. We cannot lead without risking ourselves. Indeed, it is most often out of our wounds that we bring wholeness to others. When we experience this second sign, the sign of the wounded healer, we also realize how little we can give of pastoral care and how much we ourselves need it.

CHAPTER 6

The Self-Differentiated Samaritan

JEANNE STEVENSON MOESSNER[1] (1991)

Ann was a patient on an addictive disease unit in a psychiatric facility; she entered group therapy after leaving the detoxification unit. As was customary at the beginning of each group session, the patients and counselors introduced themselves. When Ann's turn came, she had difficulty with the counselor's request: Tell us about yourself.

> ANN: I take care of people: I'm a nurse. I'm a mother; I take care of my daughter. I'm a daughter; I take care of my mother who has Alzheimer's. She lives with us.

> COUNSELOR: Tell us something about yourself.

> ANN: I can't. I don't know who I am.

The Elusive Self

Ann's comment illustrates the difficulty many women have in establishing a sense of identity. This phenomenon has been encountered by several researchers. Lillian B. Rubin, for example, studied 160 women who had difficulty answering the question, Who am I? This difficulty was attributed to the mystery about women's nature, *the elusive self*.[2] Rubin's "elusive self" is not far removed from the work of pastoral theologian Orlo Strunk, who speaks in terms of the "Secret Self,"[3] the central region of the person, a private centerpoint in each of us that is good, and the internal essence of who we authentically are that resists external demands of compliance and conformity. Lacking adequate knowledge of who they are, women often exhibit low self-esteem.

We see this problem particularly among women who have identified themselves in conformity with our culture's traditional feminine stereotypes. Women in this situation commonly describe themselves as wives, mothers, and kind, caring, and unselfish people.[4]

They have followed society's ideal of the good woman, yet society has not reciprocated by rewarding their ideal qualities. In her exemplary care of the "other," something is amiss in the woman's care of herself. Professional and paid caregivers must confront the paradoxical question, What is a useful ministry with women who have so often excelled as caregivers themselves?

Cultural Archetypes of Femininity

Much of women's caregiving, unfortunately, is intricately involved in their pleasing others. To be "pleasing," subordinate, subservient, and dependent is a *cultural archetype* of what being "feminine" means.[5] One theologian has named the characteristics that accompany such an archetype as sins; these feminine "sins" include diffuseness, dependence on others for self-definition, lack of an organizing center, and distractibility.[6] These characteristics and the tendency to be pleasing and passive have contributed to exploitation, battering, sexual abuse, psychological abuse, and role conflict.

Feminine Power

Because women have traditionally been primary caregivers, they actually wield great power over infants and children. "Mother's power" over life nurturance and death avoidance is remembered, revered, feared, and envied. The all-powerful mother can be a terrifying and capricious image, causing some women to avoid powerful authority lest they be regarded as a modern Medea.[7] Those who envy a woman's innate power can respond with reprisals. As women's power has become more obvious and organized, men have become more insecure and misogynist.[8] Pastoral caregivers may ask themselves, When ministering to women, how can we better monitor our own vulnerability to women or our own insecure and misogynist reactions to previous experiences of a woman's authority as mother?

A Paradigm for the Pastoral Care of Women

These considerations bring us to the question, What is a healthy paradigm for the pastoral care of women? This chapter offers a substitute for the prominent shepherding paradigm extracted from John 10 and presents theological foundations for the pastoral care of women.

The paradigm developed in this chapter also comes from Scripture; unabashedly, this work is an attempt to find our predominant images for healing and helping within our own discipline, even as we remain in constant relationship with the behavioral sciences. This attempt is in agreement with the sentiment of numerous pastoral theologians "that in this particular time and place, the stress should be on the second rather than the first word in the title for our field—upon theology and its relationship to the meaning of pastoral, rather than the other way around."[9]

The theological paradigm [that I set forth here] as foundational for the pastoral care of women comes from Luke 10, the parable of a Samaritan. This narrative develops the interconnection in the injunction to love God, neighbor, and self (Luke 10:27). Underscoring love of self, this chapter utilizes the parable as appropriate to women in search of the elusive self. A second type of interconnectedness essential to the Samaritan paradigm is reflected by the function of the inn and developed in this chapter as crucial in pastoral practice with those by the side of the road.

Love of God, Self, and Neighbor: A Paradigm of Interconnection

Shepherding has been one of the dominant metaphors in pastoral care and counseling. The art of shepherding as described in John 10 has been extended to pastoral care and developed by pastoral theologians such as Seward Hiltner.[10] Although other theologians such as Carroll Wise have spoken of inherent dangers in the use of this symbol, no other paradigm has been as prominent. Wise expresses his reserve over the symbol of the shepherd in this way: the symbol subtly but powerfully conveys the idea of the shepherd over the sheep.[11] Although Wise points to places in the New Testament that stressed the equality and unity of all believers, he offers no alternative paradigm to that of the good shepherd.

AN ALTERNATIVE TO THE ISOLATED SHEPHERD

Shepherding was also my favored image in the field of pastoral care until I prepared a sermon on the Good Shepherd passage in John 10. I was beguiled with the phrase "the voice of strangers."

> He who enters by the door [of the sheepfold] is the shepherd of the sheep. To him the gatekeeper opens; the sheep hear his voice, and he calls his own sheep by name and leads them out... A stranger they will not follow, but they will flee from him, for they do not know the voice of strangers. (10:2–3; 5, RSV)

In this biblical pericope, there is mention of wolves, thieves, robbers, hirelings, and gatekeepers. All of these figures are predictable within the passage. The mysterious grouping is that of the strangers. The "voice of strangers" stands in tension with the voice of the Good Shepherd.

In the biblical setting, Jesus talks to the Pharisees about himself. He speaks about leadership and uses the shepherd as a type. The Pharisees, the religious leaders of that day, could not comprehend the christological import of his metaphor. Yet, I as a pastoral theologian understand it so well. I often imagine myself as a shepherd, standing in the door of the classroom or church, greeting the flock by name, feeling responsible for their nurture, becoming so identified with shepherding that it takes all I have. I and others in pastoral ministry give our lives for the sheep. We give exemplary care to others. We become the good shepherd. In doing so, however, we, like the Pharisees, miss the christological import of the metaphor. In becoming the good shepherd of our flock, *we* are the voice of strangers.

With the traditional male developmental emphases on autonomy, individuation, and self-sufficiency as goals of maturity, usurping the place of the Good Shepherd is not difficult for the individual. To warn religious leaders against this propensity, Jesus reiterates twice in John 10 that he is the door of the sheep and that he is the Good Shepherd.

A paradigm other than that of the good shepherd, one with less inherent danger of lone external hierarchical authority, is crucial for the pastoral care of women. As more women in transition move away from reliance on external authority figures, away from passivity, and into a comfort with their own internal authority, we seek a paradigm that avoids the risk of the lone shepherd who can control, cajole, and cavort with the sheep. To see how the isolated shepherd can ravish the flock, we need only glance at the recent documentation of a scandal in the early 1980s in which a winsome and adored pastor sexually abused at least six women parishioners over a four-year period.[12] In the allegations against their pastor, the six women acknowledged they were caught off guard by the attention given them by a male, religious authority. Although the recent book *Is Nothing Sacred?* exposes sexual misconduct, we have yet to document the more prevalent psychological abuse between male authority figures and their parishioners.

A CALL TO INTERCONNECTEDNESS

With the emerging emphases and goals in female developmental theory on mutuality and interdependence, a paradigm that is appropriate in the pastoral care of women needs to underscore interconnectedness in the helping dimensions of ministry. Two types of interconnectedness are essential. One type is discussed later as relatedness to other disciplines in healing. The other type of interconnectedness is the interplay of love of neighbor, God, and self. North American pastoral theology has been criticized for lack of attention to this interconnection;[13] German theology after World War II has been stamped by the conviction that interpersonal disturbances between people are intimately tied up with disturbances between people and God. Friedrich Wintzer reminds us that the question about the relationship of a person to God, self, and neighbor is a central one to pastoral care and counseling.[14] Surely such an interconnection is present in the injunction in Luke 10:27 to love God with all our heart, and with all our soul, and with all our mind, and our neighbor as ourselves. It is followed by a parable of a Samaritan who stopped to help a wounded person. The parable has been understood by commentators to be an elaboration of what it means to "love your neighbor." The parable also implies that love of neighbor is intimately tied up with love of God. Pastoral care of women must concern itself with the more subtle interconnection implied in the text: love your neighbor as yourself.

Carol Gilligan, in her ground-breaking *In a Different Voice*, has worked with the complex interplay of self and other.[15] She suggests that women's development moves through three phases in this interplay. The first phase pivots on care for oneself. A person cares for the self in order to ensure survival. A transition occurs when this first position is seen as egoistic. A concept of responsibility develops in a growing understanding between self and other. In the second phase of Gilligan's sequence, caring for others is equated with what is good. A disequilibrium occurs as the woman neglects to give care to herself and to receive care. Caring is confused with self-sacrifice that hurts and neglects the self of the caregiver. A transition occurs when this dilemma is recognized. In Gilligan's third caring pattern, a new connection develops between self and other. Self-knowledge is essential for this perspective and leads to healthy relationships. It involves concern with the interrelationship between self and other but a condemnation of self-exploitation.

The movement in Gilligan's sequence is from a narcissism to an altruism to an interdependence between self and other. Using the parable of the Samaritan as a paradigm for interconnectedness, one can understand the sequence within the text as follows: The robber represents the infantile position: what is yours is mine. The priest and Levite depict the narcissistic worldview: what is mine is mine. The Samaritan, in caring for the neighbor, exhibits the traditionally "feminine" altruistic posture: what is mine is yours.

FINISHING THE JOURNEY

In our customary way of reading this biblical text, we women have not acknowledged a crucial aspect to the narrative, an aspect so significant that it shatters the previous sequence: the Samaritan finished his journey. The Samaritan finished his journey while meeting the need of a wounded and marginal person. The Samaritan did not give everything away; in this enigmatic parable, he did not injure, hurt, or neglect the self. He loved himself, and he loved his neighbor. He relied in a sense on the communal, on a type of teamwork as represented by the inn and by the host at the inn. In the pastoral care of women, we can appropriately interpret this last and preferred phase in the complex interplay of self and other as: what is mine is mine, but I have enough to share. Thus, the Samaritan as paradigm represents love of self and neighbor, with love of God understood in the parable. This paradigm can be utilized to describe developmentally mature women from the perspective of the Christian faith. It reinforces recent research in women's development that underscores the fact that all psychological growth for women occurs within emotional connections and not separate from them.[16] This paradigm supports the notion that in genuine caretaking the caretaker is not submerged. The paradigm can be utilized in the new understanding of women's development, which is called "self-in-relation" theory or "being-in-relationship." This theory posits that the core self-structure in women is the relational self.[17]

Love of self for a woman is the conviction and perception that she is of infinitely great value and immense worth. This understanding may run counter to society's or her family's attempt to grant her relative value. Diogenes Allen, a philosophical theologian, utilizes the Samaritan parable to illustrate the absolute value of a person, in contrast to a person's relative value. The Samaritan acknowledges the intrinsic worth and great value of the one stripped, beaten, and left for half-dead. This compassion is a mirroring of God's perfect love.[18] This kind of compassion in the Samaritan passage is described as "being moved to pity."

> To love a thing is to see a thing as existing in its own right—to go out to its existence. And to go out to a thing in this way when it is a living thing, and particularly when it is a living person, is *fundamentally to have pity for it*...The insight into its existence is at the same time an insight into its suffering, its defenselessness, its profound vulnerability.[19]

The loved self is a self-in-Relation. We have absolute value because we have been created to receive God's presence.[20] Our absolute value is based on God, who alone is wholly good. This philosophical and theological premise offers another dimension to the title *Good Samaritan*.

Interconnectedness and the Inn

The second type of interconnectedness essential to the Samaritan paradigm is reflected by the function of the inn. As pastoral counselors, pastors, laity, and seminarians, we must sometimes take the wounded to the inn. The inn may be a battered woman's shelter, a Resolve meeting, a Bosom Buddies' support group, a round of chemotherapy. The inn may be represented by other disciplines in healing, such as the behavioral sciences. The inn may be the church. Again, we must acknowledge that some women have been so neglected by the Levite and the priest that the inn as synagogue or church will not be a timely place for restoration. These women recall the damage done when institutional religion fostered the beliefs of male (particularly white) supremacy, women as evil, glorification of suffering, an unquestioning stance toward religious authority, a passive and nondiscerning acceptance of all hardships, and deification of the work ethic.[21] Women who have been devastated by one or more of these distortions understandably view religion as "only for superstitious and sheeplike types."[22] The inn as a place of spirituality and a spiritual shelter (*Herberge*) has more appeal to women scarred by institutional religion. In our exegetical attempt to understand the inn in the Lukan passage containing the Samaritan parable, we do know that the inn was a temporary lodging place, a place where a journeying person found room for the night.

CONNECTIONS IN A MODERN INN

As a chaplain on an addictive disease unit in a psychiatric hospital, I experienced an "inn" and I witnessed the recovery of Ann, the patient mentioned at the beginning of this chapter. "Restoration at the inn" in this location involved the Alcoholics Anonymous recovery program and a multidisciplinary team of health care providers. Our team was composed of a psychiatrist, a nurse, two patient counselors, one family therapist, one aftercare counselor, and one activities therapist. We had access to the evaluations of a clinical psychologist. The team met three mornings a week to discuss patients before making rounds together. The spiritual component was central to the treatment. As a therapeutic team, although our proximate professional goals sometimes differed, we were united by an ultimate goal: love of Higher Power, love of self, love of neighbor as encouraged by the peer networking of AA. Both types of interconnectedness under discussion in this chapter are displayed here: the interplay of love of God, neighbor, and self; and our relatedness as pastors and pastoral counselors to other disciplines in healing.

Ann made considerable progress under the care of this multidisciplinary team. After leaving the hospital, Ann lived in a halfway house with other professionals in recovery as addicts. While Ann was still an inpatient, I met her on a Sunday after a hospital worship service. She had heard a poem about a great craftsman that went like this: At an auction, no one bid on a battered, weathered old violin. Just as the auctioneer announced, "Going once, going twice," a person entered the room, mounted the podium, took the bow, and played the instrument. A thrilling sound came from the violin; the audience was spellbound. After the person finished playing, the bidding escalated to unheard-of amounts simply because the discarded violin had been touched by the crafter's hand. Ann identified with the battered, weathered violin and had what we called in that facility a "spiritual awakening."

Ann's experience encapsulates a cyclical movement within the Samaritan paradigm.

> And Ann, once half-dead and beaten,
> will go back eventually
> to a helping profession and family relationships in love
> of neighbor,
> stronger for having been restored at the inn,
> for having learned to love herself on the journey,
> for experiencing the touch of the Crafter's Hand.

PART TWO

PARADOXICAL
IMAGES *of* CARE

Introduction

The authors in this section employ paradox and paradoxical imagery to address the perils and predicaments of pastoral ministry. A number of them juxtapose seemingly contradictory terms in an effort to capture the complex array of internal conflicts and external role expectations that routinely beset ministers. The six chapters that follow portray ministers as personally wounded yet responding to others as healers, as sometimes wise though often playing the fool, and as those strangers at times being called to enter the most intimate recesses of another's life; they are wounded healers, wise fools, and intimate strangers. In these essays, a minister's own feelings of doubt and inadequacy come to the fore but are viewed less as debilitating handicaps than as essential tools of the pastoral trade. The wounded healer and wise fool in particular stand alongside images of the living human document and solicitous shepherd as arguably the most enduring and influential metaphors for ministry in contemporary pastoral theology.

Henri J. M. Nouwen

The Wounded Healer is a thin, best-selling book by Henri J. M. Nouwen, first published in the early 1970s and still assigned in seminary classrooms today. Nouwen, who died in 1996, was a widely known Roman Catholic priest, psychologist, and pastoral theologian from Holland. He taught for many years at Notre Dame and in the divinity schools at Yale and Harvard. In the portion of his book found in chapter 7, he suggests that even as Jesus' broken body became a source of consolation and healing for countless generations of Christians, so a minister's own innermost wounds may become means by which others find comfort and hope. These wounds, however, must be reminiscent of those tended by the good Samaritan, carefully and consistently bound.

Primary among these wounds for Nouwen is the minister's loneliness, both personal and professional, especially as the vocation of ministry has become increasingly marginal in contemporary society. While invariably painful, loneliness is not something to be shrouded or excised from one's life. Various attempts to do so, Nouwen claims, only place "exhausting demands" on those persons or objects sought out to fill the void. Instead, the "deep incision" of one's loneliness, like that of the Grand Canyon, can prove "an inexhaustible source of beauty and self-understanding."[1]

Just how, though, can a minister's loneliness accomplish healing in another's life? While some critics charge that the image of the wounded healer promotes an excess of morbid self-concern, Nouwen resoundingly rejects any inclinations to "spiritual exhibitionism." "A minister who talks in the pulpit about his own personal problems is of no help to his congregation, for no suffering human being is helped by someone who tells him that he has the same problems."[2] Rather, attending to their loneliness reminds ministers of what they hold in common with everyone else.

They need not so much share *of* their loneliness but, by accepting loneliness as an integral part of themselves, share *in* the loneliness of others. Nouwen calls this sharing-*in* process the source of *hospitality*, whereby growing comfortable in one's own house allows for opening that house to strangers, "paying attention without intention"[3] of molding guests to some preconceived ideal. "Paradoxically, by withdrawing into ourselves, not out of self-pity but out of humility, we create the space for another to be himself and to come to us on his own terms,"[4] Nouwen writes, reclaiming for pastoral ministry a staple of religious mysticism. "The paradox indeed is that hospitality asks for the creation of an empty space where the guest can find his own soul."[5]

Heije Faber

Just prior to the publication of Nouwen's *The Wounded Healer*, a book on hospital ministry written by another Dutch pastoral theologian, Heije Faber, was translated into English. Faber, a minister of the Dutch Reformed Church and active in the underground resistance movement in World War II, studied for a brief period under Seward Hiltner in Chicago and was instrumental in introducing clinical pastoral education to the Netherlands.

In a section from *Pastoral Care in the Modern Hospital* (1968, 1971), found here in chapter 8, he argues that a minister in the hospital setting functions much as does a clown in the modern circus. Faber's image of minister as circus clown has shown considerable staying power in contemporary pastoral theology, particularly as an impetus for another metaphor for ministry, the wise fool, developed by Alastair Campbell and Donald Capps in the two decades that followed. Seward Hiltner, writing in the foreword to Faber's book, calls his circus clown "the most original metaphor about ministry of the modern age."[6]

With Nouwen, Faber recognizes that ministers of his day are no longer afforded the social standing and moral authority assumed by their predecessors. Instead, much like the idiot in Dostoevsky's novel of the same title or the whisky priest in Graham Greene's *The Power and the Glory*, ministers are relegated to the sidelines of society. If they are seen to possess any wisdom at all, it is likely the wisdom of one playing the fool. In the context especially of the modern hospital, with its dazzling acrobatics of cutting-edge science and technological wizardry, any gifts a minister brings to bear on behalf of healing appear only to pale by comparison.

Such appearances, however, can be deceiving. The seemingly amateur but in fact highly skilled clown plays a crucial role as an outlet for emotional expression and release in the circus, mediating between the breathtaking feats of superhuman grandeur by the performers high above and the awestruck terror of the audience down below. Even so, Faber observes, does the seemingly marginal presence of the minister change the emotional climate of the hospital. Like the circus clown, the minister mediates between patient-as-audience and physician-as-performer and at the boundaries of a healing understood as at once human and divine.

The minister, for Faber, becomes that clown who, though clearly a part of the circus even while standing at its margins, brings its amazing acts down to human scale. The sensational acrobats "make us feel tense and frightened, but the clown puts it back in perspective," he writes. "In a childish way [the clown] makes these stunt-men look a little foolish; he makes us feel that they are, after all, only human and ordinary, and thus re-establishes a sort of spiritual balance."[7]

Alastair V. Campbell

In chapter 9, Alastair V. Campbell expands on Faber's image by suggesting that even outside the world of the hospital, ministers could do worse than to occasionally play the fool. Citing Paul's injunction to the church in Corinth, where he instructs those considered wise by the world's standards to instead "become fools so that you may become wise" (1 Cor. 3:18), Campbell discusses the sweeping heritage of the fool in folklore, literature, theology, and political life. The consequential role of the court jester, the village idiot, or the circus clown becomes clear. The fool often possesses more wisdom than the wise. Though terribly "vulnerable to those who hold earthly power," the fool nonetheless serves in every time and place as an "essential counterpoise to human arrogance, pomposity, and despotism."[8] Not infrequently the fool, and only the fool, is permitted, though still at grave personal risk, to speak truth to power.

The fool's inherent simplicity, loyalty, and capacity for prophecy mimic, for Campbell, qualities essential to contemporary pastoral care. Ministers who labor at the edges of society can find instructive the fool's simple "power to expose insincerity and self-deception" from the margins, in turn reclaiming childlike aspects of themselves inevitably neglected, discarded, or encrusted in the world-weariness of their adult lives. Ministers can take heart in the fool's foolhardy disregard of self in loyal deference to another of greater worth or esteem, counting their own lives as loss. They can take courage, too, in the fool's penchant for prophecy, "not in the sense of *fore*telling the future, but in the sense of *forth*telling, of pointing to the signs of the times and proclaiming divine revelations about them."[9]

For Campbell, these qualities translate in broad terms not into an "image of the 'jolly parson,' who spreads a false cheerfulness in a denial of pain," but rather into a vision for a ministry less consumed with professionalism, with office space, with appointment calendars, or with receptionists who run interference. His wise fool is that minister who delights more in silence than in speaking, who is comfortable in his or her own skin, who is little concerned with questions of success, and who is willing when necessary to tell the truth in love. Though fools, Campbell says, admirably persevere when all others have fled, they likewise know times when love empowers through laughter and letting go.[10]

Donald Capps

Faber's circus clown and Campbell's wise fool would likely have enjoyed far less longevity and continuing influence as metaphors for ministry had it not been for a popular book by Donald Capps, *Reframing: A New Method in Pastoral Care*,[11] published a decade after Campbell's work on the wise fool. Excerpts from Capps's book appear in chapter 10. Capps is a prolific, pragmatic, and iconoclastic psychologist of religion who in 1981 succeeded Seward Hiltner as a professor of pastoral theology at Princeton Theological Seminary. He grounds the images of the circus clown and wise fool—depicted by Faber and Campbell in more sweeping, broad brush strokes—in what was then an emerging new method in counseling known as reframing.

The various and usually unconventional counseling interventions that together comprise the method of reframing center on the counselor's strategic use of playful paradoxical injunctions to loosen equally paradoxical but terribly problematic emotional or relational knots or "double-binds" that have come to constrict the lives of suffering persons. Reframing thus involves, in a sense, the counselor's using carefully chosen words to infuse the counselee's predicament with a weakened "dose" of paradox, a kind of vaccine by which to immunize against or counteract those more destructive forms of paradox that led to the presenting problem in the first place.

When Capps wrote, the various techniques for this paradoxical inoculation, for reframing, were widely known and increasingly embraced by professional counselors outside the church. Capps's book, in turn, provides a biblical and theological rationale for reframing intended specifically for clergy, whose counseling styles to that point were more likely to reflect the person-centered approach of Carl Rogers that Hiltner so successfully linked to the image of the solicitous shepherd, or alternatively to reflect, in the manner of Nouwen's wounded healer, a suspicion of anything considered a *technique* of care or counseling at all.

Capps explicitly expresses no desire to undermine pastoral approaches associated with images of the solicitous shepherd or wounded healer. He nonetheless does give them a run for their money. By intentionally attaching a potent new (though, he argues, an actually ancient) method for giving counsel to Campbell's image of the wise fool, he heightens the intrigue and secures the status of what otherwise seemed destined to become a more fleeting metaphor for pastoral ministry. As a result, both the metaphor of the wise fool and the powerful techniques of reframing continue to influence and be used by ministers and pastoral counselors today.

Robert C. Dykstra

In my own essay in chapter 11,[12] I explore the possibilities of another paradoxical metaphor, the intimate stranger, specifically for informing the work of hospital chaplains in situations of sudden traumatic loss. As with the wounded healer and wise fool, the image of the intimate stranger is firmly rooted in the biblical witness, particularly in ancient Israel's historic commitment to provide hospitality to those strangers or resident aliens who sojourned in its midst.

This essay grew out of a desire to address my own escalating sense of disillusionment after several years of working as a part-time hospital chaplain while in graduate school. Of necessity, but also, I think, as a result of personal preference, this ministry often took me into the intensive care and emergency units of the hospital. There I found myself immersed in dramatic and sometimes threatening encounters with patients and family members confronting the onslaught of sudden traumatic injury, illness, or death.

Over time, the sheer accumulation of these kinds of encounters began to take their toll on my faith and ministry. In the face of steady exposure to tragedy and death, I began not only to doubt whether I had anything of substance to offer the victims and their families, but also to question God's loving and faithful nature that I had previously taken for granted. Though well-acquainted with crisis intervention techniques, I became less and less confident that going through the motions of crisis counseling, however necessary, would be enough to sustain the patients, their family members, and, of increasingly urgent personal concern, their chaplain. Confronting others' severe crises on a weekly basis, I found myself in a crisis of sorts as well.

Since the patients and their families in these moments were ordinarily strangers to me, I wondered whether I might find guidance in my predicament by studying biblical injunctions concerning hospitality to strangers. Initially, I was seeking biblical support or language for the kinds of interventions typically called for by the crisis counseling literature, that is, for approaches I was already using in the hospital, though with waning conviction and perhaps efficacy.

As I began to immerse myself, however, in biblical and other literature on the significance of strangers in ancient Israel and in contemporary American cultural life, the image of the intimate stranger became rife with possibilities. The metaphor ushered in a new awareness that those patients and family members were not the only strangers in situations of sudden loss, but that I, too, was a stranger at such times, not only to them but increasingly to myself. I realized that God seemed to become more and more a stranger to me in these moments as well. The intimate stranger, in the way of metaphors, began to open fresh venues for me to understand and approach my life and work. Ministers, I came to realize, are of necessity those familiar with the strange and who open themselves to the God-bearing power of strangeness itself.

James E. Dittes

Finally, in chapter 12, James E. Dittes offers a vision of the pastoral counselor as ascetic witness. Though his juxtaposing the terms *ascetic* and *witness* is not inherently paradoxical in the manner of some previous images of Part Two, paradox and paradoxical tension do figure prominently in Dittes's understanding of the work of the pastoral counselor. This work, for him, consists in a fiercely monastic discipline. The counselor's painful renunciations–of standards of everyday etiquette, of need for ongoing relationship or intimacy with counselees, of ordinary gauges of success or achievement, and even of any clear sense of one's own pastoral identity–open for the counselee a refreshingly disorienting, an almost surreal but, for Dittes, an actually *more* real world of safety, grace, and eschatological hope.

"The counselor's renunciation is particularly strenuous," he writes, "because, paradoxically, the counselor gives up precisely the resources he or she hopes for the counselee to discover–relationship and accomplishment–or, in Freud's abbreviated statement of the goals of therapy, love and work." Dittes does not deny that counselors come to their work with powerful personal agendas, but he insists that these motivations be held in check: "If the counselor *needs* the counseling to be successful, *needs* to achieve intense rapport, *needs* to resolve the counselee's distress, *needs* to restore the counselee to abundant life, then the counselor will be driven to forsake the attentive witnessing and to yield to the world's ways of commanding and cajoling."[13]

For Dittes, pastoral counselors voluntarily, paradoxically, and at a severe but essential cost to themselves surrender the very qualities of selfhood they hope that counselees may discover in the parallel universe of the counseling room. This encounter constitutes an alternative reality, a whole new world where counselees simply cannot fail but instead experience their lives unfiltered, uncensored, without possibility of judgment, evaluation, or even of receiving good advice from their counselor.

What pastoral counselors do instead, Dittes says, is *witness*: "The counselor is content to be a witness, not a player,"[14] in the counselee's life. The counselor attempts not to *do*, to *save*, or to *resolve*, Dittes maintains, but rather to simply and intensely *regard* the counselee. The counselor's costly vocational asceticism is in service to witnessing the counselee's life *as is*, a "rare and strenuous gift"[15] that sends both minister and counselee alike into uncharted territory devoid of "expectations, demands, performances, and checklists," and eliciting instead the other's "uncalculated, unmeasured, even reckless trust."[16] "Sometimes beginning pastoral counselors think of pastoral counseling as a set of supremely refined skills," Dittes concludes. "It is really much simpler than that. To undertake pastoral counseling is not to pile on norms and expectations of yourself, but to strip them away."[17] In this regard, at least, we may actually have come full circle in this section back to Henri Nouwen's vision of the wounded healer. For both Nouwen and Dittes, one-time colleagues in pastoral theology at Yale Divinity School, counseling becomes the paradoxical, perhaps cruciform art of withdrawing oneself, of making oneself somehow *less*, for the sake of making space for others, for enabling them to become something *more*.

CHAPTER 7

The Wounded Healer

Henri J. M. Nouwen[1] (1972)

In the middle of our convulsive world men and women raise their voices time and again to announce with incredible boldness that we are waiting for a Liberator. We are waiting, they announce, for a Messiah who will free us from hatred and oppression, from racism and war–a Messiah who will let peace and justice take their rightful place.

If the ministry is meant to hold the promise of this Messiah, then whatever we can learn of His coming will give us a deeper understanding of what is called for in ministry today.

How does our Liberator come? I found an old legend in the Talmud which may suggest to us the beginning of an answer:

> Rabbi Yoshua ben Levi came upon Elijah the prophet while he was standing at the entrance of Rabbi Simeron ben Yohai's cave... He asked Elijah, "When will the Messiah come?" Elijah replied,
> "Go and ask him yourself."
> "Where is he?"
> "Sitting at the gates of the city."
> "How shall I know him?"
> "He is sitting among the poor covered with wounds. The others unbind all their wounds at the same time and then bind them up again. But he unbinds one at a time and binds it up again, saying to himself, 'Perhaps I shall be needed: if so I must always be ready so as not to delay for a moment.'" (Taken from the tractate Sanhedrin.)

The Messiah, the story tells us, is sitting among the poor, binding his wounds one at a time, waiting for the moment when he will be needed. So it is too with the minister. Since it is his task to make visible the first vestiges of liberation for others, he must bind his own wounds carefully in anticipation of the moment when he will be needed. He is called to be the wounded healer, the one who must look after his own wounds but at the same time be prepared to heal the wounds of others.

He is both the wounded minister and the healing minister, two concepts I would like to explore in this chapter.

The Wounded Minister

The Talmud story suggests that, because he binds his own wounds one at a time, the Messiah would not have to take time to prepare himself if asked to help someone else. He would be ready to help. Jesus has given this story a new fullness by making his own broken body the way to health, to liberation and new life. Thus like Jesus, he who proclaims liberation is called not only to care for his own wounds and the wounds of others, but also to make his wounds into a major source of his healing power.

The Minister's Wounds

But what are our wounds? They have been spoken about in many ways by many voices. Words such as "alienation," "separation," "isolation" and "loneliness" have been used as the names of our wounded condition. Maybe the word "loneliness" best expresses our immediate experience and therefore most fittingly enables us to understand our brokenness. The loneliness of the minister is especially painful; for over and above his experience as a man in modern society, he feels an added loneliness, resulting from the changing meaning of the ministerial profession itself.

PERSONAL LONELINESS

We live in a society in which loneliness has become one of the most painful human wounds. The growing competition and rivalry which pervade our lives from birth have created in us an acute awareness of our isolation. This awareness has in turn left many with a heightened anxiety and an intense search for the experience of unity and community. It has also led people to ask anew how love, friendship, brotherhood and sisterhood can free them from isolation and offer them a sense of intimacy and belonging. All around us we see the many ways by which the people of the western world are trying to escape this loneliness. Psychotherapy, the many institutes which offer group experiences with verbal and nonverbal communication techniques, summer courses and conferences supported by scholars, trainers and "huggers" where people can share common problems, and the many experiments which seek to create intimate liturgies where peace is not only announced but also felt—these increasingly popular phenomena are all signs of a painful attempt to break through the immobilizing wall of loneliness.

But the more I think about loneliness, the more I think that the wound of loneliness is like the Grand Canyon—a deep incision in the surface of our existence which has become an inexhaustible source of beauty and self-understanding.

Therefore I would like to voice loudly and clearly what might seem unpopular and maybe even disturbing: The Christian way of life does not take away our loneliness; it protects and cherishes it as a precious gift. Sometimes it seems as if we do everything possible to avoid the painful confrontation with our basic human loneliness, and allow ourselves to be trapped by false gods promising immediate satisfaction and quick relief. But perhaps the painful awareness of loneliness is an invitation to transcend our limitations and look beyond the boundaries of our existence. The awareness of loneliness might be a gift we must protect and guard, because our loneliness reveals to us an inner emptiness that can be destructive when misunderstood, but filled with promise for him who can tolerate its sweet pain.

When we are impatient, when we want to give up our loneliness and try to overcome the separation and incompleteness we feel, too soon, we easily relate to our human world with devastating expectations. We ignore what we already know with a deep-seated, intuitive knowledge—that no love or friendship, no intimate embrace or tender kiss, no community, commune or collective, no man or woman, will ever be able to satisfy our desire to be released from our lonely condition. This truth is so disconcerting and painful that we are more prone to play games with our fantasies than to face the truth of our existence. Thus we keep hoping that one day we will find the man who really understands our experiences, the woman who will bring peace to our restless life, the job where we can fulfill our potentials, the book which will explain everything, and the place where we can feel at home. Such false hope leads us to make exhausting demands and prepares us for bitterness and dangerous hostility when we start discovering that nobody, and nothing, can live up to our absolute expectations.

Many marriages are ruined because neither partner was able to fulfill the often hidden hope that the other would take his or her loneliness away. And many celibates live with the naïve dream that in the intimacy of marriage their loneliness will be taken away.

When the minister lives with these false expectations and illusions, he prevents himself from claiming his own loneliness as a source of human understanding and is unable to offer any real service to the many who do not understand their own suffering.

PROFESSIONAL LONELINESS

The wound of loneliness in the life of the minister hurts all the more, since he not only shares in the human condition of isolation, but also finds that his professional impact on others is diminishing. The minister is called to speak to the ultimate concerns of life: birth and death, union and separation, love and hate. He has an urgent desire to give meaning to people's lives. But he finds himself standing on the edges of events and only reluctantly admitted to the spot where the decisions are made.

In hospitals, where many utter their first cry as well as their last words, ministers are often more tolerated than required. In prisons, where men's desire for liberation and freedom is most painfully felt, a chaplain feels like a guilty bystander whose words hardly move the wardens. In the cities, where children play between buildings and old people die isolated and forgotten, the protests of priests are hardly taken seriously and their demands hang in the air like rhetorical questions. Many churches decorated with words announcing salvation and new life are often little more than parlors for those who feel quite comfortable with the old life and who are not likely to let the minister's words change their stone hearts into furnaces where swords can be cast into plowshares and spears into pruning hooks.

The painful irony is that the minister, who wants to touch the center of men's lives, finds himself on the periphery, often pleading in vain for admission. He never seems to be where the action is, where the plans are made and the strategies discussed. He always seems to arrive at the wrong places at the wrong times with the wrong people, outside the walls of the city when the feast is over, with a few crying women.

A few years ago, when I was chaplain of the Holland-America line, I was standing on the bridge of a huge Dutch ocean liner which was trying to find its way through a thick fog into the port of Rotterdam. The fog was so thick, in fact, that the steersman could not even see the bow of the ship. The captain, carefully listening to a radar station operator who was explaining his position between other ships, walked nervously up and down the bridge and shouted his orders to the steersman. When he suddenly stumbled over me, he blurted out, "God damn it, Father, get out of my way." But when I was ready to run away, filled with feelings of incompetence and guilt, he came back and said, "Why don't you just stay around. This might be the only time I really need you."

There was a time, not too long ago, when we felt like captains running our own ships with a great sense of power and self-confidence. Now we are standing in the way. That is our lonely position: We are powerless, on the side, liked maybe by a few crew members who swab the decks and goof off to drink a beer with us, but not taken very seriously when the weather is fine.

The wound of our loneliness is indeed deep. Maybe we had forgotten it, since there were so many distractions. But our failure to change the world with our good intentions and sincere actions and our undesired displacement to the edges of life have made us aware that the wound is still there.

So we see how loneliness is the minister's wound not only because he shares in the human condition, but also because of the unique predicament of his profession. It is this wound which he is called to bind with more care and attention than others usually do. For a deep understanding of his own pain makes it possible for him to convert his weakness into strength and to offer his own experience as a source of healing to those who are often lost in the darkness of their own misunderstood sufferings. This is a very hard call, because for a minister who is committed to forming a community of faith, loneliness is a very painful wound which is easily subject to denial and neglect. But once the pain is accepted and understood, a denial is no longer necessary, and ministry can become a healing service.

The Healing Minister

How can wounds become a source of healing? This is a question which requires careful consideration. For when we want to put our wounded selves in the service of others, we must consider the relationship between our professional and personal lives.

Personal and Professional Lives

On the one hand, no minister can keep his own experience of life hidden from those he wants to help. Nor should he want to keep it hidden. While a doctor can still be a good doctor even when his private life is severely disrupted, no minister can offer service without a constant and vital acknowledgment of his own experiences. On the other hand, it would be very easy to misuse the concept of the wounded healer by defending a form of spiritual exhibitionism. A minister who talks in the pulpit about his own personal problems is of no help to his congregation, for no suffering human being is helped by someone who tells him that he has the same problems. Remarks such as, "Don't worry because I suffer from the same depression, confusion and anxiety as you do," help no one. This spiritual exhibitionism adds little faith to little faith and creates narrow-mindedness instead of new perspectives. Open wounds stink and do not heal.

Making one's own wounds a source of healing, therefore, does not call for a sharing of superficial personal pains but for a constant willingness to see one's own pain and suffering as rising from the depth of the human condition which all men share.

To some, the concept of the wounded healer might sound morbid and unhealthy. They might feel that the ideal of self-fulfillment is replaced by an ideal of self-castigation and that pain is romanticized instead of criticized. I would like to show how the idea of the wounded healer does not contradict the concept of self-realization, or self-fulfillment, but deepens and broadens it.

Healing and Hospitality

How does healing take place? Many words, such as care and compassion, understanding and forgiveness, fellowship and community, have been used for the healing task of the Christian minister. I like to use the word hospitality, not only because it has such deep roots in the Judaeo-Christian tradition, but also, and primarily, because it gives us more insight into the nature of response to the human condition of loneliness. Hospitality is the virtue which allows us to break through the narrowness of our own fears and to open our houses to the stranger, with the intuition that salvation comes to us in the form of a tired traveler. Hospitality makes anxious disciples into powerful witnesses, makes suspicious owners into generous givers, and makes close-minded sectarians into interested recipients of new ideas and insights.

But it has become very difficult for us today to fully understand the implications of hospitality. Like the Semitic nomads, we live in a desert with many lonely travelers who are looking for a moment of peace, for a fresh drink and for a sign of encouragement so that they can continue their mysterious search for freedom.

What does hospitality as a healing power require? It requires first of all that the host feel at home in his own house, and secondly that he create a free and fearless place for the unexpected visitor. Therefore, hospitality embraces two concepts: concentration and community.

HOSPITALITY AND CONCENTRATION

Hospitality is the ability to pay attention to the guest. This is very difficult, since we are preoccupied with our own needs, worries and tensions which prevent us from taking distance from ourselves in order to pay attention to others.

Not long ago I met a parish priest. After describing his hectic daily schedule–religious services, classroom teaching, luncheon and dinner engagements, and organizational meetings–he said apologetically: "Yes...but there are so many problems..." When I asked, "Whose problems?" he was silent for a few minutes, and then more or less reluctantly said, "I guess–my own." Indeed, his incredible activities seemed in large part motivated by fear of what he would discover when he came to a standstill. He actually said: "I guess I am busy in order to avoid a painful self-concentration."

So we find it extremely hard to pay attention because of our intentions. As soon as our intentions take over, the question no longer is, "Who is he?" but, "What can I get from him?"–and then we no longer listen to what he is saying but to what we can do with what he is saying. Then the fulfillment of our unrecognized need for sympathy, friendship, popularity, success, understanding, money or a career becomes our concern, and instead of paying attention to the other person we impose ourselves upon him with intrusive curiosity.[2]

Anyone who wants to pay attention without intention has to be at home in his own house–that is, he has to discover the center of his life in his own heart. Concentration, which leads to meditation and contemplation, is therefore the necessary precondition for true hospitality. When our souls are restless, when we are driven by thousands of different and often conflicting stimuli, when we are always "over there" between people, ideas and the worries of this world, how can we possibly create the room and space where someone else can enter freely without feeling himself an unlawful intruder?

Paradoxically, by withdrawing into ourselves, not out of self-pity but out of humility, we create the space for another to be himself and to come to us on his own terms. James Hillman, director of studies at the C. G. Jung Institute in Zurich, speaking about counseling, writes:

> For the other person to open and talk requires a withdrawal of the counselor. I must withdraw to make room for the other...This withdrawal, rather than going-out-to-meet the other, is an intense act of concentration, a model for which can be found in the Jewish mystical doctrine of Tsimtsum. God as omnipresent and omnipotent was everywhere. He filled the universe with his Being. How then could the creation come about?...God had to create by withdrawal; He created the not-Him, the other, by self-concentration...On the human level, withdrawal of myself aids the other to come into being.[3]

But human withdrawal is a very painful and lonely process, because it forces us to face directly our own condition in all its beauty as well as misery. When we are not afraid to enter into our own center and to concentrate on the stirrings of our own soul, we come to know that being alive means being loved. This experience tells us that we can only love because we are born out of love, that we can only give because our life is a gift, and that we can only make others free because we are set free by Him whose heart is greater than ours. When we have found the anchor places for our lives in our own center, we can be free to let others enter into the space created for them and allow them to dance their own dance, sing their own song and speak their own language without fear. Then our presence is no longer threatening and demanding but inviting and liberating.

HOSPITALITY AND COMMUNITY

The minister who has come to terms with his own loneliness and is at home in his own house is a host who offers hospitality to his guests. He gives them a friendly space, where they may feel free to come and go, to be close and distant, to rest and to play, to talk and to be silent, to eat and to fast. The paradox indeed is that hospitality asks for the creation of an empty space where the guest can find his own soul.

Why is this a healing ministry? It is healing because it takes away the false illusion that wholeness can be given by one to another. It is healing because it does not take away the loneliness and the pain of another, but invites him to recognize his loneliness on a level where it can be shared. Many people in this life suffer because they are anxiously searching for the man or woman, the event or encounter, which will take their loneliness away. But when they enter a house with real hospitality they soon see that their own wounds must be understood not as sources of despair and bitterness, but as signs that they have to travel on in obedience to the calling sounds of their own wounds.

From this we get an idea of the kind of help a minister may offer. A minister is not a doctor whose primary task is to take away pain. Rather, he deepens the pain to a level where it can be shared. When someone comes with his loneliness to the minister, he can only expect that his loneliness will be understood and felt, so that he no longer has to run away from it but can accept it as an expression of his basic human condition. When a woman suffers the loss of her child, the minister is not called upon to comfort her by telling her that she still has two beautiful healthy children at home; he is challenged to help her realize that the death of her child reveals her own mortal condition, the same human condition which he and others share with her.

Perhaps the main task of the minister is to prevent people from suffering for the wrong reasons. Many people suffer because of the false supposition on which they have based their lives. That supposition is that there should be no fear or loneliness, no confusion or doubt. But these sufferings can only be dealt with creatively when they are understood as wounds integral to our human condition. Therefore ministry is a very confronting service. It does not allow people to live with illusions of immortality and wholeness. It keeps reminding others that they are mortal and broken, but also that with the recognition of this condition, liberation starts.

No minister can save anyone. He can only offer himself as a guide to fearful people. Yet, paradoxically, it is precisely in this guidance that the first signs of hope become visible. This is so because a shared pain is no longer paralyzing but mobilizing, when understood as a way to liberation. When we become aware that we do not have to escape our pains, but that we can mobilize them into a common search for life, those very pains are transformed from expressions of despair into signs of hope.

Through this common search, hospitality becomes community. Hospitality becomes community as it creates a unity based on the shared confession of our basic brokenness and on a shared hope. This hope in turn leads us far beyond the boundaries of human togetherness to Him who calls His people away from the land of slavery to the land of freedom. It belongs to the central insight of the Judaeo-Christian tradition, that it is the call of God which forms the people of God.

A Christian community is therefore a healing community not because wounds are cured and pains are alleviated, but because wounds and pains become openings or occasions for a new vision. Mutual confession then becomes a mutual deepening of hope, and sharing weakness becomes a reminder to one and all of the coming strength.

When loneliness is among the chief wounds of the minister, hospitality can convert that wound into a source of healing. Concentration prevents the minister from burdening others with his pain and allows him to accept his wounds as helpful teachers of his own and his neighbor's condition. Community arises where the sharing of pain takes place, not as a stifling form of self-complaint, but as a recognition of God's saving promises.

Conclusion

I started this chapter with the story of Rabbi Joshua ben Levi, who asked Elijah, "When will the Messiah come?" There is an important conclusion to this story. When Elijah had explained to him how he could find the Messiah sitting among the poor at the gates of the city, Rabbi Joshua ben Levi went to the Messiah and said to him:

"Peace unto you, my master and teacher."
> The Messiah answered, "Peace unto you, son of Levi."
> He asked, "When is the master coming?"
> "Today," he answered.
> Rabbi Yoshua returned to Elijah, who asked, "What did he tell you?"
> "He indeed has deceived me, for he said 'Today I am coming' and he has not come."
> Elijah said, "This is what he told you: 'Today if you would listen to His voice.'" (Psalm 95.7)

Even when we know that we are called to be wounded healers, it is still very difficult to acknowledge that healing has to take place today. Because we are living in days when our wounds have become all too visible. Our loneliness and isolation has become so much a part of our daily experience, that we cry out for a Liberator who will take us away from our misery and bring us justice and peace.

To announce, however, that the Liberator is sitting among the poor and that the wounds are signs of hope and that today is the day of liberation, is a step very few can take. But this is exactly the announcement of the wounded healer: "The master is coming—not tomorrow, but today, not next year, but this year, not after all our misery is passed, but in the middle of it, not in another place but right here where we are standing."

And with a challenging confrontation he says:

O that today you would listen to his voice!
Harden not your heart as at Meribah,
as on that day at Massah in the desert
when they tried me, though they saw
my work. (Psalm 95.7–9)

If indeed we listen to the voice and believe that ministry is a sign of hope, because it makes visible the first rays of light of the coming Messiah, we can make ourselves and others understand that we already carry in us the source of our own search. Thus ministry can indeed be a witness to the living truth that the wound, which causes us to suffer now, will be revealed to us later as the place where God intimated his new creation.

CHAPTER 8

The Circus Clown

Heije Faber[1] (1971)

If we are to give a true account of what it is we do and what we have to say as ministers in the hospital, then we must look at the minister's contribution and sketch his relationship to the other members of the [hospital] staff. I intend to do this through the somewhat unusual comparison of the minister in a hospital with the clown in a circus. I trust that it will become quite clear that this comparison is not a trivial one, but has a deep significance.

I would argue that the clown is a necessity in the circus, without whom the circus is no longer a circus but is reduced to a string of numbers, and that the clown occupies a unique place among the other artists in the circus. There are three tensions in the life of the clown: first, the tension between being a member of a team and being in isolation; secondly, the tension of appearing to be and feeling like an amateur among acknowledged experts; and finally, the tension between the need for study and training on the one hand and the necessity to be original and creative on the other. It should not prove difficult to make the connection with the minister's position.

In his striking novel *The Clown*,[2] German author Heinrich Böll has drawn a moving picture of the clown. The book describes the thoughts and feelings of a professional clown who has been deserted by the woman who has shared his life for some years and with whom he has been deeply in love. She has left to marry a man who is a social "success," a leading member of his church.

The Character of Clowning

In his reaction to this the clown makes clear to us what the essential character of clowning is about. The clown is one who cannot feel at home among those who are so successful; they make him feel powerless, weak. In the standards and clichés of normal life he senses the superficial and the spurious. He lives, as it were, on a different wavelength; he is one who, despite all his outward clumsiness and failure, nevertheless comes across to us as a man who comes close to what life is really about. He knows the meaning of love, of sorrow, of solidarity. These are things that those who make a fortune or a name for themselves, who sit in the front row, never find. The clown makes us feel nostalgic. We find him pathetic and laughable, but he represents something in ourselves; we somehow see in him something of what we ought really to be like.

Charlie Chaplin and Buziau spoke to thousands because they managed to show the ability to find the genuine, the authentic on the edges of life: the wry smile in the face of failure; the strange victory of the man who recognizes his weakness, his powerlessness in failure, and accepts it as part of the scheme of things; the little man who continues to have faith in something indestructible. Why *did* people flock to see the films of Chaplin and the revues featuring Buziau? Is it not because in the midst of this overpowering world with its armies and wars, its churches and politics, business empires and industries, and its vast cities, man still knows in his heart that he is only small, and he wants to recognize his small and powerless self in those little, funny people who play this part with a smile, who, playing like children amongst big guns, suddenly allow what is threatening to be seen for what it is, powerless and ridiculous. In this case the clown has a clear function. He puts things in perspective. He shows that there are more sides to life than those grasped by the big battalions. It is no accident that in the courts of the mighty the jester alone had the freedom to say what he liked. The jester reduced the ruler, who might have absolute power over life and death, to the stature of a man like others, and so made life bearable for the courtiers and, one suspects, for the ruler himself. Jesters fulfilled, in modern parlance, a psycho-hygienic function.

This is also the function of the clown in the circus itself; that is why he belongs to it, this place in which people perform great feats, tame wild animals and do hair-raising stunts on the trapeze. They make us feel tense and frightened, but the clown puts it back in perspective. In a childish way he makes these stunt-men look a little foolish; he makes us feel that they are, after all, only human and ordinary, and thus re-establishes a sort of spiritual balance.

We have seen, then, that the clown has his own place in our world. He is much more than a joker, a funny guy. He brings home to us an aspect of life which we need to make the world tolerable. He has his own wavelength, his own pattern.

The Changing Image of the Minister

One of the remarkable phenomena of our time is the change which has overtaken the image of the priest and minister. They used to be regarded as the pillars of an ordered society, the upholders of morality, guardians of respectability, people of social standing, men of unmistakable authority. These features are gradually fading and giving way to a newly emerging shape, which bears a remarkable resemblance to the figure of the clown. How clearly this is captured in the Chaplinesque character of Don Camillo, known through books and films all over the world.

Already in a previous century the famous Danish theologian, Kierkegaard, made use of this imagery in a now famous passage. We find clownish features in the novels of Bernanos and Graham Greene (e.g., the whisky-soaked priest in *The Power and the Glory*). Many will be familiar with the figure of the idiot in Dostoevsky's novel of the same name. We are beginning to get a feel for "the foolishness of God" in our world. How this can work out in reality is shown, for example, by the non-violent protest movement against racial segregation in the United States. To fight without resort to violence shows a touch of the clown.

The Foolishness of God

There are words in the New Testament which point to the reality of this "foolishness of God." In the first letter to the Corinthians, Paul speaks of the divine foolishness of the cross of Christ, who has allowed himself to be crucified: "the foolishness of God is wiser than men, and the weakness of God is stronger than men" (1:25, RSV). And a little later, he observes that the Christian community does not consist of many influential or important people: "God chose what is foolish in the world to shame the wise" (1:27a, RSV). Christians are, therefore, according to Paul, called to be "fools for Christ's sake." Did Christ himself perhaps hint at this when he spoke of the need to be converted and become like little children? We are undoubtedly touching here on a real aspect of the New Testament understanding of faith.

It is not so easy to capture this aspect definitively in words. We can indicate it as follows: a character which is slightly anti-social; openness and sympathy in love; a feel for the fringes of human life; a kind of irresponsibility, carelessness and inner freedom; the ability to share suffering, compassion; humor (but normally not satirical humor!); a great deal of patience and wisdom. And we are to note that these are not experienced as normal human qualities but as a pattern of life of another order, on another wavelength. This is the life of a "saint," in its deepest sense.

Tensions in the Lives of Clowns and of Ministers

We noted earlier a threefold tension in the life of the clown, and also remarked that there was clearly a parallel here with the tensions of the minister in a hospital. We must now look at the latter.

Belonging and Isolation

First, there is the tension between belonging to a team and a measure of isolation. The clown is a member of a team: they value one another and have a certain sense of solidarity; they respect each other's skills. At the same time, the clown has his own place, his "number"; he is different from the others. Essentially he stands alone in the circus. In his work, he has little contact with the others. He represents a personal "dimension." Clergy also find that it seems difficult for the medical staff to grasp the nature of their work, even when they make a real effort to do so.

For the clown, the public is much more than an object of his prowess, as it is for the other circus artistes. He has a kind of solidarity with the public in the boundary situations of our existence: sorrow, the absurd, setbacks. Chaplin and Buziau have a relationship with the public which is peculiar to them. The clown tries to get the audience "with him" in smiling in the midst of tragedy: he shows his littleness, but in so doing points to real greatness. In the same sort of way the minister in the hospital is other than the medical men, for whom the patients become objects of their medical skills, to be "treated." Of course there is an element of solidarity with the patient, but the role of the doctor towards the patient demands objectivity. Here lies a real difference in the role of the minister. His solidarity with the patient is peculiarly his own, different from that of the doctor; it springs from a familiarity with the boundary situation. The solidarity of the doctor and patient is that of comrades-in-arms; that of the minister is that of standing with the patient in the difficulties and opportunities of boundary situations. In this solidarity the minister, like the clown, will seek to make himself small, but in so doing he will point towards the great things, which can set the sick man free, show him the (divine) humor of the situation, so that in the midst of his suffering he will raise a smile.

Like the clown, the minister also represents a different order, a separate wavelength, the world of faith, i.e., that of the man who discovers God at the center of his life. Perhaps we may say that the world of the clown is that of the one who in the ultimate decaying of life asserts himself as truly human. It may well be that the two worlds are much closer to each other than one suspects.

An Amateur among Experts

The second tension experienced by the clown is between the awareness that he is amongst "experts" and the fact that by comparison he is an "amateur." They do their stunts; he seems to contribute no such feats. In the hospital the minister experiences a similar contrast. Increasingly, the hospital is the scene of tremendous feats; between these walls great strides are made in the march of science and technology. Those working there are all experts in their own fields who have had a special training for their task. The specialists, nurses, social workers, analysts, physiotherapists—they are all trapeze-artistes, but the poor clergyman is the clown. He presents a clear contrast to all of them. Paul, in the same letter to the Corinthians from which we quoted above, writes that his work among them in Corinth was not marked "by plausible words of wisdom." He does not trust that kind of stunt; he wants the work to be God's, and for that reason he must avoid putting himself in the limelight through cleverness.

The minister has a different sort of contact with the patient from that of other members of the team. He does not wear a white coat, is not conspicuous. In the hospital he is just an "ordinary" person. He may not rely on his learning or training, on a sympathetic personality, on a straightforward easy manner, nor on his seriousness, or the warmth of his approach, or his good reputation or even on his modesty. All these things can at any time get in the way of that which needs to come into being between him and the patient. The minister is only true to his calling when he does not draw attention to himself in any way whatever, but by his actions and his words points a way to the one in whose service he stands, whom he represents and seeks to make present to the man in his sickness. There must be an *innocence* about him, though not gullible ignorance; he must be the one who knows the powers of darkness and temptation—indeed, no aspect of life should be foreign to him—yet also knows he can see and point to a way which surmounts them. He must therefore be naive, in the sense in which Christ spoke of becoming a child, an attitude constantly aware of its own opposite, fully understanding it. The minister who is just naive will not be able to understand and accept the other as he needs to be understood, as someone who has run to a stand-still in the blind alleys of existence. Paul could write about the value of "foolishness," because his Jewish upbringing has instilled the experience of "wisdom" and its lure into every fiber of his being.

Study and Creativity

The third tension is that between the necessity of study and training on the one hand and of originality and creativity on the other. If the minister is to be compared with the clown, he is not to overlook how Grock, one of the greatest of clowns, would study his act almost daily, frequently giving it fresh slants, and taking care to note the reactions of the audience. He realized that a clown had to be professional. The pastoral ministry is also a trade one has to learn and make one's own by study and training. It is encouraging to find that an increasing number of ministers in the Netherlands are now preparing for their ministry by taking part in a "clinical training" course. Neither clown nor minister are innocents; they know what they are doing. Yet clergy will have to realize that too often their knowledge is not enough. They have too little insight into the patient and the way in which he has to wrestle with the problems of being ill; they realize too little that the business of creating a relationship with the sick is deliberate and a matter of continuous self-examination; more generally, they are too little aware of the fact that in purely professional terms they fall short of the mark in certain respects.

And yet, at the same time, the pastoral ministry can never be a question of routine and familiar ruts; at least it ought not to be. The minister, like the clown, must in the depths of his being remain original and creative. What does that mean in practice? For me it means that the minister also experiences the pangs of doubt and unbelief which the patient faces on his sickbed. It is when the minister thinks that his belief is a possession, to be handed out at will, that his ministry becomes a routine. He will only be able to listen to the doubt and the hidden unbelief in others (and without that he simply cannot be of help!) if he is also tuned to listen to the doubts and unbelief in himself.

It follows from this that he will need a community–preferably in the setting of his work, i.e., of colleagues–in which he can discuss the personal aspects of his work with others. Such exchange will shed light on points where he will not be able to provide such light himself, and where study and self-imposed meditation are also not likely to do so. Indeed, true study and real meditation are more likely to spring from such conversations. The isolation of the minister is on the one hand a condition of his ministry, but it can also endanger the reality of his work.

The Inner Life of the Minister

The reader will have noticed that my aim is to create a measure of understanding of the minister and his task among the other members of the team by sketching the lines of the pastoral ministry as it were from within, to show how being a minister is experienced inwardly. In other words, we are not just looking at the task of the minister but also at the minister himself. The picture will therefore not be complete unless we go further and attempt to depict how the minister experiences this threefold tension and copes or fails to cope with it. I want to draw attention to three points, which need to be grasped by those who have dealings with the minister, if they are to have a clear understanding of him.

Sense of Inferiority

First, many clergy who come to work in institutions such as hospitals or prisons will, initially at any rate, suffer under a sense of inferiority. The others in the team seem to be so much better at their job; they can point to results; they are often more efficient. The minister is then exposed to the temptation to imitate the others and in some way or other to conform. He also tries to conduct his conversations after the manner of the psychiatrist or the social worker. He does not realize that in so doing he is, in missionary terms, "going native." He ceases to be himself.

If he does not try this, he may fall into an opposite trap, in that he attempts to mark off his position in too self-assertive a fashion. He compensates for his unsureness through a show of authority; he makes it clear that he has rights and can expect cooperation. Alternatively he quickly feels himself slighted and complains far more than is reasonable. It is simply a necessary aspect of working in a team that one has to learn to fit in with the work of others and that this involves a certain amount of "give"; nurses and medical staff have to learn a similar lesson.

I am not sure how frequently such compensation occurs. Probably there is a great deal less of it than I might seem to suggest. What I am concerned to stress is that the position of the minister in the hospital not only creates uncertainty for the hospital staff but also for him. He is not always capable of judging his place, status and role clearly amongst the various experts in the hospital. The older man will probably have less difficulty, but the younger clergy especially will often not find their way around hospital life without problems.

Cultural Shifts

The second point we must note is that in coping with the tensions indicated, the minister is also affected by the vast shifts which occur throughout our modern culture, creating difficulties in assessing his actual task and opportunities. Not only in the hospital but everywhere in modern society we meet a growing re-thinking of "the place and task of the clergy in a new world."[3] Some ministers sense this shift as an erosion of the pastoral ministry: the role, task and structure of the ministry seem to become diffused. The church and consequently the ministry suffer a loss of function in comparison with an earlier age; they are being penned into a small and clearly marked off area.

More and more other social agencies are taking over work which used to be part of the church's task. There is a consequent and inevitable loss of authority. For example, when the Pope makes pronouncements in the field of modern scientific developments, these carry much less weight than they would have done in the last century. For some clergy this can result in a loss of belief in their contribution. We pointed this out in another connection. Everywhere in the church one finds the same discussion: What is the essence of the pastoral ministry? What is irreplaceable about it? And what, in the light of this, are the possibilities open to us of realizing this essential ministry?

It is clear enough that the work of the minister is different from that of the psychiatrist and the medical social worker. Of course there are points of contact, but it possesses something peculiarly its own, its own focal point. I believe that we will best grasp this if we say simply that the minister is the representative of the church. More is involved in this than the words might suggest, and it is here more than anywhere that we come on the track of the true character of pastoral ministry.

As a representative of the church the minister in fact seeks to represent Christ. It is true, of course, that every person may in his dealings with others and therefore with the sick know himself to be a follower of Christ. One can see one's work as nurse or doctor as service to Christ. Indeed, in a famous poem, Guillaume van der Graft says of the surgeon that, even if he himself does not believe in Christ, in the poet's eyes he still brings relief from pain for the sake of Christ. The minister, however, has been explicitly appointed by his church to represent Christ.

At the Second Vatican Council, the Roman Catholic Church produced some new definitions of the church which appeal to me. The church is there described as the people of God, which in its earthly pilgrimage is being led by Christ into a future in the light. If to represent Christ means to make him present, then the consequence for the ministry is that the minister so stands by the other (i.e., more is involved than proclaiming the message or distributing the sacraments) that the other comes to accept that he belongs, that in the solidarity offered him by the minister he finds the courage to entrust himself to Christ and to the light. The pastoral ministry is therefore pastoral solidarity with the other, supporting him in the quest to become one who dares to believe in himself, because he has discovered through the minister, *experienced* through him, that Christ believes in him. As a result, he begins to look for that light in hope and in turn finds himself wanting and able to be in solidarity with others.

To represent Christ is therefore essentially a way of being (i.e., an interaction of word and deed), in the deepest sense an attitude. When we grasp this, we can see that the presence of the minister changes the "climate" of the hospital: instead of being an institution it becomes a home. It becomes much more than a factory, a place in which "feats' are performed. This happens in the same way in which the "climate" of the circus changes through the presence of the clown, who by his performance puts the "feats" of the others in perspective.

In a discussion about the significance of the pastoral ministry in the hospital a surgeon remarked that we need the minister for the climate, the spirit of the hospital. It is not that we want to have a certain reputation, that with us, as in church hospitals, there are services and that we therefore meet the wishes of those patients who value them; it is, rather, that we recognize that our medical work comes to stand in a different framework when the minister works beside us, a framework which we sense to be right.

The hospital must be more than a factory. We could perhaps say that, just as the clown makes the circus what it truly is, so the presence of the minister makes the hospital truly itself. Through his place in it he sets the experts in a different perspective. He represents a different wavelength, another order, in which man is no longer only an object of treatment, but a person, who struggles in his suffering to remain man, perhaps man with a relationship to God.

Activity and Presence

There is a third point. The minister can attempt to resolve the tensions inherent in his position by excessive activity. He thinks that he can justify his place in the hospital by *much doing*. The hospital is increasingly becoming a place in which people are busy with the patient. In earlier days, one of the features of the process of recovery was the rest which the hospital afforded the patient. The modern hospital, by contrast, is a beehive humming with endless activity.

One of the prime considerations has become the need to shorten the average stay of the patient. This can only be achieved through being constantly and efficiently busy with the patient. It is tempting for the minister to try to compensate for his lack of certainty by also being busy with all sorts of things, lots of conversations, lectures, study groups, services, leaflets, in short, by being able to produce a long and impressive work list. Sometimes he feels he needs to justify his existence in this way.

Of course a minister needs to map out his work efficiently and to make good use of his time. Yet he must never forget that, in his ministry, what he *is* is more important than what he *does*. Decisive for the "success" of his ministry is his ability to recognize that pastoral relationship in which he stands and on that basis to seek to create proper and good relationships. What matters is his attitude, whether he has a real interest in (which means "being among") the patients, the staff, in all concerned, in the institution itself and–never forget!– in himself.

CHAPTER 9

The Wise Fool

Alastair V. Campbell[1] (1981)

> All things counter, original, spare, strange;
>   Whatever is fickle, freckled (who knows how?)
>   With swift, slow; sweet, sour; adazzle, dim;
> He fathers-forth whose beauty is past change:
>   Praise him.

Gerard Manley Hopkins[2]

The paradoxical insight that we heal most effectively by sharing our vulnerability leads to [another] image by which pastoral care can be rediscovered: the disheveled, gauche, tragicomic figure of the fool. Paul's advice to the Corinthian church effectively dismisses worldly wisdom as a guideline for Christians:

> If anyone among you thinks he is wise by this world's standards, he should become a fool, in order to be really wise. (1 Cor. 3:18, TEV)

The fool is especially vulnerable to those who hold earthly power: easily derided and exploited, used as a scapegoat, treated (as Paul says in describing his own "folly for Christ's sake") as "the offal of the world...the scum of the earth" (1 Cor. 4:13, JB).

The Fool: A Necessary Figure

Yet in all societies and all ages the fool has been a necessary and significant figure.[3] He appears as the essential counterpoise to human arrogance, pomposity, and despotism. His unruly behavior questions the limits of order; his "crazy," outspoken talk probes the meaning of "common sense"; his unconventional appearance exposes the pride and vanity of those around him; his foolhardy loyalty to "lost" causes undercuts prudence and self-interest.

The more we examine it, the more complex and ambiguous the image of the fool becomes. Folly is often two-edged, making mockery of good and ill alike, provoking malicious and cruel laughter at times, yet also using humor and ridicule to evoke love and concern. Since folly steps outside order, we cannot expect to control it easily—more often it takes us over in a holy or unholy madness. In this chapter I shall try to impose some order on the fool's image in order to see its significance for pastoral care, suggesting three dimensions of such care: folly as simplicity, folly as loyalty, and folly as prophecy; but the feeling must remain that somewhere in the wings the fool is having the last laugh!

Folly as Simplicity

Søren Kierkegaard, reflecting in his journals upon the significance of the incarnation of Christ, remarked, "One is sickened by the chatter of fussy go-betweens about Christ being the greatest hero, etc., etc., the humorous interpretation is far better."[4] Kierkegaard had in mind the central paradox of Christianity that "the eternal is the historical."[5] He realized that to the logically minded such an idea must be plainly absurd, laughable, a cosmic joke.

So it was that when Paul debated with the Epicurean and Stoic philosophers in Athens, some of them said contemptuously, "Does this parrot know what he is talking about?" (Acts 17:18, JB). Similarly, Festus, the Roman governor of Caesarea, shouts out to Paul, when he declares that the Messiah had to suffer and then rise from the dead, "Paul, you are raving; too much study is driving you mad" (Acts 26:24, NEB). Such reactions illustrate well Paul's own description of the effect his preaching had: "We proclaim the crucified Christ, a message that is offensive to the Jews and nonsense to the Gentiles" (1 Cor. 1:23, TEV).

Folly as Wisdom or Nonsense?

How do we know when folly is a kind of wisdom and when it is simply nonsense? This is the first question which the ambiguous figure of the fool poses. In *The Exploits of the Incomparable Mulla Nasrudin*, Idries Shah has popularized an ancient figure of wise folly who originates in the mystical and intuitive insights of the Sufis of Islam. The Mulla is a highly entertaining character whose "foolishness" often works to his advantage:

> Time and again Nasrudin passed from Persia to Greece on donkey-back. Each time he had two panniers of straw, and trudged back without them. Every time the guards searched him for contraband. They never found any.
>
> "What are you carrying, Nasrudin?"

"I am a smuggler."

Years later, more and more prosperous in appearance, Nasrudin moved to Egypt. One of the customs men met him there.

"Tell me, Mulla, now that you are out of the jurisdiction of Greece and Persia, living here in such luxury—what was it you were smuggling when we could never catch you?"

"Donkeys."[6]

The wisdom of Mulla Nasrudin derives from the clever way in which his folly reveals the unexpected, the overlooked. The description of Touchstone in *As You Like It* fits the Mulla well: "He uses his folly like a stalking horse and under the presentation of that he shoots his wit."[7]

Such folly is undoubtedly a kind of wisdom and (as we shall see in a later section) the odd and surprising behavior of the fool can provide a form of prophetic insight.

The Folly of Christianity

But the folly of Christianity is less cunning, less contrived, than the type of witty perception which is the stock-in-trade of the professional fool. Perhaps Erasmus is nearer the mark when he argues in his famous work *Praise of Folly*[8] that Christianity is close to a kind of natural simplicity. (We note that his remarks would now be viewed as deplorably sexist and "ageist"):

> The very young and the very old, women and simpletons are the people who take the greatest delight in sacred and holy things, and are therefore always found nearest the altars, led there doubtless solely by their natural instinct.[9]

Erasmus' reference to the simpleton or "*natural* fool" (a term used from medieval times to draw a contrast with the "artificial fool," i.e., the professional court jester) heightens the ambiguity of the gospel's folly. For the natural fool lacks the *capacity* to reason. He speaks out of an intellectual innocence, unaware of the complexity of rational discourse. An obvious comparison may be drawn with Jesus' exhortation to his disciples to receive the Kingdom of God like little children (Lk. 18:17), and with the simplicity of Jesus' own teaching, which depended not on complicated arguments but on vivid stories and dramatic actions. Thus Erasmus is prepared to describe Jesus himself as "something of a fool":

> Christ, too, though he is the wisdom of the Father, was made something of a fool himself in order to help the folly of mankind, when he assumed the nature of man and was seen in man's form.[10]

Now we are indeed closer to the "folly of the cross," for how are we to distinguish the naiveté and intellectual incompetence of little children or of the mentally retarded from nonsense? Can we really say that such untutored simplicity is a form of wisdom? The question cannot be answered unambiguously.

"Natural fools" *do* lack knowledge and reasoning ability. They frequently fail to understand the more complex aspects of human experience, and their lack of ability to predict consequences can at times endanger themselves and others. Yet this same lack of sophistication gives a refreshing directness to the simpler person's ways of relating to others. There is a physical immediacy in responses of affection and anger and a lack of hypocrisy in the things said. (One can understand how the "natural fool" was the precursor of the professional court fool, who had a license to speak hard truths to the king.)[11]

The Effect of the Fool

Dostoevsky's novel *The Idiot* provides an interesting portrayal of the effect which an (apparently) simple-minded person can have on those around him. The principal character, Prince Myshkin (who is an epileptic, as Dostoevsky himself was), appears slow-witted and socially gauche. His open simplicity of manner leads people to regard him as an idiot, especially since he does not conform to the insincerities and cynical self-seeking of the upper-class society to which he belongs. His honesty and simplicity expose the corruptions of the people around him, yet in a gentle and perceptive manner which seems to offer them a way back to their true selves. The effect he creates on people is well summed up by Ganya, a character who is at once fascinated by Prince Myshkin and furious at his simple honesty:

> What made me think this morning that you were an idiot? You notice things other people never notice. One could have a real talk to you, though, perhaps, one had better not.[12]

The wisdom of such simplicity lies in its power to expose insincerity and self-deception. Often simple persons are unaware of the effect they are having on those around them, and (unlike the professional fool) they are not acting the way they do *in order* to create an effect. Yet they mediate singleness and honesty to those who have ears to hear and eyes to see. It is as though they hold up a mirror in which we can see a reflection of our society's and our own hypocrisy.

Those of us who are adult and in full possession of our faculties cannot, of course, pretend to possess the simplicity of the natural fool. We cannot make ourselves into innocent little children or dispossess ourselves of our reasoning powers. Indeed, it would be a strange denial of ourselves to want to do so.

Rediscovering the Losses of Adult Wisdom

But the image of folly as simplicity can help us rediscover parts of ourselves which have been lost as we learned "adult wisdom," thus opening up more spontaneous ways of relating to ourselves and others. That same simplicity can remind us that faith is a product of trust, not of reason, and that such trust comes more easily to those who do not insist on intellectualizing every experience. Rediscovering simplicity can also make us less afraid of speaking nonsense in the world's estimation, for such "nonsense" can often strike at the heart of truth.

How these aspects of the simplicity of folly may improve our pastoral care will be discussed at the end of the chapter, after we have examined two other dimensions of folly: loyalty and prophecy.

Folly as Loyalty

A second dimension of folly brings us to the notion of *foolhardiness.* The folly of the cross, and therefore of those who try to obey Jesus' call to take up *their* cross and follow him, is the sheer lack of self-interest which such action entails. As Paul continues to pursue the theme of folly in his first letter to the Corinthians, he is moved to draw some invidious comparisons between his converts' life and his own:

> It seems to me that God has given the very last place to us apostles...For Christ's sake we are fools; but you are wise in union with Christ! We are weak, but you are strong! We are despised, but you are honored! To this very moment we go hungry and thirsty; we are clothed in rags; we are beaten; we wander from place to place; we wear ourselves out with hard work...We are no more than this world's garbage. (1 Cor. 4:9–13, TEV)

Loyalty as Enigma

Paul had a tendency to get carried away with self-admiration when describing the rigors of his life, as he himself was aware (2 Cor. 11:17); but the purpose of this "boasting" was to remind his fellow Christians that loyalty to Christ must mean hardship and the risking of self: "I am content with weaknesses, insults, hardships, persecutions, and difficulties for Christ's sake. For when I am weak, then I am strong" (2 Cor. 12:10, TEV). The loyalty of the fool who follows Christ is an enigma in the world's eyes–the greater the loyalty, the greater the suffering which ensues. Why then remain loyal, if there is no advantage to it?

The same enigma is presented in dramatic form by the character of the Fool in Shakespeare's *King Lear.* The play depicts the sharp contrast between the misunderstood loyalty of Cordelia, Kent, and the Fool, and the falsely trusted flattery of Goneril, Regan, and Edmund. The King discovers too late who his real enemies are; and, as his madness mounts, the fury of a stormy night matches his inner turmoil. Now, cast out into the storm by his heartless daughters, the half-crazed old man finds that his only companion is the Fool who "labors to outjest his heart-struck injuries."[13] Why does the Fool stay by the King's side when everyone else deserts him? In typical style, the Fool explains himself in a little ditty:

> That sir which serves and seeks for gain,
> And follows but for form,

Will pack when it begins to rain,
    And leave thee in the storm.
But I will tarry; the Fool will stay,
    And let the wise man fly.
The knave turns fool that runs away;
    The Fool, no knave, perdy.[14]

Against the greed, treachery, and callous disregard for others which now dominates Lear's former kingdom, the Fool presents the simple virtue of an unheroic but persistent loyalty. Shame lies not in being a fool, but in being a knave.[15]

Jesus and the Enigma of Loyalty

This enigma—the strange willingness to disregard self out of a higher loyalty—can be found at the center of Jesus' life and death. The taunting of the dying Jesus by the chief priests, scribes, and elders focuses on the helpless state of the one who, it was claimed, was King of Israel and Son of God: "He saved others; himself he cannot save... He trusted in God; let him deliver him now" (Mt. 27:42–43, KJV). The mockery echoes the temptations in the wilderness when Jesus refused to seek power and safety by supernatural means (Lk. 4:1–13 and par.). Instead, he chose the foolhardy way, the unprotected path that led to danger and death.

Such foolhardiness is also a prominent feature of Jesus' teaching. Some of his sayings and stories draw attention to the *wrong* kind of foolishness: There is the fool who builds a house on sand instead of on rock (Mt. 7:24–27 and par.); the fool who enlarges his barns and neglects his soul (Lk. 12:13–21); and the five female fools who are caught unprepared for the coming of the bridegroom (Mt. 25:1–13). Yet at the same time Jesus encourages a quite outrageous improvidence in his followers: they must deny themselves to follow him (Mt. 16:24); a man cannot stay to bury his father or turn back to say good-by to his family (Lk. 9:59–62); the rich young man must sell all he had (Mt. 19:16–22); family and possessions are rightly left behind for the Kingdom's sake (Mk. 10:29 and par.); and no thought is to be taken for the morrow (Lk. 12:22–23).

The force of all this teaching may be summed up in the mysterious saying of Jesus: "Whosoever will save his life shall lose it: and whosoever will lose his life for my sake shall find it" (Mt. 16:25, AV). It is useless to try to take away the sharpness of this saying by the glib explanation that since faith brings a higher fulfillment, there is really no danger of loss for the Christian. Such an easy solution translates following Jesus into enlightened self-interest, and thereby removes the folly of the cross.

The Fool's Lack of Self-interest

The whole point of fools' loyalty is that they *cannot* be sure it will be to their advantage. Their loyalty is the very opposite of prudence, because, on the face of it, they are risking comfort and life itself for some unattainable ideal. They would not be fools at all if they already knew that everything would turn out all right. (One of the lessons the first Christians had to learn was that their hopes for an early coming of the Kingdom of God, when love and justice would finally prevail, were mistaken. No such easy reassurance presented itself.)

All that fools for Christ's sake can know is that to be true to themselves they must try to be loyal to Christ and that this must mean putting love and service to others first in life. The enigma of such loyalty finds its ultimate expression in the crazy logic of loving those who do you harm:

> Love your enemies, do good to those who hate you, bless those who curse you, and pray for those who mistreat you. (Lk. 6:27–28, TEV)

Jesus surely appears to be the greatest of fools when he asks God to forgive his accusers and executioners even as they mock him in his suffering. How could a person allow himself to be so exploited, unless he trusted beyond reason, in the ultimate triumph of love? As we shall see, the same question faces those who try to be the givers of care in much less extreme situations of mockery and hurt. There is nothing more easily exploited than the loyalty of the fool.[16]

Folly as Prophecy

So far we have been examining what may be called the "pathetic" aspects of the fool's image, the fool as a simpleton, and the fool as a loyal, easily exploited friend. But there is also a more active, rumbustious, resilient aspect to the fool, which must not be neglected. This comic aspect gives a quite different perspective to the nature of folly. It reveals it to be a form of *prophecy*, not in the sense of *fore*telling the future, but in the sense of *forth*telling, of pointing to the signs of the times and proclaiming divine revelations about them.

Prophetic Folly as Challenge to Norms and Authorities

The prophetic aspect of folly has, throughout the ages, functioned as a form of challenge to the accepted norms, conventions, and authorities within a society. Thus Wolfgang Zucker can argue that the modern circus clown is a vehicle of God's laughter at our arrogance and self-importance:

> Who laughs? Is it the clown, the marginal outsider; or is it the audience when it is taken to and beyond the limits of its own restricting order? Or still another possibility: is not the clown perhaps himself the laughter of the Infinite about the Finite when it pretends to be absolute? The laughter of God?[17]

An interesting historical example of the use of folly as a challenge to ecclesiastical authority is found in the medieval *Narrenfest*, the Feast of Fools. This was a kind of anti-Mass celebrated by the younger clergy in defiance of the bishop and his established orders. Beginning on the first day of January (the Day of Circumcision), it continued until Epiphany. The "celebrants" wore masks and fantastic costumes, banqueted at the altar, celebrated an obscene parody of the ritual of the Mass, and even, on occasion, worshiped an ass as the "Lord of Disorder."

Despite official opposition the practice was followed in many European cathedral churches from the twelfth to the fifteenth century, and vestiges of it can be found as late as the seventeenth century.[18] Such frolics can be regarded as a kind of safety valve, allowing the expression of forbidden wishes which the usual pomp and solemnity of religious ritual cannot allow, but they also have a deeper significance. They raise questions about the undue importance with which religious institutions invest themselves.

Foolery of Old Testament Prophets

Thus such dramatic foolery is moving in the direction of the Old Testament prophets' challenge to the practice of cultic sacrifices:

> What shall I bring when I approach the LORD?
> How shall I stoop before God on high?
> Am I to approach him with whole-offerings or yearling calves?
> Will the LORD accept thousands of rams
> > or ten thousand rivers of oil?
> Shall I offer my eldest son for my wrongdoing,
> > my children for my own sin? (Mic. 6:6–7, NEB)

The dramatic exaggeration of Micah's descriptions, culminating in the horror of human sacrifice, creates a parody of priestly worship and prepares the hearer for the contrast of the prophet's own message:

> God has told you what is good;
> > and what is it that the LORD asks of you?
> > Only to act justly, to love loyalty,
> > to walk wisely before your God. (Mic. 6:8, NEB)

The creation of such dramatic effects is still more evident in the bizarre *behavior* of the Old Testament prophets. By means of symbolic actions,[19] reminiscent of the "crazy" antics of the professional clown, they drew attention to God's judgment on Israel. For example, Isaiah went naked and barefoot for three years to warn of the impending humiliation and captivity of Egypt and Cush (Isa. 20:1–6); Hosea married a prostitute and gave ominous names to her children (Hos. 1:2–9). Jeremiah hid a waist-cloth in a crevice among rocks (Jer. 13:1–11); walked around with a yoke on his back (Jer. 27:1–11); and threw a book containing prophecies of disaster into the Euphrates, weighting it with a stone (Jer. 51:59–64). Ezekiel cut off his hair and beard, burned some in the center of the city, cut some up, and scattered the rest to the wind (Ezek. 5:1–14); he packed his belongings and left the city like an exile (Ezek. 12:1–11); and he failed to show signs of mourning when his wife died (Ezek. 24:15–24).

When we add to these strange actions of the prophets their ecstatic utterances and dramatic visions, it is no surprise to read that Hosea was accused of being a crazy fool (Hos. 9:7) or that Jeremiah was in danger of being locked up as a madman (Jer. 29:26f.). Such strange behavior, however, is madness only to those who are too set in their ways to hear the prophet's message. The whole point of prophecy is that it does not fit in with the "common-sense" assumptions of the day: it cuts cross-grained to earthly power and authority, announcing God's judgment upon it. Thus it is often misunderstood, ridiculed, or simply ignored. There is something elusive about such incongruity. You need to have ears to hear it and eyes to see it (see Isa. 6).

Jesus' Prophetic Foolery

The same element of incongruity may be seen in the prophetic words and actions of Jesus. He reverses the accepted religious values of his day, making the humble tax-gatherer more righteous than the law-abiding Pharisee (Lk. 18:10–14), the Samaritan more loving than the priest and the Levite (Lk. 10:25–37), the rich man less acceptable than the poor (Lk. 18:25 and par.). He associates with the "wrong" company (Lk. 15:1f) and fails to fast and abstain from wine like other prophets (Lk. 7:34). He defies the legalism of the Sabbath laws by allowing his disciples to pluck ears of corn and by healing a man with a paralyzed hand (Lk. 6:1–11 and par.).

The drama of Jesus' prophetic actions and the colorful and paradoxical imagery of his teachings have been captured in an attractive way in the musical *Godspell*, which portrays Jesus and his followers as a troupe of playful and irreverent clowns. *Godspell* succeeds in restoring humor and gaiety in the life of Jesus, which (in view of the criticisms made by the religious authorities of his time) must have been present, but was quickly lost in the solemnity of pious memories.

The guise of the clown also conveys some of the pathos of the gospel narrative, for the clown's appearance is at once both comic and tragic. But the clown's costume is also an inadequate portrayal of the depth of folly in the passion of Jesus. Here Jesus' words about the strange appearance of John the Baptist apply:

> "What was the spectacle that drew you to the wilderness? A reed-bed swept by the wind? No? Then what did you go out to see? A man dressed in silks and satins? (Lk. 7:24–25, NEB)

The appearance which Jesus presents as his death approaches vividly conveys the reversal of values which his whole life represented: "He had no beauty, no majesty to draw our eyes" (Isa. 53:2, NEB). Before his betrayal and arrest, he strips off his clothing and, wearing only a cloth around his waist, like the humblest slave, he washes the feet of his disciples (John 13:3ff.). Then before he is led out to be crucified, the Roman soldiers strip off his clothes once more, and, in mockery of his kingship, dress him in a purple robe and a crown of thorny branches. The "Kingly" costume forced onto Jesus makes mockery of his accusers, not of him, since his kingship was not of this world and the humility of a condemned prisoner was his royal choice. Jesus, incongruously clad as a slave and as mock king, challenges all who arrogate to themselves a place of special importance in this world or the next.

Non-prophetic Foolery

Thus folly can function as a potent form of prophecy, because, by its startling reversal of the shaft of ridicule, it allows us to see ourselves in a clearer light and prevents us from giving to fallible human institutions the honor they are *not* due. Yet we must beware of supposing that *all* folly is prophetic in this way. Clowning, buffoonery, and satire can often be heartless, destructive of human values, a weapon to protect the perpetrator against any genuine involvement with others. Frequently, professional fools function merely as mouthpieces for the hidden desires of their audiences, allowing them to identify with an excess of vulgarity and violence without feeling a sense of responsibility for it themselves.

Again, much professional foolery finds its origin in a cruel mockery of "freaks," that is, the mentally subnormal, physically deformed, or emotionally damaged members of society. In fact, the human capacity for laughter and for delight in the unusual can be used in an amazing variety of ways, for good or ill. But the capacity to laugh also points to an essentially human attribute, the ability to reflect upon experience. It is this self-reflective ability which makes *homo ridens* into a creature who can respond to the challenge of prophecy, and, in turn, allows us to regard prophetic folly as an aspect of pastoral care.

Pastoral Care as Folly

In *Pastoral Care in the Modern Hospital,* Heije Faber suggests that we can compare the minister working in a hospital with the clown in the circus. The clown's role, according to Faber, contains three tensions: he is one of many circus acts, yet he has a certain uniqueness, setting him apart from the others; he appears and feels like an amateur amongst highly skilled professionals; and his act is one of creative spontaneity, yet it demands study and training. Faber implies that the clown to be truly a clown must never seem quite at home in the circus, and he has little difficulty in showing that a minister in the modern hospital is (or should be) in that same position. What the minister has to offer is different in kind from the many professional skills encompassed by the health care professions.[20]

The analogy drawn by Faber can be broadened out to apply to pastoral care as a whole, not simply to the pastoral work of ministers working in hospital settings. Just as the clown act is unique in the circus, so pastoral care must be *in* the world, but not *of* the world. It must operate within modern society, recognizing its powerful effects on people, but it can never fit comfortably into it. A caring which is pastoral must always seem a little bizarre, a little naive, and not a little irreverent, in the context of the values which our materialistic culture worships.

Moreover, pastoral care must avoid the temptation to turn its "clown act" into the polished performance of the trapeze artist, the lion tamer, or the juggler. The folly, the scandal, of pastoral care is that it describes the stumbling efforts of the nonprofessional to care for others. Some words about the sense of identification which the circus clown evokes in his audience might equally be applied to the attractiveness and fallibility of ordinary human caring:

> In him, in his ludicrous contradictions of dignity and embarrassment,
> of pomp and rags, of assurance and collapse, of sentiment and sadness,
> of innocence and guile, we learn to see ourselves.[21]

The Danger of Losing Professionalism

Thus the tendency in recent pastoral care literature to focus almost exclusively on "counseling skills" and to encourage the development of a cadre of professional "pastoral counselors" must be viewed with some alarm. Such developments create a "competence gap" between professional, trained counselors and the "ordinary" church member and easily result in a loss of the uniquely *foolish* aspects of pastoral care.

On the other hand, the foolish aspects of caring are not to be equated with the blundering (if well-meant) incompetence of those who have not troubled to prepare themselves for the task of helping others. As Faber reminds us, the clown's refreshing spontaneity is the product of careful preparation and training. The same must be true of the folly of our pastoral care. It will be helpful to others only when we learn how to acquire the simplicity, loyal love, and releasing laughter of God's "foolishness." Such qualities rarely come naturally to us. They need some kind of learning.

Simplicity

Let us, then, return to the simplicity of the fool and consider how we might try to identify with it. The greatest hazard facing us in trying to help others is our verbosity. We use words to distance ourselves from experience—our own and other people's—and so to lose the simple sense of *nearness*—nearness of nature, of other people, and of God. The loss of this unitary vision permits us to be seduced into playing verbal games with people instead of seeking with them that which brings them peace.

Avenues to Simplicity

In Kahlil Gibran's words: "Thought is a bird of space, that in a cage of words may indeed unfold its wings, but cannot fly."[22] To rediscover the simplicity of the natural fool we need to find ways of release from the "cage of words." Thus preparation for caring means learning to enjoy the richness of silence, not as a hard ascetic discipline, but as a refreshment and a delight. From this grounding in silence we can learn to respond in simpler ways to our own bodies, learning to be more at home in them and to rejoice in the richness of sense experience which is continually offered to us through them. This in turn can open up our vision of the outer world, preventing us from constantly snatching from it only that which will serve our immediate purposes, restoring a childlike vision.

Music offers another avenue to simplicity, since it communicates both spontaneity and order at a level which words cannot reach. In responding to its mysterious powers of rhythm, sound, and silence, we are released from the domination of clock time, with its measured reminders of passing minutes and hours, and are free to enter the world of the simple fool, where all is immediacy and where anxiety has no sway over us. We no longer need to justify each moment by what has been achieved in it, but can appreciate time, not as demand, but as gift.

Foolish Ways as Rich Resources

If we are willing to prepare ourselves in these foolish ways, we can bring rich resources of help to others. Those who know silence and immediacy as friends will no longer feel worried about knowing the right *words* to say to others. They will not need to justify themselves in their own eyes by being "successful" and admired helpers of the needy.

Their help will emanate from a simple enjoyment of getting close to a fellow human being who welcomes their company. (To the little man perched up a tree, Jesus says, "Hurry down, Zacchaeus, because I must stay in your house today" [Lk. 19:5, TEV]. How could a busy man like Jesus spare such time?) The simple fool carries no baggage when another seeks help, no techniques, no "pastoral medicine bag." When pretense is stripped aside, all we fools have to offer one another is "a condition of complete simplicity, costing not less than everything."[23] Few of us manage to be so foolish.

Loyal Love

But now a great worry must face us when we consider so simplified an approach to pastoral care: the fear of loss of control. When care is offered by a professional agency, in the form of social casework, medical care, educational assistance, legal advice, etc., there are numerous devices for protecting professional helpers (and to a lesser extent, their clients) against exploitation. Access to help is controlled by appointment systems, by cost limitations, and by referrals to other agencies; the liability of the helper is limited to the area of claimed professional competence and the personal life of the helper is strictly segregated from professional life. These devices protect both professional and client against the hazards of overinvolvement. Thus, even in the intense encounters of professional psychotherapy, the helping relationship remains strictly a business one, offered within stated hours and according to a defined set of rules.

A Foolish Offer of Love

The folly of pastoral care, at least as I have been describing it, is that it refuses to operate within these protective limitations. It foolishly offers love. It is therefore a foolhardy activity which may result in the exploitation of both helper and helped. This danger is seen most clearly in the tendency for helping relationships to foster a destructive form of dependency. Such dependency is always mutual: not only does the person seeking help make childish and unrealistic demands on the time and attention of the helper; the helper (consciously or unconsciously) encourages such dependency, acquiescing in and even encouraging each unreasonable demand.

Helper and helped alike are caught within a ring of fear, each one as frightened as the other of being left alone and unloved. (Of course, helpers rationalize their overattentiveness by saying that it is the other's need to which they respond, failing to see the forces of anxiety which prevent them from saying no to the other's demands.) In view of such dangers it is important to distinguish the loyalty of the fool from such mutual evasions of responsibility, masquerading under the name of care. The fool is vulnerable precisely because of refusal to take part in such self-protective maneuvers. "Prithee, nuncle," says Lear's Fool, "keep a schoolmaster that can teach thy Fool to lie. I would fain learn to lie."[24]

A Compulsion to Speak the Truth

Fools can be hurt and exploited because they must speak the truth even if this inevitably brings anger on their own heads. There is nothing collusive about the loving loyalty of fools: not for them the easy comfort of the appeaser and flatterer. The fool for Christ's sake trusts in love, and that must mean the love that lets go, not the overprotectiveness which denies reality and coddles the other person.

Perhaps this is the hardest lesson to learn in the art of caring, because it means setting our own limits on relationships, without the aid of receptionists, office hours, or professional codes of practice. We often confuse overinvolvement in others' troubles with Christian love and fail to risk the unpopularity of refusing to meet others' expectations of us. Yet Jesus resisted the insatiable demands of the crowds in order to pray in solitude (Lk. 9:18); and his love for his disciples meant leaving them without a leader (but not without the comfort of his Spirit) to face persecution and ridicule.[25] For us, loving loyalty will often mean staying close to others, when they need us and when others have turned their backs on them; but equally loving loyalty can mean trusting in God's all-pervading love, when we see that the best way to help others is to enable them to reject us and let go of us. Then we seem poor fools indeed, since our loving heaps coals of fire on *our* heads.

Laughter in Heaven

Yet how serious the folly of pastoral care is now becoming, it seems! Fortunately for us and for those we try to help, our folly need not always be such a solemn matter. (It would be, no doubt, if we really believed that the cure of all the world's woes depended on the success of our erratic efforts to care.) It seems more realistic to suggest that our folly can at best save people from putting their trust in false idols, helping them to question any grandiose claims for the betterment of humankind.

In a discussion of Paul Tillich's use of terms like "depth of being" and "ultimate concern," Alan Watts wonders whether joy in the presence of God has got to be such an awesome experience:

> Does anyone really want the End, the Final Ground of all things, to be *completely* serious? No twinkle? No gaiety? Something rigid and overwhelming and ponderously real? Such a profound seriousness might be the ante-room, but not the presence chamber.[26]

Encouraging the Laughter of Fools

If instead there is laughter in heaven, as Watts suggests, then a major part of our witness to love is to encourage laughter on earth. In saying this, I am not seeking to invoke the image of the "jolly parson," who spreads a false cheerfulness in a denial of pain. Rather, it is the carefree image of the fool which must reappear, as an expression of the joyousness of faith. Such a reappearance of laughter might help us to save the churches from their obsession with decency, order, and respectability and allow them to offer a genuine alternative to the images of power and material prosperity which dominate "developed" societies.

Pastoral care needs to become prophetic, mediating a new and strangely different attitude to life, leaving people wondering whether to laugh *at* it or *with* it, tapping into the well of laughter of God's revelation of himself. Churches that are capable of laughing at themselves, of admitting their fallibility and frequent descents into the ridiculous, will be better able to speak with a prophetic voice to the alienating and dehumanizing powers of our age. And individuals who have a lightness of touch, an informality based on amusement at their own ineptitude, bring the simplest of gifts to others—the releasing power of laughter.

CHAPTER 10

The Wise Fool Reframed

Donald Capps[1] (1990)

The pastoral care and counseling movement of the 1950s and 1960s has been roundly attacked in recent years. Some critics have claimed that it is virtually bankrupt, that the movement has overemphasized the secular psychotherapies and psychological sciences and has neglected the theological sciences. Some have charged that the movement has bought into individualism and the therapeutic culture and has given the faith community very short shrift, that it has subscribed to the values of contemporary society, and has failed to give adequate attention to Christian ethical and moral principles. These critics—proponents of the "new" pastoral theology, including Charles Gerkin, Don Browning, and James Poling—see themselves as providing pastoral care and counseling with a much-needed theological, ecclesial, and ethical foundation.

Some of this criticism of the pastoral counseling movement is unfair and overdrawn, based on a somewhat inaccurate picture of what was actually written and practiced in the 1950s and 1960s. Much of it, however, is warranted and welcome. The enterprise of pastoral theology is currently experiencing a renaissance, and promising new directions are being charted. Yet, in spite of these new developments, nothing new has emerged at the basic level of technique.

One of the most exciting features of the pastoral care and counseling movement of the 1950s and 1960s was that new methods and techniques were being proposed, experimented with, assessed, and evaluated. By the mid-1960s, there were enough techniques available for Howard Clinebell to write a basic textbook in pastoral counseling that set forth a variety of them: supportive counseling, crisis counseling, educative counseling, and so forth.[2] Clinebell's text was revised in 1984, and while it includes a new theological rationale for the earlier project, it adds no new methods to those already in the earlier text.[3]

It is true that many pastoral counseling specialists have been using a variety of methods, including some not addressed in either edition of Clinebell's textbook. For most parish pastors, however, the techniques they employ in their pastoral care and counseling work have been, and remain, those described by Clinebell. Thus, for all the discussion currently taking place at more theoretical levels, we have seen virtually no innovation at the basic level of method and technique. If new winds are blowing in the field of pastoral theology, shouldn't more be happening at the basic level of methods? Shouldn't pastors be testing and refining new care and counseling techniques as they were in the 1960s? If such innovation is not taking place today at the grass roots, what will be the outcome of current theorizing? Will it prove to have been merely an academic exercise?

A New Pastoral Method

[I propose to take] a step toward addressing these questions, [arguing] for the addition of a single method to the techniques that are already available to parish pastors. [My approach] emphatically does not propose the elimination of any of the existing methods and is not offered as a replacement for any one. At the same time, I view it as a significant addition because it can be used in a variety of pastoral care and counseling contexts and with virtually any parishioner. Moreover, it reflects some of the new directions in pastoral theology, especially the effort to develop a biblically grounded approach to pastoral care and counseling.

This method, while emerging out of recent developments in psychotherapy, has much affinity and compatibility with certain biblical forms, experiences, and ideas. Thus, in recommending it, I hope to contribute to the discussion in pastoral theology circles of more adequate theological foundations for pastoral care and counseling. But I do so more from the level of method than the level of theory.

The method is "reframing," a technique widely used in psychotherapy over the past two decades. Reframing has been employed by many of the major therapists of our time, including Milton Erickson, Virginia Satir, Carl Whitaker, and Jay Haley. For the general reading public, Richard Bandler and John Grinder have made reframing readily accessible through their popular books.[4] I make particular use of the writings of Paul Watzlawick and his colleagues, John Weakland and Richard Fisch, primarily because their discussion of reframing is both philosophically sophisticated and extremely practical. Their book *Change: Principles of Problem Formation and Problem Resolution* is especially valuable because it treats reframing within the context of a philosophically based theory of change.[5]

First-Order and Second-Order Change

Watzlawick, Weakland, and Fisch propose that there are two kinds of change: *first-order change* that occurs within a given system which itself remains unchanged; and *second-order change* that alters the system itself. To illustrate the difference they cite the case of a person who is having a nightmare. This person can do many things *in* the dream—run, hide, fight, jump off a cliff—but no shift from any one of these behaviors to another would ever terminate the nightmare. This is first-order change. Second-order change involves a shift from dreaming to waking. Waking is not a part of the dream but a change to an altogether different state. Second-order change is a *change of change.* What occurs in second-order change is not merely a shift from stasis to change, but a fundamental alteration in change itself. In first-order change, the more things change, the more they remain the same. In second-order change, everything is different because the system itself is no longer the same.[6]

There are many situations in life in which first-order change is all that we require. When the temperature in the room falls to an uncomfortable level, we can adjust the thermostat until we are comfortable again. *More of the same* eventually achieves the desired effect. But in other situations of life, first-order change is insufficient. In these cases it may become the problem, making matters worse than they were before remedial efforts were tried.

An illustration is the United States' experience with prohibiting the consumption of alcohol. At first, necessary restrictions were placed on alcohol consumption, but when these did not reduce the problem, *more of the same* was carried to its ultimate—the elimination of the problem through prohibition. Prohibition, however, turned out to be worse than the problem it was designed to eliminate: "Alcoholism rises, a whole clandestine industry comes into existence, the low quality of its products makes alcohol into even more of a public health problem, a special police force is needed to hunt down the bootleggers and in the process becomes unusually corrupt, etc., etc."[7]

A common approach to the reduction or elimination of a problem is to introduce its opposite as the logical solution. If a friend is depressed, we try to cheer her up. If our spouse is uncommunicative, perhaps even secretive, we try to get him to "open up." But these attempted solutions rarely, if ever, work. In fact, they increase the original problem and eventually become a problem in their own right.

Efforts to get the husband to communicate make him more withholding and more secretive, even to the point where he refuses to make disclosures that are harmless and irrelevant, "just to teach her that she need not know everything." This behavior, in turn, adds further fuel to her worries: "If he refuses to talk to me about these little things, there *must* be something the matter." The less information he gives her, the more persistently she will seek it, and the more she seeks it, the less he will give her. In time, this very pattern of interaction becomes, itself, the problem.

So, efforts to deal with a perceived problem by introducing its opposite result in a first-order change, where the more things change, the more they remain the same. What is required here is second-order change—an action that alters the interactional system itself.

The Mishandling of Difficulties

From this basic distinction between first- and second-order change, Watzlawick and his coauthors conclude that there are *difficulties* and there are *problems*. *Difficulties* are a fact of human existence. Some difficulties can be reduced or eliminated, while others are inescapable and have to be accepted as the price we pay for existing at all. Suffering, evil, and death are difficulties. Diseases, oppression, and poverty are problems. *Problems* are situations that are created and maintained through the mishandling of difficulties. There are basically three ways in which this mishandling can occur:

1. A difficulty exists for which action is necessary, but none is taken. This mishandling is called *simplification*. There are two forms of simplification. One is denial that a difficulty exists, often accompanied by an attack on those who disagree and who believe action should be initiated. The second is to acknowledge that there is a small difficulty, but to insist that it may be disposed of by a quick or simple solution. Such mishandling produces problems that not only fail to reduce or eliminate the difficulty but also have their own negative effects.

2. Change is attempted regarding a difficulty that, for all practical purposes, is either unchangeable or nonexistent. Here, action is taken when it should not be. This mishandling is called *utopianism*. It, too, can take one of two possible forms.

The first is introjective utopianism, where we have deep, painful feelings of personal inadequacy for being unable to reach what are, in fact, unattainable goals (e.g., the goal of perfect happiness). Here, "the very act of setting this goal creates a situation in which the unattainability of the goal is not likely to be blamed on its utopian nature but rather on one's ineptitude: my life should be rich and rewarding, but I am living in banality and boredom; I should have intense feelings but cannot awaken them in myself."[8] Symptoms of this form of utopianism are depression, dropping out, withdrawal, suicidal thoughts, divorce, alienation, and nihilistic world views.

The second is projective utopianism. Its basic ingredient "is a moral, righteous stance based on the conviction of having found the truth and sustained by the resulting missionary responsibility of changing the world."[9] In this view, the failure to attain unattainable goals is not a negative reflection on us; the problem is with those who do not share our vision. Symptoms of this form of utopianism are righteous self-justification, paranoia, and the illusion of originality. The belief that we have the solution to difficulties that are actually unsolvable justifies hostile and uncivil attitudes toward others, causes us to become paranoid when others condemn or take our solution lightly, and leads us to entertain the false notion that this solution is new, that nothing of this sort has ever been attempted (and failed) in the past.

These two forms of utopianism are similar in one important respect: the premises on which they are based are considered to be more real or genuine than reality as we know it. Thus, the idea that we might attain perfect happiness or solve the unsolvable is more real to us than experiential evidence that these goals cannot be achieved.

The point is not that goals should not be set, worked toward, and realized. What the authors are challenging is the setting of unattainable goals, or envisioning change in difficulties that are, for all practical purposes, unchangeable. Unattainable goals do not reduce or eliminate difficulties. Instead, they create problems that did not previously exist. The failure to attain perfect happiness leads to feelings of inadequacy that would not have developed if the impossible goal had not been entertained. By setting goals that require actions by others that they are unlikely to perform, we create unnecessary and unproductive animosities between ourselves and others.

3. A first-order change is attempted in regard to a difficulty that can be changed only at the second-order level, or a second-order change is attempted when a first-order change would be appropriate. Action is taken at the wrong level—a mishandling called paradox. The attempted solutions are inherently paradoxical and incapable of producing second-order change. Instead, they imprison people in first-order change. When the paradoxical nature of these attempted solutions is revealed for what it is, a paradox, another paradox can be introduced that enables the desired second-order change to occur. In this case, the second paradox has practical or therapeutic effects. Thus, unrecognized or unacknowledged paradoxes usually effect only first-order change, while the self-conscious use of paradox achieves second-order change.

A mother was trying to change the behavior of her eight-year-old son, who did not like to do his homework. She told the therapist: "I want Andy to learn to do things, and I want him to do things—but I want him to want to do them...I want him to want to do things, but I realize it's going to be something that we have to teach him."[10] Here, the mother has caught herself and her son in a paradox. She wants him to want to do things, that is, to want to do them not because she wants him to do them. This paradox is the classic double bind. The more she tries to teach her son to want to do things, the less he will perceive the doing of these things as something he wants to do. The more he does them, the more he does them because she wants him to do them. The desired change— from acting because she wants to acting because he wants—does not occur. The mother and son are locked into first-order change; the more things change, the more they remain the same.

Here are other examples of paradoxical communications: "I want you to dominate me." "Don't be so obedient." "Be spontaneous." "You should enjoy playing with the children, like other fathers do." "You know that you are free to go, and please don't worry if I start to cry." "Don't think about me at home alone tonight; just go out and have a good time."[11] A counseling session involves an unhappily married couple and their college-age son: The mother looks at her son with love and admiration and exclaims, "After all, it's a simple matter. All we want in the world is for George to have as happy a marriage as we have."[12] A husband who was challenging his wife's resistance to hiring household help explained, "I want her to be free enough to do what she wants."

A vast number of attempted solutions to difficulties are paradoxical and therefore place individuals in impossible dilemmas, binds, impasses, and deadlocks. They are damned if they do, and damned if they don't. First-order changes are achieved, but these only make for greater frustration and hopelessness. The son who would not do his homework now does it, but his mother knows that he does not want to do it, that he is doing it only because she is making him do it. Or, alternatively, he refuses to do his homework not just for the original reason (not wanting to do it) but also because he is now very aware that she wants him to do it. In either case, what began as the difficulty of unfinished homework has become a problem between mother and son: a mutually frustrating interpersonal conflict.

But paradox, when used with self-conscious intention, can also effect second-order change. Watzlawick's team develops this point in their theory of second-order change, which introduces the concept and method of reframing.[13]

The Wise Fool Reframes

I contend that the method of reframing and the pastoral identity of the "wise fool" have a great deal in common. This term is from Alastair V. Campbell who identified three pastoral self-images—the shepherd, the wounded healer, and the wise fool. All three represent legitimate ways of being a pastoral caregiver.[14] Yet, there is a rather strong affinity between the wise-fool image and the reframing method. The reframing method is tailor-made for the wise fool, and the wise-fool image will find greater acceptance as the reframing method is accorded a place among existing pastoral care and counseling methods.

The pastoral image of the shepherd, once dominant, was especially congenial to the methods and techniques that first emerged in our field. It was joined in the 1970s by the wounded-healer type, which is suspicious of methods and techniques, favoring instead a ministry of "presence." Now, decades later, the wise fool is taking its place alongside the shepherd and wounded-healer images, and it is only natural that at least one pastoral care and counseling method suitable to this image would result.

The shepherd [image] is associated with the views of Seward Hiltner, who emphasized the shepherding perspective in *The Christian Shepherd* and *Preface to Pastoral Theology*.[15] The wounded healer is the image proposed by Henri Nouwen in his book entitled *The Wounded Healer*.[16] The wise fool image is based on Heije Faber's comparison of the minister in the hospital to the clown in the circus.[17] Campbell expands on Faber's insightful metaphor in his discussion of the ministry of wise folly.

As one reads this discussion, one sees that the art of reframing is most congenial to the wise fool approach to pastoral care. As shepherds guide and wounded healers empathize, wise fools reframe. Reframing is the very lifeblood of wise-fool ministry.

Like the pastoral images of shepherd and wounded healer, the wise-fool image is profoundly biblical. As Campbell points out, Paul dismisses worldly wisdom as a guide for Christians and elevates the fool instead: "If any among you think they are wise by this world's standards, they should become fools, in order to be really wise" (1 Cor. 3:18). These fools are vulnerable to earthly powers, are often derided and exploited, are treated as scapegoats, and viewed as "the offal of the world, the scum of the earth" (1 Cor. 4:13). Yet, in all societies and all ages, fools have been "the essential counterpoise to human arrogance, pomposity, and despotism." The fool's "unruly behavior questions the limits of order," the fool's "crazy" outspoken talk probes the meaning of "common sense," the fool's unconventional appearance exposes pride and vanity, and the fool's loyalty to "lost causes" undercuts prudence and self-interest.[18]

The Ambiguous Image of the Fool

The more we examine such folly, however, the more ambiguous the image of the fool becomes: "Folly is often two-edged, making mockery of good and ill alike, providing malicious and cruel laughter at times, yet also using humor and ridicule to evoke love and concern. Since folly steps outside order, we cannot expect to control it easily—more often it takes us over in a holy or unholy madness."[19]

On the other hand, Campbell wants to "impose some order on the fool's image in order to see its significance for pastoral care." He identifies three aspects or dimensions to the wise-fool image: simplicity, loyalty, and prophecy. I suggest that these three dimensions oppose the mishandlings of difficulties identified by Watzlawick and his colleagues; because they do, the wise-fool image favors the reframing method.

Folly as Simplicity: Beyond Simplification

How do we know when folly is wisdom and not simply nonsense? One way we know this is that something unexpected or overlooked becomes disclosed. Sometimes the disclosure of the unexpected or overlooked involves seeing complexities that others were unable to see. But the disclosures that we normally associate with wise folly usually result from taking a simpler view of the situation than others have done. This is not the fallacy of *simplification*, which sees no problem when in fact there is one. Instead, this is the ability to recognize that the problem is actually simpler than it has been perceived to be.

Suppose, for example, that a group of co-workers are discussing one of their colleagues and offering a number of explanations for why Bill is the way he is. One colleague ventures the opinion that Bill "has narcissistic tendencies reflected in his grandiose self-image." Another observes that Bill "has a problem with authority, especially in situations where he is expected to be deferential to persons who hold positions of legitimate authority over him." Another adds that there are "paranoid" features to Bill's personality which cause him to be on guard, especially in situations where the power he holds is unequal to that of the person with whom he is dealing. Then suppose that after these observations have been offered and solemnly affirmed by the group, another of Bill's co-workers, silent to this point, were to blurt out in obvious anger, "The trouble with Bill is that he's a damned liar. I doubt that he's ever told the truth in his life."

Creating a New Frame of Analysis

This statement breaks the diagnostic frame which had prevailed to this point and places Bill in a wholly different frame of analysis. Where the original frame was "psychological assessment," the new frame is "moral evaluation." The new frame directs attention to something that was overlooked by the psychological assessments of Bill—the simple but important fact that Bill never tells the truth about anything, that nothing he says is credible. This is a simpler view of Bill than the other diagnoses provided, but it is not simplistic.

To say that Bill is a "damned liar" is certainly not to minimize the group's frustrations with Bill. On the contrary, it is to challenge the group to look at the problem from an entirely different standpoint and to see another dimension of it. Yet, the force of this particular challenge is that, when viewed psychologically, certain behaviors may look very complex, but when viewed morally, they are simple and straightforward. Could it be that claims to such complexity are little more than rationalizations for duplicitous behavior? The statement, "Bill is a damned liar," in fact challenges the assumption of the psychological assessments that Bill is a very complex person. The statement says, in effect, "I do not believe that Bill is complex. Instead, he is merely duplicitous."

Thus, one characteristic of the "wise fool" is the capacity to see situations as simpler than others have thought them to be. Other pastoral types tend to see situations as complex, involved, or deep-seated. Shepherds focus on the various contextual and systematic factors that may be responsible for the problem, and wounded healers seek to plumb the depths of deep and painful difficulties. Wise fools tend to see problems as much less intricate and complicated. Truth is remarkably simple. Error and falsity are unnecessarily complex.

Resolving the Problem

This does not mean, however, that once the problem's inherent simplicity has been disclosed, it will necessarily be easy to resolve. Often there is an inverse relationship between a simple problem and an easy solution. Suppose that the survival of a couple's marriage depends on the husband's ability to remain faithful to his wife. This is simple: Be faithful, and you will save your marriage. But for this particular husband, who has had a series of affairs, this prescription is not easy at all. In fact, being faithful is actually much harder for him than devising intricate game plans and complicated stories designed to deceive his wife about his sexual behavior. The problem itself is quite simple, but the solution is very difficult.

It is like the story of Naaman, who was instructed by the prophet to wash in the Jordan River and he would be cured of leprosy. By assuring Naaman that everyone knew he could do difficult things, his servant reframed the situation for Naaman, enabling him to do the simple thing which was otherwise so hard for him.

No doubt, the wise fool will fail to perceive certain facts about situations which shepherds, with their appreciation for complexity, and wounded healers, with their sensitivity to depths, will more readily recognize. It is not that the wise fool is always right and the shepherd and wounded healer types are always wrong. Rather, we are identifying a characteristic of wise fools, their tendency to view problems as simpler than they appear to others. Unless the wise fool succumbs to simplification (which is the flip side of the danger that shepherds will be guilty of complexification and wounded healers of false profundity), there is usually genuine insight in what the wise fool has to say.

Unfortunately, we tend to resent the suggestion that the truth can be remarkably simple. It offends our intelligence to be told that, where our problems are concerned, there may actually be *less* than meets the eye. Thus, the wisdom of the fool is often dismissed because we are offended by it.

Citing examples from history and literature, such as the Sufis of Islam and Prince Myshkin in Dostoevski's novel *The Idiot*, Campbell talks about wise fools' own simplicity, which enables them to expose the insincerity, self-deception, hypocrisy, and corruption of the people around them. Adults who are in full possession of their faculties cannot pretend to possess the simplicity of natural fools like Prince Myshkin; it would be a strange denial of ourselves to want to do so. But the image of folly as simplicity can help us to rediscover the parts of ourselves which have been lost as we learned "adult wisdom," thus opening up more spontaneous ways of relating to ourselves and others.[20]

By recovering the child in ourselves, we discover, anew, our capacity to see problems as simpler than others see them. To perceive such simplicity in human problems, however, often requires the capacity to engage in complex analytical reasoning processes. So, the wise fool image is not an excuse for an unthinking, nonreflective approach to ministry. Wise folly calls forth simplicity, not stupidity or simple nonsense.

Folly as Loyalty: Beyond Utopianism

In discussing the simplicity of wise folly, Campbell was concerned with the question: "How do we know when folly is a kind of wisdom and when is it simple nonsense?" In approaching folly as loyalty, his concern is not a question but an enigma: the fool's willingness to disregard self out of a higher loyalty.

In Shakespeare's *King Lear*, the fool stands by the king's side when everyone else has deserted him, exhibiting "the simple virtue of an unheroic but persistent loyalty."[21] He acknowledges that he may be a fool for staying with Lear when the situation is hopeless, but he is not a knave, one who

> Serves and seeks for gain,
>> And follows but for form,
> Will pack when it begins to rain,
>> And leave thee in the storm. (Act II, Scene 4)

There is no shame in being a loyal fool. There is only shame in being a self-serving and faithless knave.

Jesus and Foolish Loyalty

This foolhardy, improvident loyalty is a prominent feature of Jesus' teaching: "Whosoever will give his life for my sake shall find it" (Mt. 16:25). For Campbell, the enigmatic character of such loyalty finds its ultimate expression in the crazy logic of loving those who do you harm: "Love your enemies, do good to those who hate you, bless those who curse you, and pray for those who mistreat you" (Lk. 6:27–28). Jesus looks like the "greatest of fools" when he asks God to forgive his accusers and their minions even as they mock him in his suffering.

No one, claims Campbell, would allow himself to be exploited in this way unless he trusted, beyond all reason, in the ultimate triumph of love. The enigma of the fool's loyalty is that he allows himself to be exploited, as Jesus' enemies exploit him: "There is nothing more easily exploited than the loyalty of a fool."[22]

Hopeless, but Not Serious

What enables fools to remain loyal, refusing to "pack when it begins to rain"? Maybe, as Campbell suggests, this is based on trust in the ultimate triumph of love. But I suspect that fools are less utopian than this. Fools do not perceive that they are involved in a situation that, while hopeless now, will somehow be turned around and ultimately lead to triumph. Instead, fools are more likely to stay with a hopeless situation because, as [a book title by Paul Watzlawick] suggests, "the situation is hopeless but not serious."[23]

Unlike the utopians who persist in hopeless situations because they believe their cause may ultimately triumph, fools persist because they refuse to take such situations seriously. To put it another way, utopians are in the business of *making* meaning, while fools are more content to let meaning arise where and when it will.

As Watzlawick and his colleagues point out, "The search for a meaning in life is central and all-pervasive" for the utopian, "so much so that the seeker may question everything under the sun, *except* his quest itself, that is, the unquestioned assumption that there *is* a meaning and that he has to discover it in order to survive." The authors challenge this overinvestment in the quest for meaning, viewing it as a prescription for a life of unhappiness. They contrast it to the attitude of the King of Hearts in *Alice in Wonderland* who, after reading the nonsensical poem of the White Rabbit, cheerfully concludes: "If there is no meaning in it, that saves a world of trouble, you know, as we needn't try to find any."[24]

Because fools are not overinvested in the quest for meaning but content to let meaning arise where and when it will, they are free to invest in situations which may or may not have an identifiable purpose, logic, or reason. Fools can remain faithful to their King Lears, no matter how crazy the situation becomes, as fools are not distressed because it makes so little sense. The situation is hopeless, but not serious.

Utopians believe that the reality they envision is truer than the reality in which they currently find themselves. Fools also envision other realities–many of them–but they are not so sure that these are any truer. They have a healthy mistrust of such envisionings, perhaps because they entertain so many; so they invest instead in the reality which is there for them to see, finding their happiness–and meaning–in it.

A young minister accepted the pastorate of a small urban parish, fully aware that the church was dying and that there was really nothing she could do to save it. However, during her pastorate there, she made the sort of long-range plans that one would make if the future of the church were assured. New programs were initiated, including youth and evangelism programs designed to expand the church's membership. At no time did she seriously entertain the idea that the church could be saved. Yet, for as long as possible, she resisted the efforts of the church's leaders to plan for its eventual demise. They asked, "Why start up new programs when you know that our days are numbered?" Any answer she gave them was unpersuasive–meaningless–to them. When the church did close its doors, she knew these leaders had hurt the congregation through their negativism. Yet she also knew that the situation had always been hopeless and that nothing could have been done to turn it around.

This pastor demonstrated the loyalty of the fool. She was not loyal out of some belief in an eventual triumph, present or future. Nor did she anticipate, either at the time or later, that the whole situation would yield some dramatic meaning. The situation was hopeless, and this is all that could be said for it. But she was loyal to it in spite of its hopelessness–and through these very trying times, there were some genuinely happy moments and some meaningful experiences for her and for other members of the congregation. In fact, she can now say that, while she would never want to go through this experience again, it was one of the happiest and truest, albeit saddest, periods in her life.

The fool's loyalty will always be something of an enigma. In hindsight, one might say that the pastor had been exploited–by the official who sent her there and by the leaders who not only undermined her efforts to minister but also tried to make her the scapegoat for the eventual failure. But, not unlike Jesus, the pastor was most exploited by her faith in God, who was the spiritual source of her unwavering loyalty in this hopeless situation. Yet, like Jesus, she did not experience this condition as exploitation. In fact, her unwavering loyalty to God was a sign that she did not consider herself above–or beneath–the playing of God's fool. And she is the happier for it. St. Francis of Assisi, often called God's greatest fool, is universally regarded as the happiest of God's saints.[25]

Challenging Common Sense

If folly as "simplicity" supports reframing by discerning that problems are simpler than they appear, folly as "loyalty" supports reframing by rejecting commonsense reasons for avoiding hopeless situations. Common sense says, "Stay away from hopeless situations because you will be dragged down by them." Folly as "loyalty" challenges such common sense and perceives the situation for what it is: a hopeless situation, but not necessarily an unhappy one. King Lear's fool reframes by exhibiting loyalty which has no justification.

The failure to extricate oneself from a hopeless situation is a common description of a fool; but through their loyalty, fools offer a different perspective on such involvement. For them, the issue is not whether we know a hopeless situation when we see it, but whether we know the difference between loyalty and knavery. The fool, for no other reason than simple loyalty, will not "pack when it begins to rain, and leave thee in the storm."

Folly as Prophecy: Espousing Paradox

If the first two dimensions of folly—simplicity and loyalty—portray the fool as a person of pathos, the third—prophecy—presents a more active, resilient, challenging, and even aggressive fool. As Campbell points out, "The prophetic aspect of folly has, through the ages, functioned as a form of challenge to the accepted norms, conventions, and authorities within a society."[26] Prophecy comes across as folly because it "does not fit in with the 'common-sense' assumptions of the day: it cuts cross-grained to earthly power and authority, announcing God's judgment upon it. Thus it is often misunderstood, ridiculed, or simply ignored."[27]

Various Hebrew prophets were viewed as crazy fools: Isaiah, who went naked for three years to warn of the impending humiliation and captivity of Egypt and Cush; Hosea, who married a prostitute and gave ominous names to his children; and Jeremiah, who walked around with a yoke on his back. It is no wonder that Hosea was accused of being a crazy fool, or that Jeremiah was in danger of being locked up as a madman.[28] And Jesus' prophetic acts—e.g., throwing the money lenders out of the temple—evoked the public judgment that he, too, was a crazy fool.

Folly's Clearer Light

Folly is a potent form of prophecy because it allows us to see ourselves in a clearer light and prevents us from giving fallible human institutions the honor they are *not* due. On the other hand, Campbell warns against assuming that all folly is prophetic: "Clowning, buffoonery, and satire can often be heartless, destructive of human values, a weapon to protect the perpetrator against any genuine involvement with others."[29]

Prophetic folly works through paradox. It involves inverting and thereby subverting the common-sense assumptions of the day. Thus, Jesus uses paradox as he reverses the accepted religious values, making the humble tax-gatherer more righteous than the law-abiding Pharisee, and the Samaritan more compassionate than the priest and Levite. For Campbell, the major vehicle for Jesus' prophetic role as teacher is his use of paradox. What makes him a wise fool, and not just anybody's fool, is that he uses it self-consciously, by design and not by accident.

The Paradox of the Wise Fool

The image of the wise fool is itself paradoxical—*wise* and *fool* are juxtaposed to one another. The wounded-healer model, which juxtaposes *wounded* and *healer*, is also paradoxical, especially as it draws attention to the power of weakness and vulnerability. But Campbell sees more of paradox in the wise fool.[30] For the wise fool, there is paradox in every facet of human existence, not only in the power of weakness, but also in the success that derives from failure, the dangers that come from playing it safe, the questions that are implied in answers, the answers implied in questions, the sorrows of joy, the joys of sorrow, and so forth.

It is not that our lives are hopelessly complex, or wondrously profound, but that they are paradoxical to the core. Among Jesus' own parables, the one that best expresses this view of life is the story of the rich fool. Just when he has achieved a life of economic security, he is told his life is in immediate jeopardy, that he will not survive the night (Lk. 12:16–20). This is paradox, and it is no academic matter. It is real. It is life itself. But the rich fool did not see the paradox, where the wise fool—the story teller—did, possibly because he knew that he faced a similar fate, that when least expected, his life, too, would be required of him. A wise fool is one who sees the paradox of her own life as clearly as she sees it in the lives of others.

God's Prophet as God's Fool

What makes prophecy paradoxical? The deepest paradox in the prophetic is simply this: The prophet who claims to speak for God cannot know what he is talking about. God's prophet is also God's fool, because God's prophet cannot speak with any certainty. Take Jonah, for example. Jonah, a prophet, knew that God could make a fool of him; by causing Jonah to eat his words, God did. Jonah prophesied that "yet forty days, and Ninevah shall be overthrown!" (3:4). Forty days came and went, but Ninevah remained as secure as ever. Wise to God, Jonah could see that he had played God's fool: "I pray thee, Lord, is not this what I said when I was yet in my country? That is why I made haste to flee to Tarshish; for I knew that thou art a gracious God and merciful, slow to anger, and abounding in steadfast love, and repentest of evil" (4:2). Unlike the self-fulfilling prophet, who avoids playing God's fool by refusing to make falsifiable predictions, Jonah had played the fool—by saying things on

God's behalf that proved utterly wrong and made Jonah look very stupid in the eyes of the public. To speak for God means taking the risk–day after day– that what we say about God, especially about God's intentions for the world, will prove utterly and shamefully mistaken.

Of course, it might be argued that Jonah was wrong only because the Ninevites heard what he had to say and repented of their evil ways. Therefore, he was wrong in fact, but was vindicated because his warnings were heeded and had their desired effect. While this argument may make sense to some of us, it does not satisfy Jonah who was not one bit impressed that his words had an effect on the Ninevites. For one thing, the Ninevites may have been insincere, cynically playing the game of repentance. For another, it was more important to Jonah–for his sense of professional integrity–to be right than to have an effect, especially one as ambiguous as this. If he had aspired only for effect–to be successful–he could have been a prophet whose predictions were so ambiguously stated as to be self-fulfilling. Rather, he wanted very much to be right, to say what is unquestionably true about his God.

But God did not allow him to experience the simple pleasure of having spoken the truth about God. Instead, Jonah was God's fool. He was placed in a position where he had no choice but to speak for God, but had to say things that he actually knew nothing about. Had he taken the opposite approach and assured the Ninevites that God would surely spare them if they repented, he had no assurance that God would do this, either. While God could be a gracious God and merciful, God could also be an exacting God who is no more impressed than Jonah had been by the Ninevites' last-minute and possibly hypocritical conversion. After all, there are times when God is not mocked and will not be played for a fool. Jonah's dilemma, of course, was that he spoke for a God whose very nature is a paradox: gracious and exacting, merciful and demanding.

Speaking for a Paradoxical God

How does one speak for a paradoxical God? We mean no disrespect for God when we say "with laughter." If God were not a paradox, God's prophets would do well just to be angry. But God is a paradox, and therefore, God's prophets cannot speak, cannot live, without laughter. The story of Jonah has been a source of amusement for countless generations. Its account of the cowardly prophet who flees his prophetic role is the most humorous tale in the Bible, illustrating Campbell's view that prophecy is often carried on the wings of laughter. While we tend to view prophets as speaking in angry and indignant voices, the Jonah story says that prophecy is also filtered with laughter.

Of course, for Jonah, the events in Ninevah were no laughing matter. He had played God's fool and was God's angry prophet–so angry, in fact, that he wanted to die (4:3). But if he could have seen himself as his audience sees him, sulking under a great tree in the middle of the desert, he might have found it within himself to laugh, to see that his own situation, while hopeless, was not as serious as he had taught himself to believe.

If he could have seen the humor of it all, he might have gone from this experience to become a very different kind of prophet: not an angry prophet, but a laughing prophet. Campbell asks: If there is laughter in heaven, isn't it part of our prophetic witness to encourage laughter on earth, and to begin by learning to laugh at ourselves? "Individuals who have a lightness of touch, an informality based on amusement at their own ineptitude, bring the simplest of gifts to others–the releasing power of laughter."[31]

The Releasing Power of Laughter

Lightness of touch and the releasing power of laughter are essential to the art of reframing. Otherwise, the art degenerates into a weapon which manipulates and mocks the very ones it means to help, and dehumanizes those who use it. Reframing is not for angry prophets, but for prophets who know the releasing power of laughter. Reframing is for prophets who are wise enough to know that God can get along perfectly well without them, and fool enough to believe that God would never try to go it alone. As the poet, Rainer Maria Rilke, in Job-like bravado, put it:

> What will you do, God, when I die?
> When I, your pitcher, broken, lie?
> When I, your drink, go stale or dry?
> I am your garb, the trade you ply,
> you lose your meaning, losing me.
> Homeless without me, you will be
>   robber of your welcome, warm and sweet.
> I am your sandals: your tired feet
> will wander bare for want of me.
> What will you do, God? I am afraid.[32]

So, wise fools embrace simplicity, not simplification, loyalty, not utopianism, and a lighthearted brand of prophecy based on a healthy appreciation and respect for the paradoxical ways of God. Wise fools may not be as indispensable as shepherds, or as deep as wounded healers, but they do not flinch from truth, they do not pack when it begins to rain, and they have an acute sense for the paradoxes of human (and divine) life. Through all this, they see the enormous potential for miracles in ordinary life and are not too proud to use techniques, like reframings, to see if they may help such miracles happen a bit more often than would otherwise occur by chance. So perhaps wise fools are to be forgiven for entertaining the thought that God will find this earth a hell of a place to be when they have gone to the place where no one cries– except, shall we say, from uncontrolled laughter?

CHAPTER 11

The Intimate Stranger

Robert C. Dykstra[1] (1990)

An eighteen-year-old high school senior, whose mother was a cancer patient only days away from death in a distant urban hospital, was at home alone with his father when the father began complaining of chest pains. He asked his son to drive him to the local emergency hospital, about twenty minutes away. The young man wisely refused, instead insisting on calling an ambulance. En route to the hospital, the father suffered a severe heart attack. When the ambulance arrived at the emergency room, the father, only hours before a vigorous and robust man, now was teetering critically on the edge of life and death. As a chaplain in the hospital, I was called by a nurse to wait with the son. I found him with tears streaming down his face, his hands visibly shaking. While he had begun to prepare himself for his mother's pending death, the sudden possibility of at once losing both parents terrified and overwhelmed him. The young man's only sister–a college student–lived in a city hours away, as did any of the nearest relatives of the family. He could think of no family friends who could be asked to support him there. His parish priest was out of town. The tension-filled five or six hours we waited together for relatives to arrive, during which the father experienced two more heart attacks, were among the most agonizing moments I have had in ministry.

This essay seeks to address situations of pastoral ministry that are of a similar genre as this one, i.e., extreme crises or boundary (life-and-death) situations in the hospital emergency room, intensive care unit, or elsewhere, in which the chaplain is called to assist and care for family members who face the unexpected immediate loss of a loved one. While the hospital chaplain frequently is involved in such situations of sudden potential or actual traumatic loss, there is a noticeable absence of pastoral theological literature and reflection dealing with ministry in these circumstances.

As I faced more and more of these situations in my own chaplaincy work in a large medical center, I eventually came to notice within myself an escalating sense of utter helplessness and inadequacy. The theological language I had relied on in "safer" moments of my ministry seemed to grow increasingly flat and unable to sustain me in what I was witnessing in these overwhelming moments of ministry.

The urgency of these situations seemed to preclude any pastoral strategizing; there was simply no time to carefully think through what one might hope to accomplish in the lives of these persons who faced irreplaceable loss and great tragedy. I had the haunting sense, however, that the minutes or hours I would spend with these people would be among the most critical of their lives in terms of at least charting the course for the future integration of, or failure to integrate, this crisis into the fabric of meaning in their lives.[2]

In my reading of the crisis and hospital ministry literature, I noticed that a theme of "the stranger" kept reappearing, usually in passing, in a number of the works. I began to wonder whether an intriguing image such as that of the stranger somehow might assist me in understanding my role as chaplain to those facing a sudden traumatic loss in the hospital. I have come to believe that metaphor of the "intimate stranger" is a useful one for linking the psychological and theological worlds that the chaplain must simultaneously and necessarily occupy in such encounters. This essay, then, is an attempt to define the chaplain's responsibilities (interventions) and to explore the theological roots for understanding what takes place in these situations through analyzing them by means of the metaphor of the intimate stranger.

Crisis as Stranger and Stranger as Crisis

Two Camps of Crisis Ministry

Crisis ministry literature can be divided roughly into two distinctive camps. Each of these approaches tends to acknowledge with gratitude the contribution of the other, while at the same time making a claim for the priority of its own position. There are, nonetheless, some tensions between the two camps that cannot be readily synthesized by polite conciliations.

One approach has a decidedly pragmatic tone, focusing on the *type of interventions*—usually quite directive and active on the part of the minister—that are thought to be necessary and helpful in relieving the immediacy of the internal tension experienced by the person in crisis and in the restoration of a state of internal equilibrium similar to the person's pre-crisis condition.[3] These authors base their studies and methods of intervention on a medical model more than a theological one, citing the formative influence of pioneering research in crisis intervention by psychiatrists such as Erich Lindemann and Gerald Caplan.[4]

The other general approach in crisis ministry literature places little emphasis on techniques for intervention, instead choosing to focus on the *type of theological reflection* required by the radical nature of the suffering experienced by the person in crisis.[5] This approach to crisis ministry emphasizes that it is impossible and in some sense even undesirable ever to "go back" to one's pre-crisis state of internal equilibrium. Instead, the nature of crisis requires a radical transformation of one's previous understanding of self or life, and crisis is at root a theological problem.[6]

Embodying Both Approaches

In working with the victims of potential or actual sudden traumatic loss, the hospital chaplain in the emergency room, intensive care unit, or elsewhere, must embody both approaches to life-and-death crisis. In situations such as that of the young man and his father, noted at the beginning of this essay, the chaplain is forced to confront the necessity for direct intervention for the psychological survival of the family members, but also to confront the sheer inadequacy of any possible intervention that is not inherently and explicitly theological in its core and language. Indeed, in the presence of a drama of such magnitude, even theological language or understanding will necessarily fall short of the mark, and the resulting silence reeks of non-intervention, which in turn completes the frustrating cycle. Intervention is required but, in any ultimate sense in these circumstances, seems impossible.

Can a metaphor such as "the stranger" or "intimate strangers" assist us at this point in breaking open such a cycle? I believe it can.

Encountering the Stranger on Two Levels

As David Switzer, for example, attempts to define "crisis," a term he admits has been confusing because of its varying usage in a wide variety of contexts, he points us to an idea of the "radical newness"—or what we might call the radical strangeness—of the crisis event in our lives. This newness or strangeness threatens our previous way of ordering our lives and creates a severe threat of disintegration of the self.[7] As we encounter sudden traumatic stress or loss, we encounter the *crisis as stranger.*

Not only is their crisis a "stranger" to persons in such a predicament, alienating them from their very selves, but the chaplain who meets them is a stranger as well. In addition, the chaplain is also encountering the stranger on at least two levels:

1. literally, for typically the chaplain has never before met the person or persons experiencing the crisis; and

2. figuratively, for being in the presence of another who is experiencing unexpected trauma and loss creates in us a fear of our own potential losses.[8] The chaplain indeed may experience the *stranger as crisis.*

The metaphor of the "stranger," like metaphors generally, begins to take on a plurality of meanings, opening potentially new perspectives on the type of crises in question. Later, we will see how this metaphor also may inform the chaplain's faith and understanding concerning the role of God in such encounters, that is, the value of understanding "God as Stranger" in hospital ministry. Although it will be impossible to exhaust all the nuances of the metaphor in this essay, my hope is to consider enough of its possibilities to demonstrate its value for guiding the chaplain's reflection and practice.

The Judeo-Christian Tradition and the Experience of Stranger as Crisis

In this section I am indebted to a recent paper by Patrick D. Miller, Jr., entitled, "Israel as Host to Strangers,"[9] and to Parker J. Palmer's *The Company of Strangers: Christians and the Renewal of America's Public Life*.[10] Both Miller and Palmer argue for the unique position of the stranger in Jewish and Christian history. Their works counter any attempts to define ministry solely in terms of cordial or inviting metaphors such as ministry to a "family" or "brothers and sisters in the faith" or a "fellowship of like-minded believers," reminding us that the stranger, too, has a unique and corrective contribution to make in the history of our faith traditions.

The Role of the Stranger in the Biblical Witness

THE STRANGER AS A MORAL CATEGORY

Miller points out that our instinctive reactions to persons who fall in the group "brothers/sisters" and in the group "strangers" are quite different. The former tends to conjure positive feelings, the latter feelings of uncertainty, fear, or hesitation. In the biblical witness, however, the stranger, like the brother/sister or neighbor, is a *moral category*, included in the same category in Israel as the widow, the orphan, and the poor.[11]

Indeed, the group designated by the Hebrew root word *ger* or *gerim*, usually translated by the English words "stranger(s)" or "sojourner(s)" and which Miller comes to call the "resident alien(s)," occasioned much teaching and moral exhortation in the Israelite community. In verb form, *gur* means "to dwell for a (definite or indefinite) time, dwell as a new-comer without original rights."[12]

Miller lists various crises as the predominant reasons for sojourning: famine and search for food, military conflicts that have evicted persons from their homes, natural disasters, and exile. Gleaning and tithing laws, inclusion in Israel's worship community, and the paradigmatic sharing of a meal were all intended to demonstrate Israel's commitment to the stranger. The point Miller wants to stress is that this person is the "outsider who comes into the midst of the community without the network of relationships that can be counted upon to insure care, protection, acceptance, the one who belongs to another group but now resides in the midst of the Israelite community."[13]

GROUNDS FOR ISRAEL'S HOSPITALITY TO STRANGERS

Why is Israel unique among the ancient near eastern cultures in its protection of the stranger? Miller suggests three primary grounds for Israel's hospitality, two of which are found in Deuteronomy 10:17–19:

a) *the theological rationale:* Israel's treatment of the stranger reflects God's way with sojourners and demonstrates the Great Commandment to love the neighbor; almost always in the biblical accounts of such sojourning stories, the reason given for caring for the sojourner is the "explicit protection of the sojourner by the Lord";[14]

b) *the historical rationale:* hospitality is a way of recalling Israel's own past and present experience as strangers; Israel's own history began with sojourners named Abraham and Sarah, who were told to leave home and live as strangers in an unknown land; and also, "You yourselves were strangers in the land of Egypt"; eventually, Israel's sojourn in Egypt became the very "paradigm of *in*hospitality for Israel, the definitive story of how *not* to treat the stranger";[15]

c) *the psychological rationale:* the fact that "hospitality to the stranger allows for surprising possibilities and wonderful happenings"–"Do not neglect to show hospitality to strangers, for thereby some have entertained angels unawares" (Heb. 13:2, author's translation); the stranger is the messenger of God in Old and New Testament accounts alike, and as such deserves the "particularities of hospitality to strangers," especially "courtesy and honor without reference to whether it is deserved or not, rest and washing, and food."[16]

THE STRANGER IN THE NEW TESTAMENT

Miller concludes this survey by turning, as in his third rationale above, to the New Testament, which he believes carries on the tradition of the Old Testament witness concerning the stranger. In the parable of the Great Judgment in Matthew 25, we learn that in welcoming with hospitality the stranger at our door, we are welcoming the King. So, too, in the post-resurrection accounts of the women at the tomb or the disciples on the road to Emmaus, it is through the welcoming of the stranger that the risen Christ becomes manifest to his followers (Jn. 20; Lk. 24).[17]

The Role of the Stranger in Contemporary American Culture

As Miller presents the biblical/historical rationale for showing hospitality to the stranger, so Parker Palmer addresses our contemporary fears of and need for the stranger. Palmer laments American trends toward isolation and privatization, and calls for an intentionally public ministry.

Public Life as the Interaction of Strangers

The heart of public life, for Palmer, is simply the interaction of strangers. By "public," Palmer is referring not to any political office but, more modestly, to the coming together of strangers in places like cafes, town squares, museums, parks, and, we might add, hospitals.[18] In the "company of strangers," we are "reminded that the foundation of life together is not the intimacy of friends but the capacity of strangers to share a common territory, common resources, common problems—without ever becoming friends"; fear of the stranger is faced and dealt with; scarce resources are shared and abundance is generated; life is given color, texture, and drama; people are drawn out of themselves, reminding us "that the universe is not egocentric"; mutual responsibility becomes evident, and mutual aid possible;[19] and people are empowered and protected against power.[20]

Needing the Stranger

Palmer insists that, contrary to the modern American dogma of privatism, we often come to see ourselves more clearly in *impersonal* relationships with strangers than we can in *personal* relationships with family and friends. We need relationships that allow us to care for persons while maintaining distance, or we can come to feel smothered and cramped.[21] So the stranger becomes the spiritual guide in the public life.

While public life is "notorious for its harshness, for its capacity to crush people under the wheels of interminable effort, of intractable problems, of public opinion," Palmer argues that in God's economy close, intimate relations are not the only ones that enrich our lives, and that self-enrichment is not the ultimate goal of the life of faith anyway.[22] He suggests that in the Jewish and Christian traditions, there is one word above all others that guides our way in encountering strangers, namely, "hospitality." For Palmer, hospitality means letting the stranger find a sanctuary of warmth, trust, and good will in our company, of "letting the stranger remain a stranger while offering acceptance nonetheless."[23]

A Preliminary Look at the Metaphor of the Stranger in Hospital Ministry

Like aliens who settled into the Israelite community following a crisis of severe magnitude, those who migrate to the emergency room in their time of crisis come as outsiders into a previously formed community—that of the hospital staff, complete with its "laws" of hospital regulations and procedures—without their usual network of protective relationships. Though they come for only a brief period of time, they come in a very real sense to sustain life—their own and that of the loved one whose death is a sudden possibility. Like the aliens of old, they are vulnerable to easy manipulation and domination by the sophisticated and technical world which they enter. At such a confusing moment in their lives, these strangers find themselves, as Miller says, "without the power or capability to ensure their own survival and well-being or without the structures to provide the same."

A Ministry of the Trenches

Although its roots are embedded in churches' ministries to the poor and homeless, the modern medical center can easily forget its heritage and become a "hospital," a place of hospital-ity, in name only.[24] Especially at a time of the threat of sudden death, the medical team is thinking solely of saving the victim's life. The patient and his or her family are not "guests" or even subjects at all, but objects of regimented life-saving medical procedures or a resource for the patient's medical history. The more hospitable tasks of listening to and making space for the strangers are left to the chaplain. Chaplaincy at those moments is a front-line pastoral ministry of the trenches, far removed from the traditional "sanctuary" of the churches.

The strangers received into this uninviting sanctuary typically conjure up feelings in the chaplain similar to the natural fear of strangers recognized in the biblical witness. The chaplain meets such strangers with ambivalence. On the positive side, the chaplain experiences much of what Palmer suggests takes place in meeting the stranger. But on the more negative valence, the chaplain must honestly confront his or her hostility toward the stranger as well.

Ministry to victims of sudden traumatic loss involves a great deal of energy, concentration, piece-meal detective work, and emotional and theological risk. The chaplain inevitably absorbs some of the inherent tension in coming face-to-face with human fragility and the sudden breaking in of death. In repeating such interventions many times in any given week, and week after week, the chaplain may come to an awareness of an increasing hostility toward these strangers. If this hostility is directed toward God, the chaplain may experience God less and less as loving Parent, more and more as Stranger or even Tyrant. If this hostility is mostly "swallowed" by the chaplain, a sense of self-estrangement may result.

Perhaps because of this natural ambivalence toward the stranger, Israel developed a code of regulations (regarding tithing, gleaning, sharing a meal, justice, and worship) to guide its conduct toward the sojourner. It is because of this ambivalence today that Palmer suggests we must be intentional in enhancing public interaction and ministry. In either case, the implication is that there are, indeed, certain things that can and must be done to create a hospitable sanctuary for the stranger in crisis. The biblical and theological legacy, however, leaves the more specific details of such hospitality in question, and especially in light of the vast cultural differences between ancient Israel and contemporary America, we are led necessarily to our other primary task, namely, to examine and critique modern crisis intervention theory in light of this kind of ministry.

Crisis Intervention Theory and the Experience of Crisis as Stranger

It is not our task here to reiterate what has been written previously concerning the role of the minister in crisis intervention. Switzer, Stone, Clinebell, and others have done so already with a notable degree of unanimity. I have identified below what I consider to be four of the prominent, recurring themes in most of these writings. These themes can be applied in a relatively straightforward way to situations of sudden traumatic loss in the hospital, one purpose of this section.

The metaphor of the stranger, however, opens up more perspectives on such a situation of ministry than a straightforward application of intervention techniques might suggest. We have already noted that the chaplain, too, faces a crisis in such an encounter and must also be welcomed as a stranger into the lives of those facing loss if any ministry is to take place. We have noted in passing as well that, in the experience of the chaplain and perhaps the family members, if God is seen to be participating at all in this event or an accumulation of such events, God increasingly may be participating as a Stranger also. If the chaplain and even God are in a kind of crisis here, some assumptions of the intervention theorists—particularly their call for a very directive, unilateral, action-oriented approach to ministry to "victims" of crisis—must be reconsidered.

Four Themes in Crisis Intervention Studies

Such an exploration will serve as a major focus in this section. We begin, though, by describing four common themes in the literature.

THEME #1
THE PHENOMENOLOGICAL EXPERIENCE OF CRISIS AS STRANGER.

Lindemann suggests five symptoms of acute grief, each typically evident in persons I encounter in hospital situations of sudden traumatic loss:

1. somatic distress;
2. preoccupation with an image of the deceased;
3. guilt;
4. hostile reactions to others; and
5. loss of patterns of conduct.[25]

THEME #2
CRISIS IS NOT THE EVENT BUT THE INTERPRETATION OF THE EVENT.

All crisis literature tends to point out that the same event may lead to a crisis for one person but not for another, that is, that the crisis experience lies in the *interpretation* or *meaning* for the individual of a given event, *not* in the event itself.[26] In situations of sudden traumatic loss, the distinction between the precipitating event and the experience of crisis is not as great as the literature seems to suggest. Nevertheless, the crisis is still an internal response to a precipitating event, and the chaplain can assist the persons involved by helping them to articulate what is most threatening to them.

THEME #3
THE GOAL OF CRISIS INTERVENTION IS QUICK RELIEF OF SYMPTOMS.

Crisis literature always calls for quite active involvement on the part of the counselor or minister.[27] The goal is said to be two-fold: to quickly relieve the internal and external symptoms; and to assist the person in integrating the crisis for the sake of future growth.[28]

The metaphor of "the stranger" challenges the goal of fast symptom or pain relief common to much crisis intervention theory. While the chaplain is tempted to "do" anything to assist the suffering person, we have already suggested that no "doing" can or even should minimize the victim's pain and loss. The chaplain should not attempt to quickly turn this person's encounter with the stranger of crisis into an encounter with a friend, as the intervention literature might be interpreted to suggest.[29]

The intervention literature's demand for an active presence on the part of the chaplain is not entirely inappropriate. This type of care *does* require a more active stance. Nevertheless, the catastrophic nature of the event of sudden traumatic loss tends to embarrass the theory's generally valid goals, and often an "active silence" may be finally all the chaplain can hope to offer.

THEME #4
THE IMPORTANCE OF LEAVING IN CRISIS WORK.

All crisis ministry literature also emphasizes the short-term nature of crisis counseling, typically suggesting that more than six counseling sessions becomes counterproductive. Delving into an involved past history is discouraged, as is an endless repetition of feelings. Clearly this theme follows from the action-oriented goals discussed above.

This is perhaps good news for the hospital chaplain, who would consider even more than *one* meeting with the victims of sudden traumatic loss a luxury. Instead, the chaplain usually expects only one meeting, which may last anywhere from fifteen minutes to eight hours or more. While the limiting factors of such a one-time meeting are apparent, what may not always be so clear are the benefits of the chaplain's "leaving" after only one encounter.

One meeting means not only intensity, but freedom to say what needs to be said (and no more, I might add). The suffering person also may feel freedom to say or do whatever he or she needs to, knowing that because the chaplain is a stranger, the victim need not be held accountable forever for it.

I remember being called as chaplain to support a woman whose 26–year-old daughter had just committed suicide. As I talked with her, she began screaming, "I hate God! I hate God! I hate him! I hate him!" When her parish priest came a few moments later, however, she was polite and cordial with him, saying to him simply, "Thank you for coming." Could her "theological freedom" with me be due in part to the fact that I was a stranger who would not hold her forever accountable for her "blasphemies" against God?[30]

Israel's Response to the Stranger as Theological Guide for Crisis Intervention

Three Primary Responsibilities in Hospitality

Israel's hospitality to the stranger involved three primary responsibilities, each of which might also be considered to involve some risk for the Israelite community.

The first of these was the meeting of the *biological needs* of the stranger (the paradigmatic "sharing of a meal," gleaning and tithing laws, regulations regarding rest and washing) and the accompanying risk of "not having enough" or at least as much for oneself.

In the hospital, making a sanctuary for persons experiencing sudden traumatic loss certainly first involves seeing to it that their physical needs are met. While persons in such distress rarely feel like sharing a meal, the chaplain can offer a cup of cold water (literally, this time) or hot coffee; a private room such as a nurse's office or similar space where the distressed person and chaplain can have at least minimal privacy; or a box of Kleenex, signifying washing. The chaplain can likewise assist the person in breathing, finding the restroom or a bed or blanket, and in dealing with other somatic responses to the crisis.

A second responsibility Israel felt toward the stranger involved the meeting of *political-cultural or justice needs* of the sojourner (cf., here, Miller's noting Israel's protection of "that group of marginal or weaker members of the community without the power...to ensure their own survival..."). Aliens or outsiders tend to be treated unjustly in any time or place; their rights are not adequately protected by the dominant culture, and those who seek to provide justice for the outsiders risk ostracism from the majority, an experience not uncommon to many chaplains who challenge some of the assumptions of the medical model and environment.

Persons who enter the bewildering world of the emergency room at a time of severe crisis have a tendency to easily forfeit their usual rights. They typically are not allowed to be present with their traumatized loved one while he or she is being treated by the medical staff; they are usually the last ones present to receive any update on the condition of the patient or how the emergency treatment is progressing; they are sometimes forgotten by the busy medical team or not consulted when alternative courses of treatment are being considered; they are often left waiting in the emergency room while their loved one is moved to other parts of the hospital.

The chaplain is one staff member who seeks "justice" for the suffering family members. As a member of the hospital community, he or she can move back and forth between the treatment team and waiting family, passing information in both directions. He or she can assist the family with the hospital telephone system, can walk the family to the next waiting area if the patient is moved, or can intervene by requesting that the doctors or nurses allow the family to see the patient. Such responses help protect the rights of family members who are uncertain of just what their rights are in this strange new world of the hospital.

Finally, Israel took *theological responsibility and risk* in opening its worship to the strangers in its midst. Much of Israel's prophetic tradition attests to the potentially tragic results of theological contamination, of losing the theological purity of one's beliefs, doctrines, and religious practices when they are opened to the scrutiny of outsiders as well as to the reality of sudden death. In a sense, this may be the most threatening risk of all to the host chaplain. Situations of sudden traumatic loss defy most any theological doctrine or pious practice we might offer by way of consolation. Our routines of prayer or scripture-reading seem to fall flat at moments like these and probably are counterproductive at this early stage of the crisis.

The theological problem is compounded by the fact that the stranger comes with a religious history completely unknown to us. As a result we need to carefully feel our way into the theological issues which both our role as chaplain and the clearly theological nature of the crisis require. In my view, although there will be moments in this crisis in which only silence is appropriate, it is not too early to probe gently into the religious resources and understanding of the person, to begin to probe the meaning of this event as this person now understands it.

The Chaplain as Stranger

Much of what I have discussed immediately above can be considered the development of a theological rationale for the types of interventions chaplains typically make in situations of sudden traumatic loss. Such interventions tend to assume that the chaplain is playing *host* to strangers, to victims of such loss, an assumption made by much of the intervention literature.

The Chaplain in Crisis

I have suggested, however, that the family members are not the *only* strangers in crisis in this situation, but that the chaplain, too, is a stranger, both to the emotionally hurting "host family" and to the realities of the crisis of sudden death. My suggestion that the chaplain may also be in crisis here, if this is accurate, challenges the one-way understanding of ministry in the literature.

When I am called by the emergency room staff to be with a person facing the sudden loss of a loved one, I often experience the types of distress described by Lindemann: somatic tension; a sense of unreality, floating, or the slowing down of time; guilt (for example, for not wanting to go into this situation, and for wanting to escape it as quickly as possible, or for my relief that this is not someone I know, or for failings in my own relationships); hostile reactions to others, including an accumulating irritability or exaggerated anger with loved ones; the loss of patterns of conduct involving a restlessness stemming from a sense that since life is short–an awareness so evident in the emergency room– it therefore must be lived "hard," with constant fervor and intensity. All of these are common companions of mine and of many other hospital chaplains I know.

The Family as Host

If the realization on the part of ancient Israel (and reflected in the teachings of Jesus and the early church)–that welcoming the stranger meant a serendipitous welcoming of God–is accurate, then the chaplain responding to a call to *welcome* victims of loss should find himself or herself not only representing God to this family, but also *welcomed* by God in this family as well. It is clear that unless the family members are willing to welcome the chaplain into the depths of their experience, the chaplain both will be powerless to assist the family and will not receive any comfort from them.

Should the family allow the stranger-chaplain to "sojourn" in their lives, however, the chaplain conceivably would experience certain needs being met by this family: biological, political-cultural, and theological needs. Again, this is often the case. As the victims begin to tell the chaplain "what happened" (if they know), of the nature of the person who may be dying or already dead and the nature of their relationship with him or her, of their confusion, guilt, helplessness, religious faith, and so forth, the chaplain may experience in their openness and vulnerability a psychosomatic soothing of the chaplain's own anxiety and tension.

Politically, the chaplain experiences a validation of his or her pastoral presence in the hospital, an awareness that the chaplain does indeed serve a necessary function even in a public institution in which the role and functioning of chaplains seem frequently misunderstood; the family's openness to the chaplain (and frequently *only* to the chaplain) "justifies" (does justice to) his or her presence.

Culturally, the chaplain also receives here exposure to traumas and deep joys isolated from the experience of many Americans, gifts from the "company of strangers" that Palmer noted. The chaplain as stranger is welcomed into a larger and more connected world of humanity when welcomed by this "host family," and life is given the color, texture, and drama so lacking in much contemporary experience.

What, though, does the chaplain receive theologically when welcomed as stranger? I would like to reflect on this question in the concluding paragraphs of this essay by considering one further facet of the metaphor of the intimate stranger, the notion of God as Stranger.

God as Stranger

A Threat to Faith

To enter into situations of sudden traumatic loss not only entails for the chaplain a heightening and then reduction of psychosomatic tension, or a "political" validation of the public function of ministry, or a widening and deepening of one's cultural horizons and sense of human relatedness. It also entails, as mentioned previously, an accumulating threat to one's faith in the power and presence of God in human affairs. As Israel was rightly concerned about threats of theological contamination, of the perversion or secularization of its unique relationship with Yahweh, in opening its worship to strangers in its midst, so should the hospital chaplain be aware of the toll that such accumulating crises in public ministry can take on one's faith in the providence of God.

In the past several months of my own emergency room ministry as a hospital chaplain, I have been exposed to the deaths of a three-year-old by hanging; tiny babies in respiratory distress; a high school student and several other persons in car accidents; a university student by self-inflicted stabs with a knife; a promising young man just completing his Ph.D. in chemistry (and other young persons) by drug overdose, as well as more expected deaths of the elderly, resulting from cardiac arrest or other traumas. There have also been many equally intense encounters, such as the one involving the young man and his father noted previously, in which the victim has survived.

The spiritual threat in such an accumulation of cases is that the chaplain begins to "go through the necessary motions" suggested by the intervention literature, while ignoring the task suggested by the more theologically focused literature, reflecting on or understanding theologically what such crises mean. Put differently, the threat to the chaplain is that he or she might enter each new situation of sudden traumatic loss *less* certain of the power and providence of God than in previous situations. As William Oglesby, Jr., has warned, quoting President Lacy of Union Theological Seminary in Virginia, "the problem is that you will handle the holy things professionally, and discover that you have become calloused to them personally."[31] While functioning flawlessly as a crisis intervention worker, the chaplain nonetheless might lose his or her *theological* or *pastoral* identity, that is, one's identity as a representative of Christian *faith*, for, after all, what kind of a loving God would allow *this*? This is the threat of contamination of one's faith.

Finding Sanctuary in Strangeness

Chaplains find themselves theologically "leveled" in such situations of ministry. Theological certitudes are suddenly all up for grabs. It is precisely here, however, that the metaphor of the stranger can provide needed guidance and support.

For the image not only of crisis as stranger, of family member as stranger, of chaplain as stranger, but now also of *God* as Stranger, suggests that in the *very strangeness of the situation itself* we may find sanctuary, for in our Judeo-Christian history God continuously has shown God's self most vividly present and active in the midst of the strange and mysterious. In the visitors at Sarah's tent door, in a wrestling match at the Jabbok, in a bush that burns but is not consumed, in a slingshot, in a Samaritan, in a Cross, in a blinding vision: the witness of the tradition again and again points to the *Strange* and the *Stranger* as the bearer of God's presence and promise.

Yes, verities are lost in traumatic crisis situations, but the theological gift that the chaplain receives in them is to be found precisely in the lost verities. That is to say, in coming as a stranger to strangers in a situation of strangeness, the chaplain can find orientation in the knowledge that he or she stands in a firm tradition that has continuously acknowledged the God-bearing power of strangeness itself.

Hospital traumas demonstrate to the chaplain that God is *not* the sum total of our most beloved social values and familiar relationships, that God's word is frequently spoken *against* the values and aspirations of humanity, and that God finally cannot be contained by human sciences, technologies, or desires. To be a chaplain who affirms the biblical witness means to become one familiar with the strange, knowing that in the strange God comes in life-shattering and life-transforming ways.

CHAPTER 12

The Ascetic Witness

James E. Dittes[1] (1999)

The ministry of pastoral counseling is the stringent ministry of witnessing. Fundamentally, the pastoral counselor does not try to "do" anything and is not struggling to make something happen, to make repairs, or to make changes. The intent of pastoral counseling is more profound than that. The pastoral counselor witnesses.

Counseling as an Act of Visioning

The conversion to which counseling aspires is not a revision of tactics, agenda, or will. It is a re-vision of the self. So the counselor's contribution to this is an act of visioning. The counselor does not intervene, strategize, mobilize. The counselor regards, reliably and steadily. The counselor does not condemn, approve, diagnose, explain, or assuage or exert any other leverage over the counselee's life. The counselor witnesses to the fullness of that life. The counselor does not save; the counselor witnesses the saving.

The pastoral counselor witnesses–steadfastly, undistracted, relentlessly–the life experience of the counselee, the harried pilgrimage of a soul that has too often scurried in shadow. Lucid listener, the counselor beholds what has been averted, attests to what has been dismissed, hopes and shames alike.

Intervening would be easier and more familiar. Witnessing is a rare and strenuous gift. Intervening would put counselor and counselee in the familiar world of negotiation, the fencing of conditional and guarded trust, the marketplace of affection. Witnessing situates counselor and counselee in a world that transcends the frenzy and the fencing. It calls the bluff of habitual posturing strategies and maneuvers; it renders them meaningless. It says, "What counts is what I see. It counts for being visible and envisonable, not for being good, right, familiar, or easy."

Witnessing to Eschatological Hope

The pastoral counselor's witness testifies to the eschatological hope in which life resides, that alternative reality in which the End of life survives its ending and becomes sovereign, in which meaning prevails over grief, wholeness over dissolution. By demeanor and conviction, more than by word, the pastoral counselor provides a reliable glimpse of a reality as yet unrealized but nonetheless real, in which counselee (and counselor) find a sure niche and blessing. This is the revisioning of life, the *con-version* of life, to which the counselor's witness testifies and invokes.

The counselee may, in timidity and fear, speak of the counseling moment as a haven from the "real world," as though harshness and treachery, hectoring and torment, by default, have the authority to define "reality." But the witness of the counselor testifies that it is just the opposite: reality, finally, is in the completion and assurance savored in the counseling moment; what we, submissively and cynically, dub the "real world" is the distortion. To this eschatological affirmation, the pastoral counselor witnesses.

A Time Set Apart

Pastoral counseling is a time set apart, in a space set apart, in a relationship that is distinctive. It provides a community (usually of two people) that is different from other communities, an alternative world unlike the conventional social world. Priorities are different, customs are different, and the etiquette and expectations of how we treat each other and by which we become a community are different.

Pastoral Counseling as Time-out

The counselor experiences pastoral counseling as a time-out, just as the counselee does. The rhythms, negotiations, and rules of the conventional world are suspended in favor of an alternative world. For both the counselor and counselee, life is moved out of the marketplace into a sanctuary, the pulse of life is converted from the racing irregular tyranny of "if" to a steady "isness."

Instead of living an insecure "as if," one can live securely "as is." No less so than the counselee, the counselor is converted from the frantic urgency of being performer, expert, merchant, and consumer to the quiet intensity of being witness. For both, it is a moratorium, a benign suspension of the social contracts and web by which human relationships are conventionally defined and structured. An alternative reality prevails. The fabric of expectations– expectations of what one should give and should get–is suspended and transcended.

For the counselee, this is a gift, often unexpected. For the counselor, it is a voluntary, self-imposed discipline, an ascetic renunciation not unlike the willing adoption of the regimen of a monastery.

Culture Shock in the New World

For the counselee, the suspension of expectations is commonly more liberating than depriving; the conventional world of expectations has become thwarting and is, for the moment, well shed. The culture shock is welcome, enticing. For the counselor, the suspension is more likely to be a deprivation; the conventional world has provided structure, identity, and satisfactions; so its loss, in the act of counseling, is grieved.

The culture shock may be traumatic. Though the counselor's suspension of the rules and roles of the conventional world is a willing choice, it is not always easy to sustain—no more so than any other renunciation and discipline chosen for the sake of religious vocation. As with the discipline accepted, for example, by priests and nuns for their religious vocations, the counselor is renouncing what has been more blessing than curse.

For the period of pastoral counseling, the counselor renounces "the world," a willing sacrifice of its benefits, and invokes an alternative reality so that the counselee can experience relief from the burdens of "the world." Because the social structure has evolved as a tumultuous compromise of many needs and demands, it has ambivalent impact on each of us; it both defines and hobbles, simultaneously supports and saps.

In telling us who we are and how to behave, the social structure confers the boon of identity, a repertory of behavior, and more or less assured membership in a community—even as it also constricts and sometimes distorts identity, and dangles membership in a community as a tease. To suspend this conventional social reality for the sake of an alternative is to lose the defining and supporting as well as the crippling. What the counselee needs—and gets—is relief, harbor, and sanctuary. But to invoke this alternative reality, the counselor sacrifices, willingly, the identity-giving support of conventional social reality.

A Meeting of Pure "Beingness"

The counseling relationship partakes of the mystical qualities of Martin Buber's I-Thou relationship, a transpersonal encounter in which the usual badges of identity and objectifying tactics of "relationship" are surrendered in favor of what can be called a meeting of pure "beingness."

The counselee is temporarily immunized from the give-and-take negotiations and bartering that maneuver us through life. The counselor renounces those satisfactions and stakes, the succoring and the savoring, that ordinarily energize and direct one's conduct. The stakes are off and the wagering and tortuous maneuvering through conditionalities are over—for the counselee because the connections are temporarily severed between conduct and payoff, for the counselor because he or she is temporarily willing to live without the payoffs.

The discipline accepted by the pastoral counselor is an astonishingly simple one. The counselor is content to be a witness, not a player. The counselor is intensely present to the counselee, but as a witness. The counselor does not crave or design to have an impact, to make a difference, or to leave his or her mark on the counselee's life. Nor does the counselor aspire to find satisfaction, community, or accomplishment. Aspirations that may be perfectly appropriate in everyday conversations–to be curious, to assuage pain, to solve problems, to master perplexities, to understand and know and explain why things are the way they are, to be loved and admired and understood–are put on hold. The pastoral counselor abstains from the normal desire to be included in another's life. The pastoral counselor "gets a life" elsewhere.

An Asymmetrical Conversation

Pastoral counseling does not have the symmetry and mutuality of conventional conversation. In conventional conversation, both persons have their own distinctive points of view and experiences to offer, and the conversation proceeds by their mutual airing and sharing. Ordinary social conversation is in the intertwining of two plots, two story lines. Therein is its fertile richness, in which personhood and relationship thrive, but also therein is the room for mischief, the seedbed in which human distress thrives.

The Sparring of Ordinary Conversation

In the usual rhythms of conversation we take turns, more or less equally. I listen to your story even while I tell my own (or prepare to). I project and protect my own image/mask/identity even while I acknowledge (or don't) yours. I say, "That reminds me...," "I agree, but...," "The way I do (or see, or believe) it is...," "No, what I meant was..." Every word uttered has two meanings–never identical–one for the speaker, one for the listener. I share the stage: with you, with your perception of me (and/or misperception), and with my (mis)perception of you–there are at least that many of us. The richness and the risks of conversation lie in the interplay of these multiple meanings.

It is in such sparring that I forge identity, build bonds, fit you into my life in a way that suits me, and fit into yours in a way that makes sense to you. It is also in such sparring that I may come to feel misfitted, used, abused, twisted, misunderstood, defensive, frustrated, hostile.

Pastoral Counseling as Grace

But pastoral counseling is one-sided. Counseling provides reprieve and redress from these skirmishes. As counselee, for the time being, I don't share the stage. I have a chance to find out what words and events mean to me, because I can drop my guard against the intrusion of your meanings and against your kidnapping of mine. I can drop my apprehension of your guardedness, my fear that I may upset or misunderstand you. I can drop my obligation to be a custodian of your meanings as well as mine.

The counselor renounces his or her own social rights to claim or assert meaning, to tell his or her own story, to claim identity. The counselor even more renounces the human privilege and need to be defensive; the counselor is willing to let an hour pass, without correcting the counselee's misperceptions of him or her. The counselor replaces the role of player or partner with the role of witness. The counselee replaces the need to engage, accommodate, and skirmish with the enlivening awareness of being closely and unconditionally regarded—a replacement of the mode of "law" with the mode of "grace."

Whatever meaning the counselee's words may have for the pastoral counselor—reminder of similar experiences or troubles, seeming gestures of affection or dislike, challenges to authority or skill, misstatement of facts, misquoting of the pastor, misinterpretation of scripture, egregiously immoral behavior—the pastoral counselor abstains from considering what it means to him or her, and focuses intensively and exclusively on what it means to the counselee.

A Crucial Test

This distinction is fundamental to pastoral counseling. Here is a crucial test, a common and typical moment in pastoral counseling: Suppose the counselee says, "You don't understand me." A conventional conversation partner is expected and entitled to defend and to smooth: "I do, too, understand... I'm sorry; forgive me...Let me try again..." Even perhaps the defensiveness becomes aggressive: "That hurts, why do you have to attack me like that?" But the pastoral counselor puts all these "I's" on hold and witnesses the counselee with a response, perhaps, like this: "That must make you feel lonely again."

Another critical defining moment in all counseling relationships: "Just tell me what to do!" In conventional conversation, that puts the spotlight on the conversation partner, who may yield to the invitation to dodge it ("I don't know what to do either," or, "Let's figure out something together.") The pastoral counselor is content to let the demand linger and to let herself or himself dangle so as to witness to the plight the counselee expresses, maybe with, "I guess you feel at your wit's end." The counselor abstains from sharing the spotlight as a player yet, more crucially, assures the counselee that he or she is closely regarded, witnessed.

The Counselor as Witness

The counselor is not required to overlook a misstatement or a moral misstep. The point is that if it is reflected ("Actually, you misheard what I said in the sermon," or "You know you crossed a line that time."), such remarks are said in the mode of witnessing the counselee. They are not for the purpose of venting or defending the counselor's views, but for the purpose of inviting the counselee to reflect on the meaning of the error. ("I must have really had X on my mind during the sermon," or "I guess I was just so mad I couldn't stop.")

That is, pastoral counseling does not conspire to cover up or deny misdoing, but probes it. The happy slogan of the 1960s, "I'm OK and you're OK," is *not* the slogan of pastoral counseling. Pastoral counseling wants to transcend the question of "OKness."

Though the counselor is not present to the counselee in the ways of conventional social interaction, the counselor is far from absent or passive. The witnessing is an act of intense energy and focus, astute and attentive. The counselee experiences this moment of focused attention not just as the freedom from social pressures, which it is, but also as a moment of immense support and affirmation, which it also is. The counselor is likely to experience this tremendous investment of energy as exhausting.

The Counselor's Renunciations

The pastoral counselor abides by a fierce ascetic discipline, relinquishing for the moment of counseling the resources that most bestow esteem and personhood. In the conventional world, status, recognition, and identity are derived primarily from two sources: from relationship, that is, from belonging to another person or group (allegedly the preferred source of female identity), and from successful performance and achievement (the alleged preference of males). But the pastoral counselor renounces both these vehicles of esteem.

The Paradox of Renunciation

Pastoral counseling is earnest of an alternative world. Finding personal worth and identity rooted elsewhere, the pastoral counselor does not depend emotionally on either the relationship with the counselee or the successful achievement of any counseling agenda. The pastoral counselor does not need warmth or effectiveness in the counseling, does not court affection or avoid rejection, and does not covet and plot achievement. Such matters are irrelevant to the counselor's self-esteem.

These are monumental acts of ascetic renunciation, essential gifts to the counselee, powerful testimonies to an alternative reality. The counselor's ascetic renunciation is at least as strenuous as that of the monk or nun. For the sake of their religious vocation, monks and nuns surrender—by taking vows of poverty, celibacy, and obedience—the values that the conventional world attaches to wealth and status, sexual intimacy, and autonomy. This is not different from the counselor's vows for the moment of counseling.

The counselor's renunciation is particularly strenuous because, paradoxically, the counselor gives up precisely the resources he or she hopes for the counselee to discover—relationship and accomplishment—or, in Freud's abbreviated statement of the goals of therapy, love and work. Powerful commitments and motivations bring the counselor to counseling, but if not checked, they will drive the counselor to distort the counseling. If the counselor *needs* the counseling to be successful, *needs* to achieve intense rapport, *needs* to resolve the counselee's distress, *needs* to restore the counselee to abundant life, then the counselor will be driven to forsake the attentive witnessing and to yield to the world's ways of commanding and cajoling.

Four Ascetic Renunciations

Four ascetic renunciations can be identified:

1. the expectations of everyday etiquette,
2. the expectations of intimate relationships,
3. the expectations of performance, proficiency, prowess, achievement, and
4. the expectations of clerical or even "pastoral" identity, as this is conventionally regarded.

For the sake of embracing the counselee with an alternative set of values and for the sake of steadfast witnessing, the pastoral counselor is ready to be regarded—by the standards of the conventional world—as impolite, impersonal, nonachieving, and nonclerical.

ETIQUETTE

The simple matter of etiquette, the customs and polity by which we all affirm our membership in society, is perhaps more difficult to relinquish than the more intense badges of relationship. Our everyday world is lubricated by social conventions. They smooth the inevitable roughness of human interaction. They keep the peace. They enable us to live our lives with each other efficiently and with decorum without the need to constantly reappraise and renegotiate, without the need to start always from square one. They signal that people are members of the same community, acting more or less from the same script. They attest to the identity and meaning that derive from belonging to a culture, or subculture. They mark the ties that bind people together, even as they also mark the boundaries that divide.

Since pastoral counseling is intended to provide occasion for just the reflective reappraisals that etiquette preempts, a chance to go back to square one, a chance to look under the lid, a reexamination of membership and exclusion that has been taken for granted, pastoral counseling tries to provide a world that is relatively barren of these lubricating conventions.

Relinquished Rules of Etiquette

Here are some of the rules of etiquette that pastoral counseling tries to do without:

1. Don't let conversation lapse into silence.

Always have something to say. Silence may imply disapproval or offense, and such things are better suppressed.

2. Practice white lies.

Questions like "How are you?" "How do you like my new car?" "How was your vacation?" are to be answered with brief positive responses.

Conversation is not to be bogged down, nor the mood depressed, with honest, careful responses. (In some subcultures, a deliberately reversed convention prevails; the responses are to be exaggeratedly negative: "It was a vacation from hell; everything went wrong." But this is still a lubricating convention, a cover-up in its own way.)

3. Reassure distress.

Don't let negative feelings or negative news linger without being balanced by a positive remark. "He's better off now." "I'm sure you'll feel better soon." "He's really a good boy."

4. Show involvement.

Perhaps it is more accurate to say "Pretend involvement." Ask questions. Offer advice. Offer to help: baking, driving, phoning. Recall similar experiences of your own. And there's always, "Let's have lunch."

5. Gather only the facts.

Deal with a situation by reciting facts or inquiring about facts. "When did it happen?" "Was she sick long?" "Have you told Jerry?" "We drove 2,700 miles." "The body count was..." The purpose, of course, is to preempt the discomfort of expressing feelings.

6. Explain.

Contain distress, distressing events, and distressing feelings by explaining them. "Boys like that do those things." "The cause of the plane crash was..." "I could see it coming."

7. Moralize.

This is a form of explanation. Pronounce the difference between right and wrong and explain how any circumstance fits into your firm moral matrix. This is a powerful social lubricant that smooths over the roughness of individual distress. Facts, explanations, and moralisms are a powerful and well-established triad of suppressors of feelings.

The Contrasting Worlds

The purpose of such etiquette is the socially necessary goal to avoid trouble, to maintain social connections. But the purpose of pastoral counseling is the personally necessary goal to face trouble, to appraise social connections. So pastoral counseling suspends these conventions, at the initiative of the counselor. The set-apart nature of the counseling makes this a relatively safe experiment, and both counselors and counselees report how satisfying and refreshing they find the change. The experience of silence is especially mentioned as a welcome surprise.

But customs and conventions are stubbornly fixed and reinforced, and even experienced counselors are startled to realize how often these forms of etiquette intrude into a counseling world they thought was safely immunized.

Counselors usually find that they resort to these conventional responses when they are feeling anxious about some aspect of the counseling.

The difference between the conventional world with its etiquette and the alternative world with its starkness is one of *function*. Each is needed for its own purpose. It will not do to call the conventional world "sick" or "evil." It is not abnormal any more than it is the norm. It is, apparently, as valid and worthwhile a venture at "civilization" as our culture is able to evolve, a social compact that balances by compromise the interests of personal and social welfare, and guarantees the individual a relatively safe niche in the social fabric. But neither will it do to call the conventional world the "real" world. For the alternative world of pastoral counseling is equally real. Indeed, some might claim that it is more "real" insofar as it is, literally, *un*civilized. It affords a glimpse, beyond the life fashioned by the negotiations and compromises of civilizing, of the life as intended by its Creator, as promised by its Redeemer, as guaranteed by its Sustainer. This is life shorn of the need for anxious maneuvers to guarantee one's niche, life blessed by trust, hope, and love.

Ascetic Relationships

Priests and members of many religious orders typically renounce active sexual relationships not because sexuality is deemed "evil," but because their religious vocation requires undistracted focus and because their pastoral role requires immunity from the confusion of even latent sexual relationships. A celibate priest is able to achieve an intimacy with others that is unthreatened and unagitated by even implicit sexuality. The parishioner is able to suspend the usual apprehensions, guardedness, and flirtatious teasing that sexuality provokes because the priest has taken sexuality out of play (insofar as a priest has succeeded in doing so persuasively), and the pastoral relationship can move on to other matters.

Removing Games and Negotiations

The pastoral counselor offers a similar gift to the counselee: removal from their relationship not just of sexual games and negotiations but of all the games and negotiations that are required to construct "relationships." The counselor is under discipline. The counselor, for the duration of the counseling, is ascetic about a "relationship" with the counselee. Just as the counselor is scrupulous, of course, about separating the counseling from any possible sexual intimacy, the counselor is also scrupulous about separating the counseling from *any* possible "relationship" intimacy.

The priest hears confessions from behind a screen and a psychoanalyst out of sight of the client—symbols of the deliberate impersonality of the event. This is decidedly *not* an occasion for building a "relationship." The two people are partnered in another project. The pastoral counselor maintains the same studied aloofness and nonchalance without the buffer of screen or notepad, but may invent other symbols of the difference, such as a distinctive location, special times, the use of certain chairs just for counseling, or a verbally stated boundary.

Suspending Relationships

"Relationships" are intimate communities (commonly of two people) that nurture, sustain, and delight selfhood; they require constant work, negotiation, and wariness. As with all the ties and constructs of society and civilization, intimate personal relationships are essential to personal well-being; they make us more than we could be otherwise.

But, as with all the ties and constructs of society and civilization, intimate personal relationships are also exhausting and eroding of personal well-being; in the compromises they require, they also make us less than we could be without them. The pastoral counselor declares a kind of unilateral disarmament from such habitual jostlings. The give-and-take repertory of "relationship skills" and "relationship building" is suspended because the counselor declines to "give" and renounces "getting."

In entering the counseling relationship, the counselor pledges to abstain from letting the counseling generate a personal relationship with the counselee, in the usual sense of "relationship." Whatever pastoral or personal relationship exists before the counseling emerges unchanged after the counseling. The relationship between counselor and counselee is of an austere disembodied quality, a virtual relationship. The counselor refrains from negotiating any of those mutual satisfactions or mutual dependencies which are the normal part of any healthy social encounter.

The counselor pledges not to "need" the counselee, in the usual but complicated way that we, social creatures that we are, normally need each other for a complete sense of selfhood. The counselee is offered a privileged moratorium on just such personal negotiations and encounters. The counselor abstains from the usual social discourse in which one person finds self-warrant and identity by finding place and regard in the eyes of another. The counselor can provide even and steady regard for the counselee only by renouncing the usual human search for regard from the counselee.

Extending Sexual Abstinence

It is an extension of the sexual abstinence. Just as the counselee is offered the privilege of time-out from sexual negotiations or games, so that honest feelings can be risked and energies redirected, so too is the counselee offered the privilege of time-out from *any* negotiations of personal relationship. "What does he think of me? How can I protect or improve his opinion of me? What does she want from me? How can I protect myself from her without losing her regard?"

This haunting undertone of all social intercourse is stilled for the counselee by the counselor's renunciation of all such personal claims from the counseling relationship. The counselor does not need the counselee to like or admire him or her, does not need esteem to be warranted or bolstered by exhibiting skills or by any outcome or performance of the counseling, does not have any agenda for the counseling fueled by personal needs.

If the counselee scowls, demands, compliments, complains, behaves aloofly or seductively, such behavior can be viewed for its meaning to the counselee, not for its meaning to the counselor. The counselor abstains from needing it to mean anything. For once, the counselee is spared from having to monitor, censor, second-guess, and ration affect and energy in order to preserve a relationship. There is none at stake.

If the counselee is late for an appointment, or misses one altogether, the counselor refrains from "taking it personally." The counselor has nothing "personal" at stake, has pledged a celibacy of such concerns. So the counselor need not brood on being inconvenienced, demeaned, abandoned—all the affective meaning that such an event might otherwise have for a person. In the pledge of "celibacy," the counselor has renounced any such meaning and is therefore free to attend to the meaning the event has for the counselee.

The counselor's abstinence, like the monk's, testifies to another order of existence; it testifies to a transcending order or world that supersedes the hungers for personal intimacy, which make us lunge and grasp for "relationships" even while leaving us hungry.

PERFORMANCE AND PROWESS

"How am I doing?" Ed Koch famously wondered aloud on the streets of New York City throughout his years as mayor. So everyone wonders constantly, often desperately. "How am I doing" in the eyes of others? "How am I doing" in my eyes? In God's eyes? What checklists of accomplishments at the end of a career, at the end of a day, at the end of a pastoral counseling session validate that career, that day, that session?

It is a fair, legitimate, and normal question. We should be responsible; we need to be accomplished in measurable ways. It is also a question that drives us to distortion as we try to make the answer come out right. We misperceive and become blind to our failings. Worse, we wrestle the events of our lives to compel outcomes that fit our expectations of success, to create outcomes that readily match our checklists. We maneuver, manipulate, and manage to make others fit our scripts for success.

The Counselor's Temptation to Achieve

Pastoral counseling is especially vulnerable to such achievement-driven maneuvering. The counselor is counseling because he or she is called by the most intense and urgent motives to bring others to wholeness and fullness of life. The counselor is afflicted with such high aspirations, such worthy but elusive goals. So the counselor is tempted to manage the counseling and the counselee in ways that yield palpable results, to impose agenda and scripts, to cajole and instruct, to be impatient with hopelessness and doubt, to settle for shortcuts and shallow resolutions, to carry away something that counts as results. The counselor's high hopes become high hoops for the counselee.

But the real intent of pastoral counseling is precisely to spare the counselee just such pressures and hoops and scripts that have badgered and distorted the counselee's life to date. Pastoral counseling provides an alternative world in which the counselee is immune to such pressures.

The counselor renounces the need for the counseling to accomplish anything measurable. It is a huge sacrifice. The counselor is honestly willing to get along without results, to go through a counseling hour, even a year of counseling hours, without knowing whether the counselee's life is bettered, whether the distress is reduced, or whether affirmatives are clarified.

Meaning for Counselee, not Counselor

If the counselee expresses satisfaction at results attained or anxiety about results unattained, these are witnessed for what they mean to the counselee, not enfolded into any calculations or assessments the counselor has. If family, friends, or parishioners admire results or fret the absence of apparent "progress," the counselor is not panicked into trafficking with the currency of results. Such remarks can be witnessed and reflected as legitimate expressions of concern ("I can tell you are concerned that things go well") but need not provoke the counselor into abandoning or defending his or her own disciplined approach without the need for results.

The counselor abstains from needing to act wisely, helpfully, or masterfully. If questions are asked, of if there is silence, the counselor doesn't need to have answers or to supply words in order to avoid feeling embarrassed or like a failure. If problems are posed or unsolved, the counselor can leave them that way, unanswered questions and unresolved problems, without feeling it a rebuke or shame.

The counselor does not need to garner all the facts before feeling comfortable with a situation; if the counselee's story is confused or incomplete, the counselor doesn't have to be curious or play detective, as most friends would, in order to avoid feeling foolish or out of touch. The counselor has no need to master the perplexities of the counselee's life and of the counseling, no need for a premature closure. The counselor conveys a faith in the validity of the counselee's life and of the counseling process that transcends the conventional but idolatrous reliance on palpable accomplishment.

THE PASTORAL ROLE

A minister is often called to give up much of the conventional worldly life, including a comfortable standard of living, privacy for self and family, convenient work hours, clear lines of accountability, immunity from irresponsible gossip and criticism, and adequate staff assistance. But the pain of such surrender is commonly eased by firm vocational identity: "I do it because I am a pastor."

And that assertion of identity as "pastor" or "minister" or "clergy" has the content of well-established vocational roles.

Sacrificing the Badges of Identity

"I know who I am because I know I am a pastor, and I know I am a pastor because I preach, build church membership, teach the Bible, live a moral and pious life, comfort the afflicted (and–that proverbial symmetry–afflict the comfortable)," and so on through the endless checklist of ministerial skills and tasks. Such clergy roles are badges of identity. To surrender these badges would be an excruciating sacrifice, these hallmarks by which one orders and justifies one's day. Yet that is exactly what a pastoral counselor is called to do for the duration of counseling: to not be a pastor in these conventional senses.

The pastoral counselor is not the guide to the moral life or the guide to God, not the expert in prayer or the Bible, not the recruiter to church membership or the leader of worship life. The pastoral counselor enters the counseling naked of the hard-won assurances of what it means to be a pastor (and usually, too, of what it means to be a counselor), stripped of the roles and rules that tell how to assuage distress and chaos.

An Agent of the Transcendent

The pastoral counselor is the agent of that transcendent dimension of life in which such expectations, demands, performances, and checklists, such provings of self, are beside the point. No more than social etiquette, intimacy, or professional success are these vocational dimensions of personhood mean or lesser. For the minister as for anyone else, work and good works are valid and necessary. But they are one-sided, and pastoral counseling represents the other side, the renewing and renewable world of uncalculated, unmeasured, even reckless trust. Pastoral counseling permits the counselor–and hence the counselee–to surrender the dead-end security and indignation of the elder brother and venture the spiritual daring of the prodigal father.

Sometimes beginning pastoral counselors think of pastoral counseling as a set of supremely refined skills. It is really much simpler than that. To undertake pastoral counseling is not to pile on norms and expectations of yourself, but to strip them away.

PART THREE

CONTEMPORARY *and* CONTEXTUAL IMAGES *of* CARE

INTRODUCTION

It may seem remarkable to us in hindsight that Hiltner's solicitous shepherd could retain its influence as the dominant metaphor for contemporary Protestant pastoral theology for over two full decades in the 1950s and 1960s. Equally surprising is that Nouwen's wounded healer and, to a lesser degree, Campbell's wise fool could so thoroughly capture the imagination of ministers and pastoral theologians through much of the 1970s and 1980s. The staying power of so limited a number of images by which to conceive of pastoral care may now strike us as quaint, if not naive or deleterious, given a burgeoning of alternative pastoral images that began to appear at the brink of the new millennium. Having already considered several of these newer images in the previous sections, we concentrate in part three on a number of others.

The Environment for Contemporary Counselors

The present generation of pastoral theologians—many of them students of the civil rights, feminist, and gay liberation movements and all heirs to technologies of globalization that make the world appear ever smaller even while magnifying its complexities—has tended to focus its attention on various social and cultural locations embodied by caregivers and individuals or communities in need. Newly emerging images and metaphors for ministry evoke questions of how interlocking political, economic, racial, and sexual dynamics come to bear on diagnosing and healing the traumas of any era or place.

Who decides or names, indeed who *should* decide or name, whether a specific individual's turmoil results from some internal biochemical, psychological, or spiritual aberration, from some systemic familial, social, or ecclesial disorder, or from some combination thereof? Who is to take the lion's share of responsibility for amelioration or change? To suggest that a conflagration of cultural structures and influences contributes to any particular person's suffering, as contemporary pastoral theologians typically do, may also be to insist that pastoral care and counseling move beyond an "exploration of the inner world" so important to Boisen and other pioneers, to consider more prophetic or encompassing roles in the larger social arena.

Even now, of course, there remains something deeply compelling and corrective in pastoral theology's historic advocacy on behalf of the spiritual and emotional well-being of individuals, and in its insisting that Christian theology and ministry take the peculiar voices of individuals into account. Many pastoral theologians today, however, express concern that, in having neglected social and environmental factors that sometimes constitute—and always come to bear on—the distress of suffering persons, the early movement's greater emphasis on individual psychology, while laudable for undermining moralistic counseling tactics, nonetheless may have inadvertently contributed to isolating and thereby further burdening those very individuals it was seeking to assist.

Widening the Horizons

So has arisen within recent decades a host of new images and models that seek to highlight specific differences of context, community, gender, and race in an effort to widen previous horizons of pastoral care. To recall Miller-McLemore's essay on the living human web, "In a word, never again will a clinical moment, whether of caring for a woman recovering from hysterectomy or attending to a woman's spiritual life, be understood on intrapsychic grounds alone."[1]

The collection of contemporary images in this concluding section speaks to a dynamic contextual pluralism within pastoral theology that, though not antithetical to the visions of its early pioneers, at least hints at a dramatic shift in emphasis and an ongoing vitality in pastoral theology that continues to build on the foundations of its forebears.

Paul W. Pruyser

In certain respects, Paul W. Pruyser's metaphor of the minister as diagnostician, found in chapter 13, stands at the crossroads of this shift from the intrapsychic to the social and contextual in pastoral theology. Published in 1976, Pruyser's essay appears at the height of the influence of Henri Nouwen's metaphor of the wounded healer. Like Nouwen, Pruyser was a native of Holland who immigrated to America, in his case after serving, as did Heije Faber, in the Dutch underground resistance movement in World War II. Like Nouwen and Faber, Pruyser too was drawn to the psychology of religion in his work as a clinical psychologist at the Menninger Foundation in Topeka, Kansas.

In *The Minister as Diagnostician,* Pruyser, a Presbyterian layperson and elder until his death in 1986, seeks to relieve ministers of the kind of professional insecurity and self-doubt that the image of the wounded healer appeared to some critics to promote. While he commends the efforts of ministers who in their work in clinical settings seek to learn the language of another profession, typically psychology or psychiatry, he expresses a concern that in this process they appear to lose track of any vocabulary of their own.

Pressed in interdisciplinary case conferences to share their unique professional understandings—their own *diagnoses*—of patients, Pruyser notes that the ministers are usually at a loss: "When urged to conceptualize their observations in their own language, using their own theological concepts and symbols, and to conduct their interviews in full awareness of their pastoral office and church setting, they [feel] greatly at sea."[2] When talking with a patient or parishioner, Pruyser asks, should not the minister want to know, "prior to unleashing his therapeutic furor, something about the person's religious situation—his state of grace, his despair, his deep or shaken loyalty, his tenets or disbeliefs, his grounds for hope?"[3]

Pruyser's work, then, serves initially as a sympathetic and influential outsider's prophetic call for ministers and pastoral theologians to reclaim their own theological voice and heritage. As a prominent Christian psychologist at what was then the nation's foremost psychiatric institution, Pruyser seeks to release pastoral theology from any exclusive attachment to psychology and the intrapsychic realm, though not by suggesting that ministers return to some pre-critical, pre-clinical, moralistic frame of reference of past eras.

Indeed, Pruyser tends to accept at face value the conceptualizations of contemporary pastoral theology as laid out by Boisen, Hiltner, and other early theorists, with whom he was personally well acquainted. Like Hiltner, for example, he understands pastoral theology to offer a particular shepherding perspective on certain acts of ministry of the church, shaped by its various concomitant Christian traditions, values, and language. Less attempting to define pastoral theology for ministers and pastoral theologians, Pruyser instead encourages them to put into practice conceptualizations already available.

He points out that persons in crisis quite frequently turn first to their ministers for help because they want to understand their suffering specifically from the perspective of a shared faith.[4] Knowing that there are many legitimate ways by which to name their problem, they intentionally choose a minister in order to help them name it in a particularly religious way. The minister therefore should find in this choice not only permission but also some sense of obligation to accommodate their desire. Pruyser presses ministers and pastoral theologians to think of themselves as theological diagnosticians co-equal to those in other healing professions, without need to apologize for the unique perspective they bring to bear. *Let ministers be ministers,* Pruyser seems to be saying. *Let them be theologians.*

Pruyser's plea, however, harbors no illusions of privileging a pastoral perspective over that of any other profession; he is not advocating for an imperial theology. To the contrary, his essay functions as pivotal in the historical development of pastoral theology precisely because it hints at an emerging postmodern perspective, in which theology, while reclaiming its rightful place at the table, is considered to offer only one among many possible informed points of view.

Certainly Pruyser wants ministers and pastoral theologians to stop apologizing for their particular lenses on the sufferings of persons or communities in the face of other, seemingly more weighty or scientific, points of view. Spousal abuse, Pruyser suggests by way of example, "is no less theological than it is psychological or sociological or criminological. It may be endocrinological for all we know. What it 'is' depends on how it is regarded."[5] Yet even as this example seeks to strengthen the hand of pastoral theology in contemporary therapeutic discourse, it simultaneously renders unstable a pastoral theological position by creating a level playing field among other relevant disciplines. Though specifically pressing pastoral theology to recover a distinctively theological prowess, Pruyser attempts to move it, perhaps paradoxically, into more collegial, collaborative, and ultimately contextual dialogue with a wide range of other fields, including, but no longer limited to, psychology and psychiatry.

Gaylord Noyce

No essay in the present book takes more at face value that portion of Pruyser's injunction calling ministers to task *as* ministers, though less his assumptions concerning the relativity of a theological perspective, than does Gaylord Noyce's essay in chapter 14 on the minister as moral coach and counselor.[6] Noyce, writing in 1989 as a pastoral theologian at Yale Divinity School, sees his work in part as an extended commentary on what Hiltner himself worried might become the most misunderstood of his three "aspects" of the shepherding perspective, namely, the *guiding* function of the minister. More than the aspects of *healing* and *sustaining* individuals in need, Hiltner sensed that his use of the term *guiding* risked being misinterpreted to suggest a return to moralistic pastoral approaches of the past. For Hiltner, guiding instead could, in one sense, be thought of as *referral*; the good Samaritan *guides* the wounded man to an inn for additional care.

More often for him, guiding meant collaborative, noncoercive, nonjudgmental moral exploration with an individual in need.[7] Along with healing and sustaining, then, Hiltner emphasized that guiding, as a distinct aspect of the shepherding perspective, necessarily involves, as previously noted, the minister's temporarily setting aside concern for the larger congregation or fellowship and focusing instead on the concerns of a particular individual or smaller group.

In his metaphor of the minister as moral coach or counselor, Noyce seeks to build on Hiltner's understanding of guiding as a function of shepherding, though he ultimately moves far afield of it. Like Hiltner, Noyce insists that pastors must not be coercive or authoritarian in their approach to moral guidance, especially given the voluntary nature of church membership. He has no interest in pressing for a return to advice-giving or the use of moralistic tactics in pastoral care. Rather, Noyce argues, moral leadership involves a mutual exploration of ideas, values, and decisions between ministers and their parishioners free from coercion or compulsion.

Despite this shared concern for mutuality in moral decision-making, Noyce conceives of his metaphor of the minister as moral coach or counselor in more sweeping terms than those of Hiltner's shepherd, as encompassing far-ranging needs of the wider congregation or community. Though Noyce envisions the minister assuming the role of a coach more of adults than of children, that is, a coach more inclined to be persuasive than directive, he nonetheless wants to expand the scope of pastoral theology beyond Hiltner's concern for individuals in need. He therefore revisits distinctive venues of Christian ministry—worship, prayer, preaching, mission, and education—as legitimate arenas for Christian moral guidance and pastoral care, a broad terrain that Hiltner would have argued ordinarily falls under the ministerial perspectives of communicating or organizing, not of shepherding.

Edward P. Wimberly

In chapter 15, Edward P. Wimberly considers the African-American minister's role as indigenous storyteller, both in terms of how stories have traditionally been used by African American pastors in communicating the gospel from the pulpit and of how stories have come to serve individuals, couples, and families in pastoral care and counseling. Wimberly, a professor of pastoral care at the Interdenominational Theological Center in Atlanta and a prolific author on pastoral theology from an African American perspective, notices that widespread recent interest in narrative theology, along with a preponderance of narrative approaches in psychotherapy, affirm what has long been known among many indigenous communities as the healing power of "storying" one's faith and life. African Americans, Wimberly writes, can "take pride that the academic and professional world of counseling is rediscovering what already was a full-blown tradition in African American culture."[8]

African American ministers often use a narrative approach in pastoral care and counseling, drawing on stories from their own lives, their ministries, and the Bible as a way of helping others articulate their own particular stories as ones caught up in the larger story of God, however problematic or painful.[9] The specific stories that a minister might share with counselees emerge from a historic core narrative in African American churches that depicts God as working to deliver persons and communities from their oppression, offering hope and healing in the face of hardship or despair.

Wimberly calls this master narrative the "eschatological plot," best exemplified in the stories of the exodus of the Hebrew children from Egypt and of the resurrection of Jesus from the dead. He notices in these master narratives certain traditional storytelling devices that he describes as the unfolding, linking, thickening, and twisting of a plot.[10] The minister as indigenous storyteller, like Noyce's moral coach, is unafraid of providing "guidance when direction is needed," but for Wimberly this guidance is more likely to come in the friendly guise of a story. The storyteller suggests by this means various "ways to motivate people to action, help them to see themselves in a new light, help them to recognize new resources, [and] to channel behavior in constructive ways."[11]

Wimberly notes possible dangers in the narrative approach as well, including the threat of pastoral "imperialism" or heavy-handedness and a potential discounting among ministers of the value of formal training or of a sense of empathy in counseling. He cautions that the minister as indigenous storyteller needs at times to utilize therapeutic approaches other than narrative ones, and he suggests, significantly, that a storytelling approach necessarily also entails story-*listening*. "It is only when the story has been fully expressed and the caregiver has attended to it with empathy that the foundation is laid for the utilization of storytelling."[12]

Donald Capps

In chapter 16, Donald Capps builds on his earlier metaphor of the wise fool and accompanying discussion of the counseling method of reframing (in chapter 10) and offers the additional image of the minister as agent of hope. Here, Capps stakes out in more detailed fashion what Pruyser may have had in mind in referring to the unique perspective that ministers bring to bear on circumstances of human suffering and need. For Capps, this perspective is *hope*.

He suggests that pastors "are *agents of hope by definition* (or calling), and often this is *all* they are."[13] Noting that while hope in large part defines the calling of ministry, he argues that the nature of hope and hoping have not themselves been topics in which ministers have become widely read or to which they have given much concentrated attention. So in his essay, Capps seeks to define in considerable detail both the experience of *hoping* and the phenomenon of *hope*, and ultimately to offer additional contributions to what he considers the hope-inspiring method and techniques of reframing for pastoral care.

Hope, for Capps, is basic not only to ministry but to life itself. Building on Erik Erikson's developmental theory, he locates the rudimentary origins of a sense of hopefulness in the earliest stage of life, based particularly on an infant's relationship with a trustworthy mother or mother-substitute. Though notoriously difficult to define, Capps suggests that hoping is "the perception that what one wants to happen will happen, a perception that is fueled by desire and in response to felt deprivation."[14] Our hopes, in turn, "are projections that envision the realizable and thus involve risk."[15] Hoping, more so than wishing or craving,

Capps says, is attuned to the hard realities of life. Thus to allow oneself to hope is to envision a realizable, though not always practical, future, to risk imagining oneself or another in some future place or state beyond present realities.

Hoping depends on the capacity to know, to say, and to trust what we desire but cannot presently see or experience. This capacity to name what we desire is not always highly developed, however, and so, Capps believes, ministers can play a vital role precisely in assisting others in this naming process. Borrowing techniques, then, from brief, solution-focused psychotherapy, he offers two specific exercises whereby ministers can help counselees reinterpret painful memories from their pasts and envision and name a more hopeful future.

Karen R. Hanson

In her essay on the minister as midwife in chapter 17, Karen R. Hanson offers an alternative to those metaphors for ministry typically associated with male gender roles. Hanson, a Lutheran minister and hospital chaplain in Minnesota, discerns a number of parallels between her calling as pastor and chaplain and that of women who attend to the birthing process as midwives. Not least among these similarities are ways in which both ministry and midwifery were devalued by the splitting apart of conceptions of mind, body, and spirit in the Enlightenment, and in which the gradual reversal of this trend in contemporary Western medicine has begun to manifest itself in part through a resurgence of interest in both chaplaincy and midwifery. Hanson notes that Anton Boisen instituted clinical pastoral training in the same year—1925—that Mary Breckenridge inaugurated a school for nurse midwives in Kentucky.[16] Today, both chaplains and midwives are again enjoying increasingly visible and revitalized roles in patient care.

She derives the metaphor of midwife for ministry from the Bible itself, noting, for example, that as the midwives Shiphrah and Puah risked their lives by saving Hebrew children from slaughter by Pharaoh (Ex. 1:15–22), so God is depicted in the book of Exodus and elsewhere as the midwife who delivered Israel from slavery in Egypt.[17] She suggests that just as a midwife is first to speak of the new life she sees—"It's a girl!"—so too Mary Magdalene first testifies to the resurrection of Jesus from the dead—"I have seen the Lord!" (Jn. 20:18).

Hanson then proceeds to offer a glimpse of the courage and plight of women who served as midwives throughout much of Western history, some among them identifying midwifery as their Christian vocation, others burned at the stake as witches for misconstruals of the ways in which, not unlike in the work of Christian ministers, "they mediated the mysteries of birth, illness, and death."[18] She concludes by affirming that ministers—particularly hospital chaplains—become spiritual midwives who assist in the process of birthing new life especially when they can recognize, stand fast in the face of, and help others in naming their travails; when as ministers they see the sick and suffering as whole persons and stand with, not against, them; when they know the experience of spiritual rebirth in their own personal lives; and when they are not surprised to discover, and then grow accustomed to dealing with, the pangs of death that, however hidden, accompany every type of new birth.[19]

Margaret Zipse Kornfeld

Margaret Zipse Kornfeld develops the metaphor of minister as gardener at points throughout her extensive textbook on pastoral care and counseling, *Cultivating Wholeness*, excerpts from which are found in chapter 18.[20] Kornfeld, a marriage and family therapist who teaches at the Blanton-Peale Institute and at Union Theological Seminary in New York City, draws the image from the meditations of Julian of Norwich and, in the way of a gardener, cultivates its possibilities for pastoral care. For her, to imagine pastoral care and counseling as a form of gardening is to underscore the intricate connection between individual plants and the ground in which they grow, that is, between individuals and the churches or communities in which they are formed and nourished. Strengths or problems in one cannot be adequately considered apart from those of the other.

Kornfeld gives considerable attention to the complex nature of "ground" itself, composed of many "soils," which signify for her the various religious traditions and practices of faith and healing in any given church or faith community. Even as master gardeners must know a great deal about the ground and its soils—when to let it lie fallow, when to fertilize or water, how to detect toxic agents—so ministers, Kornfeld says, must consider nuances of their particular faith communities as the first act of pastoral care.

What kinds of plants might thrive in this particular soil? What kinds of nutrients does this soil need to produce more vital plants? Is this congregation inclined toward a sacramental approach to healing, or does it rely on the power of music, preaching, or study groups? Does this faith community emphasize social witness at the expense of personal evangelism? These sorts of contextual considerations are central to Kornfeld's organic approach, and ministers, she affirms, are strategically situated to raise them.

Given this emphasis on community and context, it comes as no surprise that Kornfeld warns that the metaphor of gardener should not be taken to imply that ministers are the exclusive agents of healing and nurture in a congregation, the sole gardeners. Perhaps mindful of criticisms directed at Hiltner's image of the shepherd for its alleged privileging of shepherd over sheep, Kornfeld reminds her readers that individual parishioners, unlike plants (or sheep), are not mere objects to be "tended." Healing in pastoral care and counseling occurs instead through the *interaction* of minister and parishioner, of counselor and counselee, with both rooted in and "sustained by the same community."[21]

Ministers, too, are plants of sorts and need to rely on many others, often an external supervising minister or mentor of greater maturity and experience who will tend, nurture, and help to balance them.[22] Ministers who think of themselves as gardeners *and* plants, she suggests, grow into an ever-greater sense not only of their own wisdom but also of gratitude. In complex and challenging counseling scenarios, they simultaneously reassure themselves of their capacity to make a difference—"*I am enough*"—while acknowledging, too, their own reliance on others—"*It's grace that's brought me safe thus far.*"[23]

Brita L. Gill-Austern

In the final chapter, Brita L. Gill-Austern, like Karen Hanson, takes up the metaphor of the midwife. She applies it, with other metaphors of voice coach, storyteller, contemplative artist, and reticent outlaw, to feminist and womanist pedagogy. Gill-Austern, a professor of psychology and pastoral theology at the Andover Newton Theological School near Boston, seeks in this procession of metaphors to bring a feminist sensibility to the art of teaching pastoral theology in seminaries or divinity schools, for, as she puts it, "our teaching is pastoral care."[24]

Drawing on Mary Field Belenky and her coauthors' images in *Women's Ways of Knowing*,[25] Gill-Austern sees the teacher less as a banker who "deposits" knowledge into the minds of students than as a midwife who in cocreative relationship draws forth what students already have within them. Recalling a midwife who once told her, "I don't deliver the baby; I simply catch it," Gill-Austern suggests that "a feminist teacher needs to catch another's ideas and bring them to light rather than simply deliver her own."[26] The midwife teacher helps her students focus in on the essentials and relax into the moment, asking in particular open-ended questions, those without predetermined answers.

What such midwives frequently assist in bringing to birth, especially among women students, is a *voice* and a *story* all their own. The students begin to reclaim, or to find for the very first time, a subjective sense of self by which to trust and name their hopes and dreams, usually in the form of a story. They also often begin to connect especially their unique biological experiences as women—including menstruation, pregnancy, lactation, or menopause—to their spiritual awareness and sensibilities. Using the voices and stories of others in novels, poetry, video, and drama in the classroom, the teacher as voice coach and storyteller models for students in her care just how powerful their own voices and narratives can be.

Finally, Gill-Austern considers the teacher of pastoral theology as a contemplative artist and reticent outlaw. Even as a sculptor contemplates beforehand the peculiar nature of the stone or other specific medium, so the feminist pastoral theologian begins by contemplating not only her subject matter but the particular students themselves: "Whom we teach precedes what we teach. [A] beginning knowledge of who is in the classroom becomes the first act of care in teaching."[27] Such care manifests itself, for Gill-Austern, in details like determining what classroom to use for a particular course and how to arrange its chairs or desks, but more sweepingly in a willingness to approach her subject matter in continually fresh ways, incessantly taking into account the possibilities of the moment.

Such tactics, however, tend to appear suspect to colleagues accustomed to more conventional pedagogical approaches and academic standards, making the feminist pastoral theologian into an outlaw of sorts, however reticent to play the role. Indeed, Gill-Austern writes, "women pastoral theologians carry the fear of being doubly marginalized," seen "by colleagues as being in a 'soft' field, not the 'hard' (classical) disciplines" and using "nontraditional methodologies that draw from the other side of binary oppositions," oppositions that typically "value the rational over the emotive, analysis over synthesis, specialization over generalization."[28] To be a feminist, like being a teacher of pastoral theology, "means to choose the fact that you will always reside somewhat on the margins of the institution," a place, perhaps, "of creative tension, but also at times a lonely place and a place of discomfort."[29]

Especially by underscoring this sense of lonely exile, Gill-Austern brings this book full circle, from the terrifying ordeal of a marginalized minister in a Boston psychiatric hospital to the reluctant recalcitrance of a feminist pastoral theologian at the edges of the academy and just outside of town. After decades of striving, so slight a shift in metaphors–from outcast to outlaw, from a pastoral self-understanding derived from one precarious social location to another equally ominous and uninviting–may offer slim comfort to those who seek some "essence" of pastoral ministry or are concerned for the future of pastoral theology. For most ministers and pastoral theologians, though, who regularly contend with the ambiguities of their calling and the fragility of their personal and vocational identities–who know, that is to say, these metaphors and more by heart–to these, it's all just another day's work.

CHAPTER 13

The Diagnostician

PAUL W. PRUYSER[1] (1976)

Who has ever heard of ministers being engaged in *diagnostic* work? The shepherd's task is to guide his sheep, to lead them to green pastures, and to take good care of them for their owner. And in modern times, if a ram or ewe is ill, the shepherd will get a veterinarian to make a diagnosis and prescribe treatment.

Moreover, if "shepherd" and "sheep" are metaphors for people, the pastor can have his ill folk diagnosed by a medical doctor or a psychiatrist, who are alleged to know far more than he does about sizing up human beings when they complain of physical or mental problems. The pastor will gladly help his people in trouble, benefitting from the advice of the diagnosticians, but he surely will not consider himself an expert in diagnosis.

But what if some people have a desire to be assessed, evaluated, diagnosed by their pastors? What if certain persons want to make an honest assessment of themselves, and turn to their pastors for expert help in making a diagnosis of their troubles, their foibles, their stance in life, their troublesome, puzzlesome, or wayward selves? What if they want precisely their pastors, rather than some other specialists, to guide them in their search for a self-diagnosis? What if they want to place themselves in a pastoral-theological rather than a medical, psychiatric, legal, or social perspective? What if they want to be in several professional hands at one and the same time? To heed those desires would make the pastor a diagnostician in his own (and his client's) right. And to foster his client's need for self-evaluation would make the pastor a diagnostician of a special kind, using a conceptual system and practical framework without equal among other specialists in the helping professions.

[My] thesis is that pastors, like all other professional workers, possess a body of theoretical and practical knowledge that is uniquely their own, evolved over years of practice by themselves and their forebears. Adding different bits of knowledge and techniques by borrowing from other disciplines, such as psychiatry and psychology, does not undo the integrity and usefulness of their own basic and applied sciences. Adding clinical insights and skills to their pastoral work does not–should not–shake the authenticity of their pastoral outlook and performance.

I propose a concise focus: the minister as diagnostician. This focus seems natural, logical, and pointed when one considers that all helpers have to address themselves to situations that need, in the first place, some kind of definition.

The Touchstone of Professional Integrity

In what way, with what concepts, in what words, with what outlook does a practicing pastor assess the problem of a client who seeks his pastoral help? What, if anything, distinguishes a pastoral from a psychological assessment? What basic and applied sciences does a pastor use when he makes himself available to someone who seeks his help in solving some personal problem? In what terms does he describe his client and size up his problems? In making his pastoral help available, how does he proceed to heal, guide, or sustain the person who is turning to him for assistance? Does he make a prior evaluation, or does he just dash into certain helping routines which he has practiced? If he makes a diagnosis, how does he do so? And does his diagnosis have any bearing upon his helping moves, his counseling techniques or goals, his advice-giving, his encouragements, his pastoral interventions? Does he know what his clients seek of him, and does he realize what they hope to attain in selecting their pastor rather than a lawyer, doctor, or social worker as their prospective helper?

A Concern for Authenticity and Integrity

These are not spuriously abstract questions. Though they have much to do with theory, they are not merely academic. They have been forced upon my mind by diverse practical and theoretical considerations, in which the authenticity of various helping professions and the integrity of their disciplines have become important foci of concern.

To put my observations in a nutshell, [I have found that] pastors all too often use "our" psychological language, and frequently the worst selection from it–stultified words such as *depression, paranoid, hysterical.* When urged to conceptualize their observations in their own language, using their own theological concepts and symbols, and to conduct their interviews in full awareness of their pastoral office and church setting, they [feel] greatly at sea. When clients clearly [seek] pastoral answers to questions of conscience or correct belief, pastors [tend] either to ignore these questions or to translate them quickly into psychological or social-interactional subtleties. [T]he theological apperceptions in which they have been trained [give] way to a psychological ordering system.

The situation is not [entirely] bleak. I grant that most pastors [bring] pastoral warmth, dedication, zest for helping, perceptiveness, and their own religiousness to their work. Some also [bring] great natural savvy to their task, and can gently put their parishioners at ease. But despite these gifts, they [manifest], and sometimes [profess], that their basic theological disciplines [are] of little help to them in ordering their observations and planning their meliorative moves. They [do] not quite trust their parishioners' occasional use of theological language and their presentations of theological conflicts. Issues of faith [are] quickly "pulled" into issues of marital role behavior, adolescent protest against parents, or dynamics of transference in the counseling situation.

A Suspicion of Theology

There [seems] to be an implicit suspicion of the relevance of theology, both to any client's life and to the method and content of the pastor's counseling process. They also [seem] to like psychological language better than theological language, unaware that psychological terminology no less than theological words can be abused as an intellectual defense against human experience.

From the perspective I espouse, it is a jarring note when any professional person no longer knows what his basic science is, or finds no use for it. Granted that in most professions the applied science and skill aspects tend to take over in daily work and to become a substantive area of concentration. Yet the anchorage points of professional thought and action must remain clear to provide a base of identity and a source of replenishment. Granted, too, that applied sciences and techniques of practice sometimes have a way of conversely influencing the basic sciences from which they emerged. Still there remains in each discipline a foundational kind of knowledge that determines the permissible language games and the distinctions between assumptions, data, and inferences.

Pluralism in the helping professions has been so zestfully promoted, and is now so well established, that the time has come for some consideration of each profession's specificity and distinctiveness. I think the question of diagnosis is a salient starting point for tackling these issues.

A New Use for an Old Word: "Diagnosis"

The Definition

Although the words "diagnosis" and "to diagnose" seem to have been all but absorbed by medicine, it will surprise no student of Greek to hear that they are general terms. They are used to mean discerning and discriminating in any field of knowledge, distinguishing one condition from another, and, by derivation, resolving or deciding. *Diagignoskein* ("distinguish") is differentiated on the one hand from *dokein* ("seem good," "think"), which leads to opinions and eventually dogmas, and on the other hand from *aisthanesthai* ("apprehend by the senses"), which means to perceive or view close to the level of appearance.

To diagnose means grasping things as they really are, so as to do the right thing. Hence, in medicine, diagnosis at its best entails etiology, for the penetrating view arrives at causes and deals with patterns of cause-and-effect relations in the course of illness.

Obviously, these meanings of diagnosis and diagnosing are applicable to a variety of disciplines, including jurisprudence, ethics, sociology, economics and, pointedly, to all the so-called helping professions. One might say that whenever we are presented with a condition, especially one that entails stress, suffering, or unhappiness, which in turn elicits a desire for relief or melioration, the first thing to do is to diagnose that condition. Any would-be helper must know what he is dealing with, otherwise his moves are only shots in the dark. Thus regarded, diagnosis is very much a pastoral task also. It should be a substantial part of any pastor's daily activities. Who would deny that pastors need to approach their charges with a discerning knowledge of their condition, their situation, or their plight, and with discriminate ideas about desirable aid or intervention?

Theology and Diagnosis

Historically, diagnosis is indeed not foreign to the theological domain. There are at least two great landmarks of theological-diagnostic literature, very different from each other to be sure. Both abound in fine descriptions of, and subtle differentiations between, various conditions, going well beyond surface impressions to grapple with "things as they really are."

MALLEUS MALEFICARUM

The first landmark is the *Malleus Maleficarum*[2] of 1480, written by two Dominicans with the explicit intention of providing a diagnostic manual for practicing exorcists. Its focus is on the phenomena of possession and how to distinguish these from other conditions, some of which might be medical. Steeped as it is in demonology, its proximate goal can hardly be called pastoral by present-day standards, or by ancient standards for that matter, unless the burning of bodies at autos-da-fé and the premature sending of souls to their eternal home be considered pastoral activities. Yet its ultimate goal was pastoral, namely, the purification of the soul. The book was written clearly to foster the art of clerical diagnosing.

And if we are horrified by this early misdirected endeavor, we have cause to be thankful to the medical profession, which, through the efforts of such men as Johannes Weyer, did its best to come up with more humane alternatives by developing a different diagnostic system altogether. It is a pity, however, that this humanization led in effect to a shift from theological to medical thinking, which siphoned off some legitimate diagnostic functions from theology.

EDWARDS'S *A TREATISE CONCERNING RELIGIOUS AFFECTIONS*

The second landmark is Jonathan Edwards's *A Treatise Concerning Religious Affections*[3] of 1746. It, too, was written in an era of upheaval and addressed itself to phenomena of religious turmoil. The Great Awakening produced troublesome manifestations which required theological discernment, careful psychological analysis, and eventually some pastoral sorting out of religious sheep from religious goats, so to speak, to foster the cure of souls. Edwards dwelled on the "signs of gracious affections," introducing both positive and negative signs. He spoke of "distinguishing marks" of saintliness and the "qualifications of those that are in favor with God and entitled to his eternal rewards."

He was a penetrating diagnostician who went well beyond surface impressions. He distinguished between good and poor diagnostic indicators and felt that some "signs" are suspect, if not worthless. For instance, he saw no diagnostic value in the mere intensity of affections; he would not take body effects and verbosity as yardsticks of conversion. He distrusted some clients' lavish use of Biblical proof texts, and saw no diagnostic value in the mere frequency of worship attendance and profuse engagement in God-talk. By our standards, Edwards' *Treatise* lacks a direct empirical footing; it hinges more on his doctrinal convictions than on observations of living people from his own orbit. To that extent it will strike us today more as a psychologically informed doctrinal study than a pastoral-theological work. It contains no concrete case studies or even vignettes, and does not eventuate in recommendations for specific interventions. What "living documents" or specific persons Edwards refers to are Biblical personalities and a few saints of the church, both remote. Yet his thinking is undoubtedly diagnostic and specifically attuned to the concrete religious situations of his time.

SØREN KIERKEGAARD

Self-diagnosis of a theological kind was pointedly pursued a century after Edwards by Søren Kierkegaard. His written works[4] give us glimpses of an assiduous diagnostic process, at times bordering on obsessional thought. It is all the more interesting in that the trained theologian and his charge are in this case one and the same person. He artfully conducts an intrapsychic dialogue concealed by introducing two fictitious parties arguing with each other.

Kierkegaard does not introduce a diagnostic system, and there is little in his writings that will strike us as pastoral. Nevertheless, his work contains much that can be seen as a demonstration of self-diagnosing within an exquisitely theological framework. There can be no doubt that theology was Kierkegaard's basic science, albeit he never became a practicing minister, let alone a pastor to others. Discerning knowledge was his goal, starting with self-knowledge for the sake of bringing about a desirable change of heart.

Diagnosis Repudiated

This background, then, should be enough to indicate that diagnosis is not a function alien to the theological perspective. [Yet] [i]f one looks at the current pastoral-theological literature, one finds that not only the word but the very idea of diagnosis seems to be repudiated in pastoral care. Some time ago I surveyed systematically a number of currently outstanding books on pastoral care and counseling, looking for evidence of a genuinely pastoral-theological diagnostic awareness in ministers. I reported my findings elsewhere:[5] the word "diagnosis" rarely occurs in an index of any of these books, and if it appears at all, it proves to refer to psychiatric or medical usage. One instance of pastoral-diagnostic thought is illustrated by Hiltner[6] in his citation of the work of the nineteenth-century Ichabod Spencer. Hiltner reports that this minister, otherwise quite gifted and astute, seems to have approached one case of pastoral care with the wrong diagnosis, going wildly astray in his efforts to help a distraught woman.

In a much earlier work, Hiltner made at least the effort to seek an approach to the difficult issue of "spiritual diagnosis" (the quotation marks are his) by suggesting that such a diagnosis has three elements: personality diagnosis, situational diagnosis, and spiritual resources diagnosis. The latter element, however, is more an assessment of positive religious values that could be put to therapeutic use by a religious worker than a clear-cut evaluation of the person's spirituality per se, which is likely to have liabilities as well as assets.

[Today], if [clinically trained pastors] think diagnostically at all, [they] typically do so by using psychiatric categories and psychiatric language. As pastors, they apply vicariously psychiatric distinctions to their clients. I am saying this without proprietary claims and without implication of thievery. After all, some knowledge about a person's psychological condition should be important to any would-be helper. If such knowledge is freely available from other friends in the helping professions, so much the better.

But would not a pastor want to have some knowledge about the person stemming from theological or religious ordering principles? Would he not like to know beforehand, prior to unleashing his therapeutic furor, something about the person's religious situation—his state of grace, his despair, his deep or shaken loyalty, his tenets or disbeliefs, his grounds for hope, if any, his rebelliousness or his tendency to deny any responsibility for himself by the pious sheep talk of the Twenty-third Psalm? These are just a few possibilities which must affect the pastor's choice of interventions, if they are thought to have any relevance at all.

[M]ost practicing pastors today, [however,] including those with clinical pastoral training, have an anti-diagnostic bent. And those using vicariously any system of psychiatric diagnosis for a foothold seem thereby to imply that diagnosing ipso facto is not a theological or pastoral activity, but a medical prerogative. [In contrast to this,] I believe that problem-laden persons who seek help from a pastor do so for very deep reasons—from the desire to look at themselves in a theological perspective.

Why Do People Turn to Pastors?

Why do problem-laden people in such large numbers turn to their pastors first in seeking help? The answers that have been given to this question are quite diverse.

Accessibility, Economics, and Trust

In rural areas, pastors are often the only accessible source of help. Here they are forced to play many roles that are parceled out differently in urban areas. Where scarcity of resources is not the main problem, economic considerations have been advanced to answer our question. Pastors, and the churches in which they operate, tend to render personal services free or at low cost, at least in the initial stages of a person's help-seeking endeavors. Moreover, in areas where other services are available, pastors are trusted as referral channels and triage agents whose advice is appreciated when the question is, "Where can I get help?" Precisely in that capacity pastors are seen by other professionals, rightly or wrongly, as first-line mental health workers, first-line legal advisers, first-line social workers—first-line counselors and caretakers in many different respects. They are sometimes house finders for the homeless and people on the move, and are in that sense first-line real estate brokers.

A Search for a Pastoral Perspective

There is so much face validity in these answers that one would hardly dare press for deeper reasons. Yet on closer inspection the typical answers all give short shrift to the client. They reduce his motives for turning to his pastor to some set of situational variables. They suggest that the client feels caught in some way and has practically no recourse other than trying out his pastor for advice. Because of their plausibility, these answers eliminate at once any more deep-seated preference a help-seeking person may have for a pastor.

One could argue, however, that the pastoral triage situation which I have described already implies some freedom of choice for the help-seeking person. If other resources are locally available, if they are known, and if economic factors play no crucial role, why would some persons still seek pastoral advice first, even for referral? Is it not likely that they trust his judgment, his know-how, his confidentiality, or his assumed frame of reference more than somebody else's? By virtue of their choice of first seeking pastoral help, are they not asking for their problems to be placed in a pastoral perspective? In seeking a pastoral answer, even if recognizing that his may be only a first or tentative answer, are they not placing themselves voluntarily into a value system, and into an ambiance of special tradition and communion which they consider relevant?

My answer to these questions is an unhesitating yes! Granted that every pastor knows of perfunctory help-seeking behavior by parishioners, and that under the pressure of schedules his own initial response may occasionally turn out to be perfunctory. People with problems usually know that there are many sides to their predicaments, allowing their condition to be placed in different perspectives.

In turning to a pastor they give a signal—they want his perspective, and they want it first. They want it most urgently, or they would not have bothered to come. They present themselves perhaps bunglingly, for they are under some kind of stress. But they may want to confess, to open up, to lay bare a secret, to share an anguish, to be consoled, to be rescued from despair, to be taken to task, to be held responsible, to be corrected for attitudes they suspect are wrong, or to be restrained in their intentions. They may want to be blessed, encouraged, admonished, or even rebuked.

The mind of man is complex, and the heart infinitely more so. One can count on it that some self-evaluation has already been attempted before the person turns to his pastor, just as he is likely to have taken some aspirin before going to his doctor. The motives and moves of help-seeking persons should never be sold short.

Religious Counsel

So let us try our question again, this time barring expeditious reasons as answers. Why do problem-laden people in such large numbers turn to their pastors first in seeking help? One person says in a phone call to his pastor: "Yes, I know there are psychiatrists in this town, and a family service center, and several social agencies. They say there is also a very good marriage counseling center. In fact, my son goes there right now. But I want to talk things over with you first." Here is an unwavering search for pastoral help, a purposive selectivity on the client's own initiative.

[T]he point I want to make is that such clients seek, among other things, religious counsel. Their beliefs drive them into the study of their pastor. They want their problems sized up and tackled within a definite frame of reference. They want their tradition to speak to them, they want to discuss themselves in familiar terms; they want a glimpse of the light of their faith to clarify their predicament.

Whatever else they may wish from their pastor or church, they want some denominational channeling of their problem-solving efforts including, if need be, the church's permission to temporarily step out of its channel. Though the person may have a poor understanding of his faith and formulate his inquiry awkwardly, he raises a theological question and knocks for this purpose at the right door. How disappointing, then, when his pastor quickly translates his quest into psychological or social terms, and fails to give him a theological answer! Or when he foregoes the opportunity for some religious re-education, from which the client may learn to raise better theological questions!

A pastor is ipso facto a theologian, who has the right, nay, the duty, to put anything he wants in a theological perspective. He may use other perspectives besides, if helpful in his profession, or if he has a broad curiosity. But wife-beating is no less theological than it is psychological or sociological or criminological. It may be endocrinological for all we know. What it "is" depends on how it is regarded.

An Inarticulate Longing

I am convinced that a great many persons who turn to their pastor for help in solving personal problems seek assistance in some kind of religious or moral self-evaluation. They want to see some criteria of their faith applied to themselves. They may not be able to say so outright, for fear of giving the impression of piosity. They may remain silent about their longing for a religious evaluation after discovering that their pastor seems to be on a different wavelength. They may not know how to phrase their wish, hoping that their pastor will make the first move in that direction by offering the right words or making the pertinent allusions.

Some may simply wish to pray, if only the pastor would offer to do so. Some may wish to be blessed, if only their pastor would be so inclined. Others may wish to be decisively confronted with their failings or disloyalties, if only their pastor had the forthrightness to do so. What parishioners expect from their pastor emerges from a complicated mixture of hopes, fears, fantasies, ambivalent feelings, and reality testing, all charged with a double set of numinous values: on the one hand those inherent in religion and the transcendent, on the other hand the numinosity of parental power and grandeur experienced in childhood.

Pastors are transference figures par excellence, not necessarily by what they are as persons but by the projections of those who seek their counsel. [When] pastors keep their own theological viewpoint submerged, or do not know what to do with it in a personal situation, they thwart the client's efforts to use the theological approach to problems forthrightly.

Hopeful Signs

There are, however, some hopeful signs. Some hospital chaplains are trying to interview the patients in order to discover their religious or moral values and come to know their deepest beliefs. Having learned some lessons from the past, they do not proceed with checklists of virtues and vices, they do not rub in sin, and they do not preach sermonettes during their interviews.

Moreover, they do not impose bans and do not assign specific acts of penance. They could, of course, if they wished and felt strongly about these things. In fact, I know of a psychiatric hospital case in which the patient insisted that a ritual foot washing be administered to him by the brethren of his communion.[7] After the hospital chaplain had overcome staff resistance to this odd demand and had made arrangements for this rite, the whole staff agreed that this event had proved to be a turning point in the patient's course from illness to health.

In Search of Appropriate Theological Categories

But the pastors and chaplains who do want to project their theology into their pastoral work, and who wish to be clear about their professional identity, have a hard time finding appropriate theological categories for approaching their patients and responding to their needs. This difficulty is particularly prominent in regard to diagnosis, i.e., in making discerning pastoral-theological evaluations of the person's problems. By comparison, it seems easier to engage directly in pastoral acts, deeds, or rituals. These have become sufficiently stylized to engender the feeling in the pastor that when he engages in them, he is really doing something meaningful and worthwhile. Not so with pastoral diagnosis. It has very little articulate precedent in the literature; seminaries do not teach it, and the few historical examples on record are in disrepute.[8]

I believe that the first duty of any professional is to achieve clarity about the problems brought before him for the sake of guiding the interventions he is to contemplate. This is a first duty to his client or patient as well as to his science. If he does not fulfill this duty, he is a charlatan, albeit perhaps a very "nice" one—whatever his shield proclaims him to be. Or he is only a variant of the old-fashioned vendor of patent medicines standing on his soapbox in the marketplace, selling his one little vial of liquid as the remedy for "seventy-eight known diseases."

An Opportunity for a New Perspective

Diagnosis in any helping profession is the exploratory process in which the troubled person is given an opportunity to assess and evaluate himself in a defined perspective, in which certain observations are made and specific data come to light, guided by conceptual or operational tools, in a personal relationship with a resource person. This is preliminary to decisions about a remedial course of action which the parties are to take jointly.

Each perspective is unique and has its own integrity, though different perspectives may be placed on one and the same bit of raw observation or experience. However we define the psychiatrist's perspective, it is not and cannot be the same as the dentist's, the sociologist's, the pastor's. And so, whatever psychiatric diagnosis is, it is not and cannot by any stretch of goodwill or cooperativeness be the same as dental, sociological, or pastoral diagnosis. Even the most outspoken holistic ambitions, which are certainly present in today's psychiatry and have always been inherent in theology, cannot make psychiatric and theological diagnosis identical. Sharing great breadth of focus does not make two perspectives the same.

Our concern is with the authenticity of pastoral diagnostic work. This is inherent in the multitude of reasons why troubled persons turn to their pastors for help. There was a time when I absolved myself from any obligation toward the pastor's authenticity, arguing that, because I was a psychologist, this was none of my business. I was bold enough, however, to appeal to some pastors to reflect on the issue, and remedy it. Now I feel that I myself may try to make some contribution to it, in a consulting capacity, despite my different professional identity. For I have come to see that in the desired interdisciplinary pooling of resources in the helping professions, the specificity of each discipline is a great asset. Sometimes psychiatry is sold short of the uniqueness of pastoral expertise for which it opted when chaplains became collaborating team members. And conversely, some clients are sold short when they selectively and purposefully turn to their pastor for help, to find that they receive only a bit of psychological advice, however good and solid and opportune that bit of advice may be.

CHAPTER 14

The Moral Coach and Counselor

GAYLORD NOYCE[1] (1989)

[My] students and I have repeatedly struggled with the problem of vocational identity in light of all the variegated expectations laid on anyone occupying the pastoral role. In one of our most helpful approaches to the quandary, each student has attempted to sum up his or her gifts and interests with a metaphor for ministry. We have then discussed these metaphors as organizing motifs for ordering all the demands of the work. We have of course used traditional images: prophet, teacher, herald, priest, shepherd. But we have used others as well: artist, historian, coach, sheepdog. "Moral counselor" can be one more clarifying expression for pastoral ministry.

Moral Counselor as Lens and Metaphor

"Moral counselor" is both a lens for examining one aspect of ministry, and a metaphor that offers insights into the whole of our work. The use of metaphor prevents reductionism; it makes a more modest claim than an analytical formula. Yet it may at the same time offer a more creative avenue of thought. The "reflective practitioner" uses "generative metaphors" for problem-solving, says Donald Schön.[2] They provide us a new way of working a puzzle. Schön illustrates by telling a story of engineers assigned the task of designing paint-brushes with synthetic bristles, which function differently from the old natural-bristled ones. They solved their stubborn problem by thinking of a brush as a pump!

Metaphors for Church and Minister

We stimulate reflection on the nature and purpose of the church with metaphors. In its relation to the world, for example, the church may be thought about as herald, as spiritual caregiver, as retreat, as pioneer, as revolutionary cadre, as moral teacher. Each metaphor offers different insights and presents different problems; each begs different biblical and theological perspectives to warrant it. Paul Minear discusses ninety-six biblical metaphors for the church, "images" like leaven, salt, Christ's body, new Israel.[3]

In terms of the ordained minister, many possibilities present themselves. We may at one moment use an anthropological insight, for example, and consider the minister as a shaman. We then note roles all clergy serve as they express and mediate the "holy" for believers and worshipers. For better or worse, people tend to see the priest-minister-shaman as someone different, with powers to heal or bless, with special access to a spiritual realm.

Likewise, we may think of the minister as "coach," using an athletic metaphor. The minister trains the congregation for mission. This generative metaphor, like others, juxtaposes apparently inconsistent concepts and thereby provides new insight.

The coach knows a lot about the game and is usually a veteran player. The coach teaches and directs practice. But the coach also knows he or she does not star on the field. The players are the ones who win or lose the game. We are concerned about the quality of communal life inside the church of course. But the moral action we are more concerned about is out there in the world—in the board room, the shop, the city council chambers, the bedroom, the classroom, and over the backyard fence. That is the main playing field. We can only coach parishioners for their work out there and send them to it in hopeful and respectful trust. The pastor is not a moral puppeteer.

Agogy: Moral Nurture of Adults

European educators have for some years converted a half-word into a useful term for the moral nurture and guidance of adults, *agogy*. The word is familiar, of course, as part of *pedagogy* or *demagogic*. One pair of authors speak of three types of intervention in the inner life of another: psychotherapy, pastoral care, and *agogy*. Agogy means literally to give guidance—as an educator or a parent might. It "aims to...exert influence governed by ideals or normativity."[4]

But *agogy* also expresses something of the style in exerting that influence. Malcolm Knowles, an American educator, prefers *andragogy*, opposing it to pedagogy, thereby making the point that in coaching adults we are less directive than with children. We engage in mutual inquiry; we evoke self-teaching by the other. We affirm the other's moral worth by exercising such respect. We build moral self-reliance, and we coach for moral action on the playing fields where that person lives out life. In this [essay], then, we look at the agogic occasions in parish life, with special concern for developing moral maturity in the congregation.

Nurturing a Congregation

Leadership of the entire congregation presents certain analogies to counseling work with individuals. Counseling hopes to strengthen a new sense of self, accepting one's personal history, developing clear boundaries between self and the world, and a moral character that guides reflection and action. With the congregation also, we nurture the sense of strong Christian identity as a unit of God's people, with a history rooted in Israel, a people separate enough from the world, while serving it, that we can be its loving moral critic and urge it on toward God's shalom.

Worship

The most significant occasion in congregational life is the weekly service of worship. The central purpose of worship is *not* moral education, and by discussing moral nurture through worship I risk some distortion. Worship is not a pep rally for moral virtue; it is not a forum for debating pro and con the public moral dilemma of the week.

Worship celebrates the worth-ship of God. It is a human activity, to be sure, but it is directed toward God, in prayer and praise. Theologically understood, its primary actions consist of a "vertical" dialogue between God and the human community. Hymns, prayers, and offering (including bread and wine brought for Eucharist) constitute action oriented toward God; that is balanced in turn by the reading and exposition of scripture and the distribution of communion in movements toward the people from God.

Humanly speaking, what happens to us as we worship is important. In praising God we rehearse—we express and thereby reinforce our understanding of—the milieu of our human existence, which is the governance and grace of God. The governance and grace of the biblical God have moral implications. Therefore, the planner and leader of worship will attend to certain moral dimensions in the service. Lacking them, the worship may be idolatrous, directed toward a god who is not God.

1. First, the worship planner-leader will see to it that the service expresses *concern for the human neighbor*. Prayers include intercessions for the peace of the world, the welfare of the poor and disinherited.

2. *Confession* gives voice to our knowledge of moral failure, sharpening our moral sensitivities meanwhile. We fail as stewards; we fail in our sensitivity to the needs of persons close to us; we fail in our fidelity to God.

3. The service also sets forth our *commitment.* The offertory moment (best *after* the service of the Word) is much more than a collection of money, whether it includes a presentation of the communion elements or not. These are symbols of our self-offering in service to God by way of service to neighbor.

4. Preaching, of course, provides occasion for more *explicit moral instruction* and exhortation. We break open the words of a text, so that the Word may

address us. And there are moral implications. Without reverting to biblicism, we review and reflect on the meanings of the law for us. Attending to the law rehearses the claims that moral structures have on us, and it reminds us of our moral seriousness as believers. The gospel complements the law, promising reconciliation to the penitent.

STRATEGIES FOR MORAL PREACHING

There are various ways we can prevent preaching from falling into moralistic sermonizing aimed at unheeding people. Such preaching does little for moral insight or action.

Wrestling with Mutually Contradictory Texts

One strategy is to wrestle with pairs of mutually contradictory texts. The puzzle draws the listener into the dilemmas presented by the variegated scriptural language and tradition. One thinks immediately of a range of contrasting biblical statements: on divorce (Lk. 16:18; Mt. 5:31–32 or 19:9); on family allegiance (Ex. 20:12–the fifth commandment on filial loyalty; and Mt. 19:29, or Lk. 14:26–on disowning family ties); on giving (e.g., Deut. 14:22–on tithing; and Lk. 18:22, "sell all you have," or Mk. 12:42–43, on the widow's mite); on respect for the state (Rom. 13; Rev. 13); on wealth (e.g., Ps. 112–on the righteous, wealthy person; and Jesus' needle's eye warning, Mk. 10:25); on truth-telling, with a story like Rahab's deceit (Josh. 2) and injunctions against falsehoods (Ex. 23:1; or Prov. 21:28). We take this tack not to be clever, but to nurture reflection and a more nuanced understanding of moral complexity.

Topical Sermons on Current Issues without Resolution

Occasionally, the same approach may be used in a topical sermon, addressing some public issue of the day. The preacher interprets and even persuades on each side of a controversy, without resolving the tension. If this is done, however, a unifying theological affirmation must be offered, lest the proclamation be lost in the tangle of moral point and counterpoint.

For example, in a sermon on Christian truthfulness, illustrations can range from the necessity for deception in international espionage to the physician's struggle for candor with a vulnerable patient about a probably terminal cancer. It may focus on both political and personal life. It may pit a rule-oriented kind of ethics against a consequentialist, end-justifies-the-means kind. But above it all, the sermon should be announcing the quest for truth as a profound and fundamental response to God. Using John, for instance, it can stress the nonlegalistic but demanding Christian life-way, one that reflects the spirit of the Christ who says, "I am the way and the truth and the life."

CONGREGATIONAL LEARNING STRATEGIES

Some congregational learning strategies relate to preaching.

Sermon Back-talk Sessions

Ministers schedule "back-talk" sessions after service to expand the chance for the church's growth as a community of moral discourse. Preaching is a one-way kind of talk; but Christian moral reflection needs dialogue. In a sermon for a back-talk Sunday, a pastor may even raise specific points for communal discussion. Back-talk sessions invite the laity to contribute their expertise, from their work-world, civic, and family life experiences. Such sessions show respect for the laity and their moral seriousness. Rightly conducted, they can also enhance the skills of moral reflection.

Discussion in Advance of Preaching

Inviting discussion in advance of preaching is another way to achieve some of these goals. A preparation group of church members will meet early in the week to go over the text for the following Sunday. Sermon preparation groups cannot write a preacher's sermon, but they can assist in important ways–by disclosing the level of maturity that is to be addressed by the speaker, by providing illustrations, by broadening and deepening hermeneutical insight, and by training one more group of people as critical listeners and better theologians of the pew.

Teaching and Learning

The range of content in the church's teaching life is wide. Adult education committees sponsor Bible study groups, courses on church history and Christian belief, and church-and-culture series on music, play-readings, or films. Alongside these, a perennial theme is Christian morals in relation to contemporary values and contemporary society. Three caveats and some suggestions are in order, to help the coach at this point.

PROBLEMS IN MORAL TEACHING PROGRAMS

The "Ain't It Awful" Syndrome

I label one nonproductive trap in moral education the "ain't it awful" syndrome. People spend their time bemoaning the low state of public and private morality in what is little more than dignified gossip. The danger, of course, is that the group takes pride in its own virtue, like the Pharisee, praying at the temple. [I]t would be far better directly to address the standard-setting tasks of Christian love. And far better yet is a search for ways to reach out to these who have been so glibly dismissed as immoral.

A Resigned Relativism

Another danger, in more sophisticated moral reflection, is a resigned relativism. At its worst, this can amount to little more than a dogmatic assertion that all values and truth-claims are relative. (All, that is, except this one assertion, which is absolutely true!) Once one admits that there are exceptions to every rule, that there are wide differences in the mores among different cultures, that there are at least two sides to nearly every question, and that even moral standards in a culture seem to evolve and change, a person wonders where to find any solid ground. (A favorite *New Yorker* cartoon of mine shows two tormented men in hell. One says to the other, "The hell of it is, the things I'm in here for aren't sins any more.")

A Self-justifying Legalism

Moreover, once it is clear that Christians do not perform the right and the good so as to gain heaven for themselves—thus mocking, by this self-seeking, the whole idea of altruism—people feel more lost at sea. This is the trap of self-justifying legalism. If God is a forgiving God who gives full acceptance to eleventh-hour workers (Mt. 20:1–16) and the death-bed penitent, legalists say to themselves, "Why struggle now?" They ask, "What do morals matter?"

With a patient, theologically sensitive ear, the good moral counselor must be prepared to help a group grow beyond Phariseeism, beyond defeatist relativism, and beyond naive religious legalism.

METHODS IN MORAL TEACHING PROGRAMS

Because our goals are moral growth rather than the production of ethical analyses for an elite leadership, we will attend to both content and group process as we plan adult moral education. Lives change more amidst the mutual support of small groups where commitment is nurtured than they do in larger, passive audiences.

Retreats

Retreats are ideal for this coaching, because they provide the sustained time where the kinds of problems just mentioned can surface and be worked through. They also offer the kind of intimate atmosphere in which commitments can develop. Retreats can build around a theme of interest to a particular segment of a congregation: the Christian in business; sexual ethics today; pacifism and just wars in a nuclear age; parenting and teenage values.

A retreat offers time for recreation, table fellowship, private and corporate worship, and study. It should be planned with a variety of vehicles for learning—films, roleplaying, debates, various sorts of Bible study. One of the best vehicles for growth in moral insight is the open-ended case study. Such a case study is always based on a real-life dilemma, so the complexities of ordinary living enter in. Stereotyping, strawman villains, and simplistic answers are avoided. The narrative is written so as to involve any alert reader from the start. Often it is short enough to be read during the first five minutes of a session without advance preparation.

Adult Bible Studies

My emphasis on retreats does not mean the weekly or fortnightly adult study group is passé. Far from it. We need more such groups. Here also, the case study format is helpful; most cases are provocative enough that the homework will get done.

Groups with Similar Occupations

One of the best settings for moral growth comes about when a group of people with similar occupations meets regularly for long enough to trust group members to use their own stories as cases. Managers ask for help about the morality of a plant closing, about firing a man in his late 50s, about handling employee alcoholism, about bribes and "consultant" fees overseas. Parents discuss with one another their standards for homework time, the use of the family car, keeping hours, curtailing the use of alcohol, parental teaching on contraception.

Service and Action Groups

Service and action groups often provide unusually high motivation for learning. A group intent on prison reform will be forced to do homework on the nature of the corrections system, and the ethics of justice and mercy. A group taking up soup kitchen service can easily move to deeper understandings of welfare policy. Action without reflection can be misguided. Study without a least some playout in the community's life can become sterile and self-satisfied.

Controversy

Rightly exploited, the life of the congregation itself is as important a resource for coaching in moral life as the formal class or ad hoc discussion group. The congregation's degree of interpersonal honesty and compassion, its sense of stewardship and social outreach, and its pattern of decision making all combine to promote or impoverish the moral experience of those whose spiritual nourishment the church provides. So too do the ways the congregation handles conflict, large or small.

Controversy is prominent in the learning menu of congregational life. Four rules of thumb about controversy in the church will help the moral counselor.

First, use the energy generated by the controversy.

Contention means emotional involvement, and involvement is better than apathy. Controversy can be destructive, without doubt, but emotion means people care.

Second, look beneath the surface.

If an issue seems petty, we need to look more than skin deep to see what nerve is being touched. A dispute over repainting the sanctuary may be a power struggle between two committees. Or it may subtly reflect deep-seated differences about the church's style of worship or about antiquated or updated relations to modern culture. It may reflect a plurality of social class that the church could acknowledge and celebrate.

Third, use controversy for training in the art of reconciliation.

The art is necessary for lay ministry in the weekday world. Everyone meets controversy–in marriage and the family, among friends, at work, in neighbor-hood and civic life. Whether it leads to enmity or forgiveness depends on the way the parties to the disputes respond. The church can think of itself as a miniature peace academy, training its participants in conflict resolution.

In church, I first learned how to overcome my fear of argument, and my ability to speak up to someone who seemed overpowering and intimidating. I learned to say, "My friend, I think we disagree about that," instead of quietly harboring resentment and proceeding less honestly with the friendship. That learning has served me well outside the church.

In church we can learn to objectify an issue–to talk about the facts and positions in a case rather than the personalities. Extrapolated to the global scale, learning of that sort can prevent fear-mongering and demagoguery that usually precede the decay of diplomacy into war.

Fourth, exploit controversy for moral growth.

It offers fertile ground. The moral counselor can capitalize on [various] community debates, raising them for discussion in the midst of congregational life, and thus taking one more step toward improving the church as a community of moral discourse and service.

Like the grain of sand troubling an oyster but making for a pearl, a small controversy may lead to study and wider vision. Given good leadership, a potentially controversial step taken by one unit within a church can lead to a new church-wide sense of mission. As coach for the congregation's moral maturity, the pastor will not back away from controversy. Rather, he or she will expect it as one of the growing pains of parish life, and one of the potential resources in the task of moral counsel.

Coaching for Compassion and Integrity

Our moral counselor metaphor has led us to stress a person's intrinsic moral integrity–a person's autonomy–rather than mere obedience to extrinsic behavioral codes. One might charge that this position arises from necessity. In American culture, the authority of the church and its ordained ministry is moral rather than juridical. That is, its power is exercised through persuasion rather than in enforceable injunction and law. In a voluntaristic church, and in a political arrangement that separates church and state, this charge would have it that we have to go this route, that we have no other choice.

For us, however, this arrangement itself is a moral choice based on justice, respect, and a knowledge of the dangers in both political and religious autocracy. Since the days of Ernest Troeltsch, an oversimplified but useful typology has served to help describe church traditions. It ranges church groups along a spectrum from the broad and highly tolerant "church" to the narrow and highly disciplined "sect," withdrawn from society. There is little question but that today some movement by the loosely organized mainline churches away from their acculturation and in the direction of the "sect"-type end of this scale is in order. We need a more disciplined community. Should it come about, however, even that movement will mostly be a collective change arising within the community, not something engineered by clergy decree. Learned priests and pastors once taught a relatively unlearned people the rules of God and claimed to govern their moral life. In a highly literate society the clergy take a different role. They must work with people, rather than above them. In utter seriousness, but with a light heart, we coach and nurture both compassion and moral integrity in the midst of our communities of faith.

CHAPTER 15

The Indigenous Storyteller

EDWARD P. WIMBERLY[1] (1991)

I have become firmly convinced that black pastors approach pastoral care through narrative. A truly narrative style of pastoral care in the black church draws upon personal stories from the pastor's life, stories from the practice of ministry, and stories from the Bible.

Using Narratives in Pastoral Care

Genuine pastoral care from a narrative perspective involves the use of stories by pastors in ways that help persons and families to visualize how and where God is at work in their lives and thereby receive healing and wholeness.

Dangers Inherent in the Method

This method of pastoral care involves several dangers.

The primary danger is that the pastor's own life experience is so subjective and personal that it might be used imperialistically to lead some pastors to think that "my way is the only way."

Second, the narrative approach might lead some to think that a personal indigenous style is all that is needed and that formal training has no place.

Third, the narrative style might cause the pastor to be less empathetic and thereby transform counselee/parishioner-centered counseling sessions into pastor-focused counseling sessions.

Potential of Narrative Counseling

However, a narrative approach need not be imperialistic, unempathetic, or pastor-focused. For example, this approach can enable the pastor to enter the parishioner's world of experience and see things through the parishioner's own eyes. It can help the parishioner take full responsibility for making his or her own decisions. It can enable the parishioner to be specific when describing events. This approach also can help the counselor to openly discuss things that are occurring between the counselor and the parishioner. Finally, it can help the counselor to express his or her feelings about what is taking place in the parishioner's life, in ways that lead to growth.

Occasions for Using Stories

Black pastors use many types of stories—long stories, anecdotes, short sayings, metaphors—to respond to the needs of their parishioners. Most specific instances in life situations lend themselves to story formation. For example, stories can be used to address the normal crises people face daily, such as birth, a child's first day at school or at day care; transitions from childhood to adolescence, from adolescence to adulthood; mid-life, old age, and death transitions.

Likewise, story formation can occur during periods of crisis: losses such as illness, accidents, changes in residence, and a variety of other events that pose threats to someone's emotional or physical well-being. Stories also can be developed during selective phases of counseling to facilitate the counseling process.

In all these ways, stories function in the caring setting to bring healing and wholeness to the lives of persons and families within the black pastoral-care context. Henry Mitchell and Nicholas Lewter call such stories *soul theology*, the core belief-system that gives shape to the world, that shows how African American people have come to grips with the world in a meaningful way.[2] These core beliefs are embodied in narratives and stories that permeate the church life of African Americans, and black pastors and congregations draw on this narrative reservoir when caring for their members. These narratives suggest ways to motivate people to action, help them to see themselves in a new light, help them recognize new resources, enable them to channel behavior in constructive ways, sustain them in crises, bring healing and reconciliation in relationships, heal the scars of memories, and provide guidance when direction is needed. Soul theology makes up the faith story that undergirds the stories used by black pastors and parishioners in caring for others.

The Faith Story

Mitchell and Lewter point out that core beliefs are expressed spontaneously during crisis situations.[3] Core beliefs are deep metaphors, images that point to the plots or directions of life; they undergird the behaviors of people as they attempt to live their lives, and normally, they are rooted in stories. For the African American Christian, deep metaphors are related to the life, death, and resurrection of Jesus Christ, who liberates the oppressed and cares for the downtrodden. The deep metaphor is informed by the Exodus story and God's involvement with God's people. These deep metaphors and core beliefs are anchored in the story of God's relationship with God's people, as recorded in Scripture and as lived out within African American churches.

The Plot

The plot that undergirds the deep metaphors of the Christian story is important to the faith story. Plots tell us why we live on earth; they point to the direction life is taking.[4] Plot in the Christian faith story shows us how our lives are connected to God's unfolding story. The faith story, therefore, answers the question of the "ultimate why" of our existence.

The dominant plot that gives life meaning for the African American Christian is what I call an eschatological plot, one that envisions hope in the midst of suffering and oppression, because God is working out God's purposes in life on behalf of persons. The eschatological plot takes suffering and oppression very seriously without minimizing their influence in life. Yet despite the prevalence of suffering and oppression, God's story of hope and liberation is unfolding. Although the final chapter of the story of liberation awaits consummation at the end of time, during many moments along life's journey there is evidence of God's presence, bringing healing, wholeness, and liberation.

This eschatological plot which undergirds the faith story of black Christians has been referred to by Mitchell and Lewter as the providence of God:

> The most essential and inclusive of these affirmations of Black core beliefs is called the Providence of God in Western terms. Many Blacks may not have so precise a word for it, and they may not even know that the idea they cling to so naturally is called a doctrine. But in Africa and Afro-America, the most reassured and trusted word about our life here on earth is that God is in charge. This faith guarantees that everyone's life is worth living. The passage that expresses it best is Paul's famous word to the Romans: "And we know that God works in everything for the good of those who love him and are called according to his plan."[5]

The eschatological plot calls the Christian to faith because each must participate in life and in God's unfolding story, knowing that things will work out in the end. The eschatological plot is important because it does not minimize suffering and oppression, nor does it give suffering and oppression the last word.

The Goal

A goal of the narrative approach to pastoral care in the black church has been to link persons in need to the unfolding of God's story in the midst of life. The African American pastor has narrated, and continues to narrate, stories that help people catch a glimpse of hope in the midst of suffering. It is by identifying with the story that Christians have linked themselves to purposeful directions in life, despite suffering and pain.

The Functions

The eschatological plot, through which God is working out healing, wholeness, and liberation on behalf of others, has four major functions: *unfolding, linking, thickening,* and *twisting.*[6] God's plot *unfolds* one scene and one chapter at a time, and one cannot know the end of the story until the entire drama is completed. However, by identifying with faith stories, particularly stories in the Bible, one can learn to participate in God's drama, while trusting God's authorship of the drama and God's plan for the final outcome. In counseling within the black church, this often has meant that the pastor must ensure that the counselee who is identifying with a biblical story reads the whole story before coming to any conclusions. For example, it is important that one continue the story of Joseph and the coat of many colors until Joseph is occupying an important government position for a second time. To stop reading this story before its end may leave the reader feeling that life is tragic. Only at the end of the story can we see God's purposes for Joseph revealed. When one reads the entire story, one can envision hope in the midst of tragedy.

When one identifies with stories that have an eschatological plot in Scripture, one is not only pointed toward God's unfolding story in the midst of life, one is *linked* with the dynamic that undergirds the plot. God's unfolding story is more than a good story with which to identify. It is an ongoing, unfolding story, even today, so when black Christians have identified with that story, they also have linked their lives with the dynamic force behind the events of life. When people are linked to God's unfolding story, their own lives become different. Significant changes take place. People find that life has direction for them, that they have value as human beings. The slaves' identification with Israel's Exodus is illustrative of such positive outcomes. By linking their lives with the unfolding plot of Israel's Exodus, the slaves focused their attention on God, who was also working on their behalf to liberate them.

The eschatological plot also thickens. *Thickening* refers to those events that intrude into God's unfolding story and seek to change the direction of that story for the ill of all involved. The plot often can thicken when suffering stakes its claim on us. This thickening could be the intrusion of oppression and victimization which, for a time, hinder our growth and development; and it is at such times that we wonder whether God really cares. However, unfortunate negative interruptions are temporary; and the story again begins to unfold in ways that help us to envision God at work, seeking to *twist* the story back to God's original intention, despite the thickening that hindered the plot.

A pastor who understands the working of God through drama can link people with the unfolding of God's story. Such a pastor seeks to help parishioners develop *story language* and *story discernment,* in order to visualize how God's drama is unfolding in their lives. This means that telling and listening to stories become central to the caring process. It also means that people learn to follow the plots of stories, to visualize how God is seeking to engage them in the drama as it impacts their lives.

The eschatological plot, with its emphasis on God's healing presence in life despite suffering and pain, has been the driving force behind the narrative approach of the black church. By telling and listening to stories, black preachers and congregants have sought to help people envision God's work in the midst of suffering. They have sought to link people with this activity, so that their lives can have significant meaning, despite the reality of suffering.

Therapeutic Functions

In addition to the unfolding, linking, thickening, and twisting of plots, faith stories have such therapeutic functions as healing, sustaining, guiding, and reconciling.[7] These are the traditional functions of pastoral care and are very much a part of the narrative approach. However, since a narrative approach to pastoral care cannot determine the impact of a story, one cannot predetermine the impact a story might have on a parishioner or counselee. Nevertheless, stories do impact people's lives in characteristic ways: They can heal or bind up wounds caused by disease, infection, and invasion; they can sustain persons in the face of overwhelming odds and lessen the impact of suffering; they can provide guidance to those who must make decisions, as well as facilitate reconciliation for those who have been alienated from God and others.

Purposes of Storytelling

Stories are shared by pastors and congregants to call to the attention of people in need how God is at work in their lives—whether God is working through healing, sustaining, guiding, or reconciling. Pastors seek to help people discern where God is working, so that the persons may cooperate with God's unfolding story as it impacts their lives. Once the story is told, the pastor waits for clues from the parishioners and counselees to discern how God is using the story. Although the storyteller cannot predict how counselees or parishioners will be influenced by the story, the storyteller can use the gift of story for specific purposes—to make points, suggest solutions, decrease opposition to offered care, increase motivation, enlarge understanding of the problem, increase self-recognition, and discover resources.[8] All these purposes serve the primary purpose—to help the parishioners or counselees to envision God's healing and holistic activity working within their lives.

Pastoral Care, Preaching, and Worship

Storytelling in pastoral care has a different function and context than it does in preaching and worship. In preaching, the purpose is to assist in disclosing the gospel. The context is usually public worship, which uses storytelling to celebrate God's unfolding drama and invites worshipers to participate in that salvation drama. In preaching and in worship, the goals of storytelling are disclosing, inviting, and celebrating in a public context.

Pastoral care, on the other hand, uses storytelling in the context of caring relationships, to help remove the personal and interpersonal obstacles that can hinder people's ability to grow. The goal of pastoral care and counseling, from a narrative perspective, is to use storytelling to strengthen people's personal and interpersonal growth, so that they can respond to God's salvation drama as it unfolds and impacts their lives.

From a narrative perspective, pastoral care can be defined as bringing all the resources of the faith story into the context of caring relationships, to bear upon the lives of people as they face life struggles which are personal, interpersonal, and emotional. The gospel must respond to the personal needs of individuals and families as they face life struggles. This is best done in the private context of pastoral care, rather than in the public context of preaching or worship. Because the context and intent of preaching, worship, and pastoral care are different, the use of storytelling in each ministry is also different.

Story-listening

So far, this discussion has been devoted to the storytelling aspect of caring. One might conclude that the telling of stories is the main dimension of a narrative approach to pastoral care. The danger of overemphasizing storytelling, however, is that it may ignore the needs of the person facing life struggles. Story-listening is also an important dimension of African American pastoral care, and the narrative approach is a story-listening as well as a storytelling approach.

Story-listening involves empathetically hearing the story of the person involved in life struggles. Being able to communicate that the person in need is cared for and understood is a result of attending to the story of the person as he or she talks. *Empathy* means that we attend to the person with our presence, body posture, and nonverbal responses. It also means using verbal responses to communicate that we have understood and are seeking to understand the person's story as it is unfolding. The caregiver also gives attention to and acknowledges the significant feelings of the person as they are expressed in the telling of the story. It is only when the story has been fully expressed and the caregiver has attended to it with empathy that the foundation is laid for the utilization of storytelling.

The emphasis must be on story-listening to avoid the trap of shifting the focus from the needs of the person facing life struggles. There are two important ways to prevent this potential abuse of storytelling. First, a growing body of literature on storytelling within the context of counseling and psychotherapy can assist pastors in knowing how to use their own life stories in facilitative ways. Second, pastors need to grow in their own personal life so that their life stories and participation in the faith story will be a reservoir of conflict-free and anxiety-free stories.

The Limitations of a Narrative Approach

In addition to the danger that a narrative approach might focus on the pastor's needs rather than those of the parishioner or counselee, other limitations to the narrative approach must be addressed as well. First, the storytelling approach is not designed to be the only approach to the problems people face.

There are times when direct and confrontational approaches are more appropriate. Sometimes pastors in the priestly role must help people face the truth and assess whether the story the person is living out is healthy or unhealthy. The key is that the pastor must help people judge their own stories in light of the faith story. When there is some discrepancy between the person's own story and the unfolding faith story, this truth should be pointed out by the pastor. Moreover, the pastor should help the counselee to align his or her own life story with God's unfolding story.

Another limitation of the storytelling method is that it may assume that the people in need have Bible knowledge. But what about those who are unchurched or have very few roots in the institutional church? Although the storytelling approach does presuppose some familiarity with biblical stories, many such stories can be used to address the problems people present, if careful thought is given to the reason the stories are being told. One cannot assume that people will find Bible stories objectionable or irrelevant to their needs, simply because of their lack of familiarity. Nor can one assume that there is no religious interest on the part of some counselees. However, this does not give the pastoral counselor license to tell religious stories without prior thought or permission from the counselee. It is always appropriate to ask for permission prior to telling the story. And one need not confine oneself to religious stories. There is rich material in African American folklore from which to draw as well.

Indigenous Pastoral Care

Because African American oral culture has always used sharing stories in caring situations, this will remain a dominant approach in the African American church. However, the storytelling approaches that are emerging in counseling psychology might prove helpful to this indigenous approach in the future.

The spontaneous use of stories triggered in counseling relies on the right-brain processes of the caregiver's thinking. That is to say, the storytelling approach relies heavily on the intuitive and imaginative capacities of the pastor or lay person, which are cultivated in oral cultures. Oral cultures emphasize emotion, celebration, poetic expression, relationships, storytelling, and story listening.[9]

An indigenous storytelling approach to pastoral care is learned by participating and living in an oral community, where hearing and speaking are very central. However, it cannot be taken for granted that this approach will remain viable and alive without some intentional effort. The more the dominant culture becomes visual, a seeing, reading, and writing culture, the greater the likelihood that oral indigenous approaches will lose some of their influence.

Steps for Building a Story

If the need for storytelling arises, counselors need to have in mind the steps for building a story:

Step 1: Explore their own lives and situations for stories that might be similar to the desired goals that have been established.

Step 2: Choose a main character, or several main characters, who have problems and goals similar to those of the counselee.

Step 3: Choose a character or situation and build a story, developing in detail the character and/or situation that introduces the desired changes required by the counseling goal. The key is to stimulate the imagination of the listener.

Step 4: Explore in detail the consequences for the main characters in achieving or not achieving the desired goals. This step must show that there are consequences in accomplishing or not accomplishing the desired goals.

This protocol helps pastoral counselors develop stories based on the established counseling goals. It also helps the storyteller develop specific characters, contexts, and plots that can trigger the imagination of the counselee. It must be emphasized that learning to tell stories in this way requires training and supervision in basic counseling skills, including building rapport, empathy, assessment of psychological and interpersonal dynamics, and the phases of counseling. Such training should be in the form of courses, as well as in actual practice and in reflection on that practice with experienced trainers. Training will enhance pastors' ability to deliver quality care to parishioners, as well as strengthen the pastors' own personal and emotional growth.

Storytelling is an art. Some of the clues for this art already exist in African American culture. However, as we continue to be changed by technology, we will need to integrate the natural community traditions with intentional methods, in order to recover and keep alive traditions that will be influenced by technology. Storytelling within African American tradition is alive and well in black churches, yet traditional patterns of care through the use of storytelling are being challenged by such societal influences as the erosion of the extended family.

The major concern for the future is to maintain the indigenous, spontaneous form of caring through stories that exist in the African American tradition. However, we can learn to preserve and enhance this tradition through studying the emerging literature on storytelling.[10] We need to take pride that the academic and professional world of counseling is rediscovering what already was a full-blown tradition in African American culture.

CHAPTER 16

The Agent of Hope

Donald Capps[1] (1996)

In *Agents of Hope*[2] I explore the idea that what makes the pastor unique among professionals is that the pastor is fundamentally an agent or bearer of hope. Other professionals offer and support hope, but they do this as a part or aspect of other things they do. Pastors, I suggest, are *agents of hope by definition* (or calling), and often this is *all* that they are. A reason they often feel vulnerable is the fact that they have nothing other than hope to offer, and hope is a very intangible thing.

Pastors are intuitively aware that they are agents of hope. I support this intuition. However, I want here to address the problem that while pastors know intuitively that they are agents of hope, and may have some clear ideas about what hope is, theologically understood, there isn't much that pastors can read about the *experience* of hope. What does it mean to hope? What is the experience of hope about? And, more specifically, what are the main elements or constituents of hope?

I will briefly comment on the developmental origins of hope, then set forth a model of the experience of hoping and the characteristics of hope, and then briefly discuss some new strategies in psychotherapy that are supportive of hope, strategies that pastors should find adaptable to the parish context.

I should also note that the inspiration for *Agents of Hope* came from John Bunyan's classic *The Pilgrim's Progress.* Hopeful was the name of the companion who accompanied Christian, the hero of the story, throughout most of his journey to the promised land. When Christian was crossing the River Jordan, his last testing before his entry into the Celestial City, he began to sink and to cry out in despair. Hopeful was there to encourage him, to hold his head above water until Christian felt the solid ground beneath him. This is the image of the pastor that I want us to reflect on.

The Origins of Hope

Erik Erikson argues that hope is born in the earliest stage of life—in infancy—and specifically in the infant's relationship with the mother or mothering one. Hope is thus born in the experience of a reliable other who, as he says, provides "a convincing pattern of providence" in which "hopes are met and hopefulness is inherently rewarding."[3] As the infant grows into a child, hope becomes associated with the *will* and with the capacity to take initiative, so that the child becomes actively involved in realizing hopes. With increasing agency also comes a greater capacity to renounce one's hope, to "transfer disappointed hopes to better prospects," and to train our expectations "on what promises to prove possible." Hope remains aligned with the maintenance of a stable, reliable and verifiable world, but it becomes increasingly identified with change, new prospects and widening horizons.

In infancy, hope is based on specific hopes and has not yet developed into an attitude or spirit of hopefulness independent of these specific hopes. But, in childhood, hopefulness becomes inherently rewarding. Hence, even when some or many of our hopes go unmet, when it would make sense for us to abandon hope, few of us actually do. This is because we have become hopeful selves, and hopefulness has become intrinsic to who we are.

The Nature of Hope

Like those who write about love, those who have written about hope have frequently commented on the difficulty of defining or describing it. My own efforts to get at the phenomenon of hope suggest the wisdom of making a distinction between "hoping" and "hopes." "Hoping" indicates that we are concerned with a process or form of experience, one that may be compared with other experiences, like "loving," "hating," "creating," and the like. "Hope" or "hopes," on the other hand, concern a phenomenon or thing, one that may be compared with other things, like "beliefs," "judgments," or "skills."

Hoping

I suggest, as a working definition for hoping, that hoping is "the perception that what one wants to happen will happen, a perception that is fueled by desire and in response to felt deprivation."

1. HOPING AS THE PERCEPTION THAT WHAT IS WANTED WILL HAPPEN.

Alexander Solzhenitsyn, the Russian author, was arrested by the KGB in 1974 and forced into exile in the United States. Shortly after he came to the U.S. he told an interviewer, "I have no proof of it; but I have a premonition, a feeling... I think—I am sure—that I will return to Russia and still have a chance to live there." His intuition that he would someday return to Russia was an indication of hoping. He had no "proof" for it, and no specific plan for realizing it, and yet he felt sure that it would someday come to pass. As it turned out, his hoping proved to be true.

I suggest that hoping is a particular kind or type of *perception*. It is the perception (or sense) that what is wanted will happen, and it therefore involves investment of self: "*I* think—*I* am sure." Without the sense that what we want to happen will in fact happen, there is no hoping going on. Of course, our confidence that what is wanted will happen can fluctuate over time. There are times when we firmly believe that a given hope will come true, and times when our confidence sags. Students who anticipate a major exam often go through this up and down cycle. One day they are quite confident. The next day they are close to despair. The very fact that hoping produces such fluctuating emotions tells us that emotions play a role in hoping, but hoping is not primarily a matter of emotions. The sense or intuition that what is wanted will happen can persist even when we do not "feel" this to be the case. This disparity between our current feelings and our longer range intuitions suggests that hoping is primarily a perceptual phenomenon. Emotions are involved, but hoping is primarily a way of seeing or perceiving.

2. HOPING IS FUELED BY DESIRE.

Because we are created in the image of God, we are desiring beings. We have longings and yearnings, and these grow out of perceived lacks or needs. Hoping is fueled by desire. We do not hope for what we already have. But hoping is a *persisting* desire. It is more intense than wishing but less intense than craving. Its intensity is expressed in its persistence, as it continues to strive until its object is realized or proven to be unrealizable. Cravings are more urgent but not as lasting. If we crave a certain food and know that we should not have it, we can sometimes talk ourselves into the notion that the craving may pass. We are not as willing to dispense with our desires. So, too, with wishes. We normally wish about those matters whose outcome we are in no position to influence, even by the simple act of entertaining the wish itself. But when we hope, we not only anticipate that the object of our desire will come about, but we also marshal our own energies and resources to make it so. Wishes have little staying power, little persistence, because they are not so invested with desire. When a wish becomes invested with desire, it is then on its way toward becoming a hope.

3. HOPING IS IN RESPONSE TO A FELT DEPRIVATION.

The third feature of hoping is that it is a response to felt deprivation. Often, what we lack is something that we have never had experience of, but toward which we have a strong sense of wanting and needing. We want the love we have never had, the recognition that we have never been afforded, the joyful life that has never been ours. Other times, what we lack is something we once had but have since been deprived of. We long for the presence of our life's companion, now deceased. We are filled with nostalgia for our childhood home.

Our sense of deprivation may also involve something we took for granted until we lost it: our health, our work, our freedom to move about.

One reason our hoping is sometimes so difficult to identify or put our finger on is that the lack we feel is deeply personal and difficult to put into words. We sense that our lives are unfulfilled, or that our existence seems purposeless and devoid of meaning. Or we have a deep sense of personal inadequacy, of not having the capabilities we want or need. How to talk about something that we know only by its absence?

Deprivations are not synonymous with loss, yet losses are a major cause of a felt sense of deprivation and are therefore of great importance to hoping. The hoping against hope that occurs in the wake of a loss reveals how deeply related hoping is to deprivation. Death takes from us the one with whom so many hopes, large and small, were shared. It also makes us desperately aware of our deprivation. If we hope for our loved one to be restored to us, we hope in vain, and we face the stark and bitter truth that our deprivation cannot be erased however long we live. We learn instead that we must make do with secondary hopes to which we manage in time to orient our lives.

Hoping, then, is the perception that what is wanted will happen, a perception fueled by desire and in response to felt deprivation. Hoping involves all of these elements, and if any one of them is missing, we are probably witnessing something that approximates hoping but is something else (like wishing, or pining, or anticipating). On the other hand, this understanding of hoping reveals that it is not a rare thing at all. We are all creatures of desire, and all of us feel deprived in one way or another, so the necessary conditions for hoping are always present.

Yet, if this is so, why is it that we are so often despairing, so often lacking in the perception that what is wanted will happen? One obvious answer is that we cannot always have what we desire. Our desire is met by hard reality, and something has to give, and what gives, more often than not, is hope. There is another reason, however, that is more subtle and less frequently noted, and this is that we do not know what it is that we desire. If it is difficult to put our finger on why we feel deprived and what we feel deprived of, it is also difficult to know what it is that we really want. This brings us to the matter of our hopes: If hoping involves the perception that what is wanted will happen, what is the "what" that is wanted? What is the "object" of our desire?

Hopes

I suggest the following working definition for hopes: "Hopes are projections that envision the realizable and thus involve risk."

1. Hopes as projections.

Because hoping is primarily a matter of sensing or perceiving, we should expect that hopes would express themselves in imagistic form and not as concepts or ideas. If so, this invites us to consider hopes to be projections. In psychology, a projection is the unconscious act or process of ascribing to others one's own ideas or intentions, especially when such ideas or intentions are considered undesirable. We may, for example, ascribe to another person sexual fantasies or aggressive intentions that are really our own. In photography, however, projection is the process of causing an image to appear on a screen. In a sense, both types of projection are based on an illusion, and are therefore inherently false. Yet, we generally view the photographic representation on the screen as artistic, whereas the ascription of ideas or intentions to another person is viewed as inappropriate, unacceptable and often pathological. Paranoia, for example, involves the false belief that someone wants to harm me.

One reason that we take a more positive view of the photographic over the psychological projection is that we understand the photographic projection to be the work of a creative mind, whereas psychological projection is the work of a mind that is mistaken, disoriented, or disturbed. The psychological projection is based on a fundamental error, the erroneous ascription of ideas and intentions to another, and once we become aware of the error, no useful purpose is served by retaining the projection. So we set about the task of learning how to withdraw it, usually by putting something else–an accurate ascription of the other's intentions toward us–in its place. In photographic projection, the image has an artistic function not in spite of but because of its illusory character. Such projections continue to be valuable precisely because they are illusory, and thus allow us to imagine a reality other than our own everyday experience.

Hopes, then, are projections because they envision a future that is technically false and unreal, as it does not exist, and yet is profoundly true and real, as it expresses yearnings and longings that not only exist but are often more real than the objective world. When we hope, we envision eventualities that are not yet realities but nevertheless appear to us as potential realities. Also, because hope is a projection, and thus involves images that play against the screen of the future, hope is a certain way of seeing, of visualizing, or fore-seeing. We see or image forth realities that are not yet present to us, and yet are made closer–almost within reach–by the images we project. In this sense, hopes are always a future projection, but through imaging they make the future more palpably real and present to us. Of course, the flip side of this is that our capacity to project a future can also cause us to despair. As Yogi Berra, catcher and manager for the New York Yankees, is reputed to have said, "The future ain't what it used to be."

Our images of hope are also *self*-projections. By hoping, we project *ourselves* into the future and envision our existence being different from what it is at present. The fact that hoping involves self-projections has inspired some psychotherapists to focus on their counselees' current self-images and their images of themselves as future-projection (what do you see yourself being in the near and more distant future?). By helping their counselees identify these two self-images, present and future, therapists enable them to find ways to close the gap that separates them, usually by assisting them in realizing the future self, enabling it to become more real, more "present," to the counselee. So, when we image the future, envision the not-yet, we place ourselves in this scene, for, after all, it is not some abstract or impersonal future that we are projecting and envisioning; it is *our* future, and thus our own involvement in the image can always be assumed. Even when we envision a future in which we are physically absent, as when we imagine a scene in which our families have gathered to mourn our own death, we have projected ourselves into this future, as we have envisioned ourselves as deceased and as witnessing the scene that stretches out before us.

Because the future is unpredictable and has its own reality, our hopeful projections rarely fit the future with perfect accuracy. This does not mean, however, that such projections should be discouraged or suppressed, for, as Erik Erikson has argued, hope is often the decisive element in *changing* the world of facts. He writes: "Hope not only maintains itself in the face of changed facts—it proves itself able to change facts, even as faith is said to move mountains."[4] We should also keep in mind that change is inevitable. The future will not be the same as the present, even as the present is not the same as the past. Basing itself on this known fact, hope chooses to anticipate the nature of the changes that may occur. It knows that such anticipations are risky and subject to error. Yet, future projections are in fact realities, as they have impact on the current state of affairs. This is one reason why the capacity to hope was so vitally important to the prisoners in concentration camps during World War II. By projecting a future, hope alters the present. Physically, the prisoners were captives, but inwardly they achieved a margin of freedom to the extent that they were able to hope. To project hopes is to achieve some degree of autonomy in the present, and, by autonomy, Erikson means self-government rather than government by others. The margin of freedom that such projections effect may be slight, but it can be the difference between life and death.

2. HOPES AS ENVISIONINGS OF THE REALIZABLE.

If hoping involves the perception that what is wanted will happen, it follows that our projected hopes will be envisionings of what is realizable. Hopes are not projections of what we believe to be impossibilities, as the very projection of impossibilities would not make for hope but for hopelessness, and would therefore be grounds for despair. When we hope, we anticipate the realization of what is projected.

If so, this does not mean that hope only envisions *realistic* possibilities. To say that hope envisions the realizable does not mean that it is bound by the practical, the sensible, the proven, or the tried and true. In many situations, we have no way of knowing on the basis of prior experience what is or is not realizable. Sometimes, we realize more than previous experience would have indicated is possible. In other cases, we realize much less. So, hopes are not based on calculations of what is realistic on the basis of prior experience. Instead, they are based on the view that the future is open, and that the future is to some degree amenable to our efforts to make a difference.

When we tell someone to be realistic, we often plunge a knife into hope itself, as such admonitions often create a spirit of quiet despair. Parents often tell their children to be realistic—about themselves, about their abilities and capacities, about their future prospects. Pastors often tell young couples who are about to married to be realistic—about the problems they will inevitably face, about the dangers of relying on romantic love to see them through the crises of married life, and about the misplaced trust in marriage to effect change in their personalities, habits, attitudes and behavior. Certainly, children and young couples need such admonitions, and, no doubt, parents and pastors are qualified to offer them. Yet the adoption of a realistic approach can erode a hopeful approach to life, as it may cause us to settle for a less full and vital life than would in fact be accessible to us. As already noted, hopes change the world of facts. They enable our children to accomplish more than *we* ever thought possible, and they enable young couples to experience marriages that may in fact be far happier than those of the adults who are cautioning them not to expect more from marriage than they can realistically hope to experience.

There are always more possibilities than a realistic assessment of our situation recognizes or acknowledges. The question then becomes, not "What is realistic to hope for?" but "What is possible *for me?*" One reason we resent admonitions to be "realistic" is that we suspect that they are not based on intimate knowledge of ourselves, but instead on a knowledge of humanity in general, or some group or category of humans with whom we are being identified on the basis of age, gender, race, or cultural background. We feel that if the other persons really knew us, in our own unique individuality, they would not be voicing these admonitions, or would at least express them very differently.

The question, "What is possible *for me?*" points instead to the role of self-knowledge in the formulation and realization of hopes. Based on what we know about ourselves, we may anticipate that certain things are possible for us and others are not. We weigh the possibilities that are in front of us in light of our understanding of ourselves, our temperament, our traits, our motivations, our values. What we envision to be realizable is thus profoundly influenced by what we understand ourselves to be.

We know, of course, that the realization of certain possibilities does not depend entirely on us. But we also know that who we are has a powerful influence on what we can anticipate in the future. If we envision ourselves becoming medical doctors some day, but also know that we do not have the personal motivation to endure years of medical training, or that we hate science or cannot stand the sight of blood, it should become clear to us, sooner or later, that becoming a medical doctor is not a real possibility for us. On the other hand, if we know that we do have the motivation to endure prolonged medical training, and that we love science and do not hate the sight of blood, becoming a medical doctor is a real possibility for us. It is not a certainty, as there are many factors besides these that could affect the outcome, some of which are entirely outside of our control. (Keats discovered while in medical training that he was incurably ill, which is why he became a poet instead, and died in his early twenties.) But, with hope, the issue is not certainty but possibility, and genuine hope is based on what is possible *for us*. The point is not that we should be realistic about our chances for realizing this or that, but that we should make an effort to know ourselves and to entertain those hopes that are not contradicted by what we learn.

3. HOPES INVOLVE RISK.

Because they involve desires that may or may not be realized, hopes are inherently risky.

Idealizing Hope and Facing Failure

It is all too easy to idealize hopes, to declare that they are inherently good as they manifest a positive attitude toward the future. Yet, because the future is open, there is always the risk that our hopes will *not* be realized. Disappointment, demoralization, even feelings of devastation may follow. Given the risks involved, we sometimes keep our hopes to ourselves, so that if they do not materialize, we will not have the added humiliation of public failure. However, concealing hopes from others does not work because our hopes are revealed more by the way we live our lives than by what we say. A couple who have been dating for several months do not have to tell us in words that certain hopes are associated with this relationship. If, in time, we no longer see them together, we know without being told that certain hopes have not been fulfilled.

To hope, then, is to place ourselves at risk. We risk the failure of our hopes and the shame and humiliation that often accompany the failure of hopes. When our hopes fail, we take it very personally because in hoping we invest ourselves, putting our very existence on the line.

Directed to Unworthy Goals

If one risk of hopes is that they set us up for possible failure, another danger is that they may direct us to unworthy goals or cause us to overlook other objectives that are more desirable. We can become captive to certain hopes precisely because we judge them to be more realizable than others. Some hopes are realizable, but the price is too high.

One may become the top salesperson in the firm—a long desired goal—but find that the price in terms of shattered personal relationships, weakened personal integrity and broken personal health was far too high. Or one finds that the achievement of professional success does not bring the anticipated personal satisfaction of financial security. There are also instances when the realization of some cherished hope leaves us confused or apathetic, as we no longer have the goal that previously energized us. Unfulfilled hopes cause despair, but fulfilled hopes often cause depression, apathy, and boredom. People who discern that they are especially prone to such reactions in the wake of hope's fulfillment–people with self-knowledge–will often entertain more than one hope, or hopes that build on one another, so that when one hope is realized they have already oriented their lives toward another. As Erikson puts it, "it is in the nature of our maturation that concrete hopes will, at a time when a hoped-for event or state comes to pass, prove to have been quietly superceded by a more advanced set of hopes."[5]

Neglecting Present Satisfactions

Another risk is that we become so oriented toward the attainment of our hopes that we neglect the satisfactions our present situation already affords. This is often used as an argument for curbing our desires and for being content with what we have. But a more useful perspective is to realize that our current situation is, in part, the fruit of various past hopes that have been fulfilled, and we should not therefore neglect their continuing meaning for us. We may need a hope-beyond-hope to sustain us through the period of depression or apathy that follows the realization of a given desire, but there are also times when our envisioning of still another hope causes us to overlook the satisfactions that previously realized desires afford.

Hope has a restless quality to it. By definition, it is oriented to the future. It should not automatically be curbed or stifled, but it is not everything, and sometimes it needs to be balanced by other perceptions and experiences. When we experience satisfaction in our present reality, we allow love an equally significant place in our lives. Where hope is always oriented to the realizable, love is appreciation for what we already have. So a discerning life–a life of wisdom–is based on our capacity to balance our hopes and our loves, and not to allow our lives to be dominated by one or the other.

Consequences for Others

Still another risk in hopes is their consequences for others. There are times when our hopes, if realized, will make life more difficult for others, especially those who are dependent on us. Knowing that our hopes may carry risks for others, we may decide they are not worth the price that others may have to pay for them, and we resign ourselves to their unfulfillment. We may continue to harbor resentments against those who inhibited the realization of these hopes. Some people carry such resentments to their graves: "If only Jim had been more courageous and less practical." "If only I had trusted my own judgment instead of listening to Liz, with all her objections and 'what ifs.'" In turn, children of parents who sacrificed their own hopes for "the sake of the children" may carry through life the sense that they were the unwitting cause of a parent's disappointment, or were made the scapegoat for a parent's inability to take the necessary personal risks involved.

Thus, as future projections that envision the realizable, hopes are risky, and are typically experienced as such. Hopes can be exciting, scary, or unnerving. Unlike reveries, musings, and daydreamings, hopes anticipate real changes, and because they do, we should not romanticize hope as though it were an utterly harmless activity. Hopes can have tremendously positive outcomes, but they are also responsible for harm. One test of our maturity as persons is our ability to hope in ways that do not put other individuals at unacceptable levels of risk. Other tests of our maturity are the willingness to accept higher levels of risk for ourselves than will be required of others, and our ability to make intentional, self-conscious efforts to minimize the costs of our hopes to others.

Hope and the Reframing of Time

I want now to comment briefly on methods that are currently in use in psychotherapy that encourage hopefulness for the future. These methods fit within the category of reframing methods, which I discussed at some length in my book entitled *Reframing: A New Method in Pastoral Care.*[6] The two methods that have particular bearing on my reflections are presented in a book by two Finnish psychotherapists, Ben Furman and Tapani Ahola, entitled *Solution Talk.*[7] The one method is called "future visioning," the other is called "revising the past."

Future Visioning

In "future visioning" the counselees are asked to project themselves into the future (several weeks, six months, a year from now) and to describe their life now that their problem has been resolved, and to explain what they believe made the change possible. The method of "future visioning" is revealing for what it precludes. By focusing on a time in the future when the problem has been "overcome" rather than upon the past where the problem is assumed to have originated, the persons involved in the situation can be seen as mutual helpers rather than as obstacles. They are not the objects of blame, as usually occurs when the therapy focuses on underlying causes of the current problem. Also, the counselees' own narrative of how the problem got resolved is potentially as worthy of a plan for its resolution as anything the therapist might have proposed. The therapist may simply give the plan his or her blessing.

For example, one of the authors was a consultant to a mental health facility. The health team met with a teenage boy whose treatment wasn't going well. When he was asked to envision himself six months from now—doing much better—and to explain how these positive results came about, he mentioned that a particular staff psychiatrist had befriended him and helped him get better. This was not, however, the psychiatrist who had been assigned to this boy; it was one he watched working with other patients. So on the basis of the boy's future visioning, this psychiatrist was assigned to him, and he began to show improvement immediately.

Theologically informed readers of Furman's and Ahola's book are often quick to note that what underlies their future visioning method is a kind of realized eschatology. The future is already here, in the present, so that what we have been hoping for—our heartfelt desires—are already being met. What their cases show is that clients are quite willing to engage in the imaginative act of future visioning, and that, when they do so, they have a lively perception of having made the future present.

Revising the Past

The other method that involves a reframing of time for the sake of a more hopeful future is Furman's and Ahola's notion of "revising the past." They note that we tend to view our past as the source of our problems, and argue that as long as we view it this way we set up an adversarial relationship with ourselves because our history is an integral part of us. This adversarial relationship with ourselves can be reduced, if not overcome completely, by viewing our past as "a resource, a store of memories, good and bad, and a source of wisdom emanating from life experience."

The past is no longer viewed as "the source of our problems" but is seen instead as "resource for solutions." The authors relate how they encourage their counselees to see past events that they have interpreted as liabilities as being, rather, sources of strength. They tell about a woman whose mother put her in a dark closet for hours when she was a child. This woman had gone on to become a gifted art teacher, helping children use their imaginations through drawing. When she related how her mother had confined her to the dark closet, the counselor (one of the authors of the book) did not minimize the trauma she had suffered, namely, that she was the victim of child abuse. But he asked her the question: "What did you do in the closet to keep yourself from going crazy with fear?" She answered, "I used my imagination. I thought of myself being somewhere else, out in the fields, or in a park." Then he said, "And isn't this what you are now doing for the children you teach? Isn't your experience of coping with being locked in a closet a source of your gift as a teacher?" She had not previously made this connection in her mind.

The method of "revising the past" is designed to change a person's perception of what is possible for him or her as far as the future is concerned, this change being made possible by changing the meaning of certain past events. This method is also based on the rather odd assumption that the past is as open and as possibility-filled as the future is. This may seem utter nonsense, for only a fool believes that the past can be other than what it was. Yet there is also wisdom—a kind of foolish wisdom—in the affirmation of the openness and revisability of the past, for it says that what is open about the past is the meaning or significance we assign to it in the present.

In support of this view, we have the biblical Joseph's contention that the turning of his brothers' act of treachery into something providential was an act of God. "Revising the past" may also be theologically understood as being grounded in the boundless mercy of God, who is able to take sinful actions that we or others committed in the past and make of them something better than we would ever have imagined.

Which is to say that God is the original and eternally Hopeful Self, who uses the agency that is God's own to keep the future ever open for new possibilities. That the world and we ourselves exist at all is because it is God's nature to be hopeful. We exist because God, in response to God's own felt deprivation, was fueled by desire, and perceived that something new could come into being. As James Weldon Johnson, author of the poem "The Creation," puts it, "And God walked out on space and said, 'I'm lonely, I'll make me a world.'"[8] This world that God made is a *self*-projection, a world into which God, from the very beginning until now and forever after, has projected God's very own self.

But this was a self-projection that carried great risk for God, as hopes, once realized, take on a life of their own, having effects that were not originally intended. Hopes are wonderful things, but they are also dangerous, a fact to which the world, and especially the history of humankind, is tragic testimony. This is why it is so essential for us to believe that God remains a Reliable Other who has not abandoned us, and why it is important that some of us be pastors, ones who assist others in their struggles to maintain hope–helping them keep their heads above water–and who testify to, and carry in their very being, the ambiguities that are inherent in hope itself.

CHAPTER 17

The Midwife

KAREN R. HANSON[1] (1996)

My ministry as a [hospital] chaplain [in] a Level One trauma center is intense and challenging. Our department responds to all critical cases that come into the Emergency Department, as well as critical incidents and deaths that occur throughout the hospital. [This] work requires a solid sense of identity and purpose. For me, the image of minister, or chaplain, as spiritual midwife has provided some of that identity and has helped me to frame the import of what I do.

The Birth of the Model

I first explored this model when I was in my Clinical Pastoral Education residency, assigned to the perinatal units of my hospital. One day early in my residency, I was called to the birthing room to attend a very premature birth and to baptize the baby upon delivery. Donning mask and gown, I went in to find the mom, dad, and medical staff already working hard to deliver the baby. As I watched, it occurred to me that my pastoral role here was to be a spiritual midwife. Though the medical staff present that day may have been spiritual people, they did not pray, at least not out loud. But I did. I prayed and watched and encouraged and was simply present with them through the birth. As the baby drew her first and last breaths, I baptized her. And then I was a midwife to the parents in another sense, being with, waiting, and praying as the travail of grief began.

In the years since that time, I have found that the image of ministry as spiritual midwifery has expanded to fit many of the travails of trauma and grief that I have encountered in hospital ministry. It has continued to enrich and enhance how I envision what it is that I do as a chaplain. In this essay, through the sharing of biblical, historical, and experiential insights, I offer this image to colleagues in the hope that their own ministries will also be enriched by the powerful metaphor of midwife.

Parallel Professions

Midwives and ministers, as professionals in hospital settings, have much in common. Although both midwives and Christian ministers already had long histories of being valued as healers, both vocations suffered devaluation as reason and the scientific method were elevated in the Enlightenment. The healing tradition that had held throughout the ages—of the intimate connection between mind, body, and spirit—split apart. Now there were specialists who dealt with each of these areas, and the ministrations of practitioners of the cure of souls were subordinated to those licensed to cure physical ailments. Likewise, women midwives were pushed out of the realm of official healers. Only men could be trained and certified as physicians. All other healers were marginalized.

In this century in the United States, this split is being healed. The pastoral care movement was midwifed into being by visionaries like Anton Boisen in the 1920s. Clinical training programs in ministry were established in hospitals and institutions, where both head and heart were enlisted to reflect on pastoral care ministry and one's own person as caregiver. Likewise, people like Mary Breckenridge came to the United States and in 1925 pioneered the Frontier Nursing Service in Kentucky, a school for midwives, and the beginning of the nurse-midwife movement.

More recently, both chaplains and midwives have begun to be seen as integral parts of the team of healers in hospitals and other care settings. Clinical pastoral training programs continue to emerge, many of them in hospitals. Likewise, giving birth came to be viewed not as a pathological process, but a normal, if sometimes critical, life experience. Certified nurse-midwife programs sprouted, and midwives were once again taking their rightful place in their long tradition as healers.

From my perspective, then, I see many parallels in the professional development of both chaplains and midwives. We are colleagues with great affinity, both in the practice of tending to births, the physical and the spiritual kind, and in our involvement as a part of the healing team in hospitals. The most striking parallel for me, however, is our stance—the intent of both professions is to be with people, to attend people in a process. The focus is not so much on doing, but on being with people in travail, on using our skills and our personhood to focus on the unique context and process of the patients and families we are privileged to attend. Ministry as midwifery evokes an important part of who I am as a chaplain. I attend to people in travail, in any kind of tribulation or anguish, as God does the miraculous work of delivering new life in its myriad forms.

The midwife model of ministry is helpful in expanding our repertoire beyond the usual male models of ministry—shepherd, prophet, priest. Its resurrection highlights the breadth of imagery used in the Bible to speak of God, for scripture is rich with midwife imagery.

The Midwife in Scripture

Known more by their deeds than by name, Shiphrah and Puah are named in the first chapter of Exodus as having risked their own lives by saving Hebrew males from being killed at birth by order of Pharaoh. When confronted about this, Shiphrah and Puah shrewdly sidestepped Pharaoh by declaring that Hebrew women are so hardy that they give birth before the midwife reaches them. For their role in helping the people of Israel grow many and strong, these midwives were blessed by God and are remembered by name as part of our spiritual heritage.

The image of people suffering affliction and of God delivering is a powerful midwife image. For example, Exodus 3:7–8 conveys God's intent to "midwife" the people of Israel out of their affliction, or travail, and to deliver them out of bondage into a land flowing with milk and honey. The passage of deliverance is a channel through the waters of the Red Sea, through which God births the people into new life. Wherever there is affliction and suffering, and wherever God delivers, these biblical references hold the potential for evoking this midwife image.

Ezekiel 16:4 mentions some things that would be done by the midwife attending a birth—cutting the umbilical cord, washing the baby, sterilizing it with a salt water solution, wrapping it in a receiving blanket, and then presumably connecting the mother and child. With these actions in mind, apply the metaphor to illustrate God's role of midwifing the creation of the world and the birth of Israel:

> *Delivering*—"Who shut in the sea with doors when it burst out of the womb?" (Job 38:8); "Shall I, the one who delivers, shut the womb?" (Isa. 66:9);
>
> *Bathing*—"I will sprinkle clean water upon you..." (Ezek. 36:25);
>
> *Clothing*—"You clothed me with skin and flesh, and knit me together with bones and sinews" (Job 10:11); "And the LORD God made garments of skin for Adam and for his wife, and clothed them" (Gen. 3:21);
>
> *Connecting mother and child*—"You...took me from the womb...kept me safe on my mother's breasts" (Ps. 22:9).

Don Benjamin makes an interesting case for the midwife's practice of "calling the fetus" as being the imagery behind certain birth or resurrection stories in the Bible.[2] In some births where labor was protracted, it was assumed that the fetus was delaying its own birth. At that point, the midwife asked the mother to name the child. Then the midwife called the fetus by name using the formula, "Lazarus, come forth" (Jn. 11:43f., KJV). Once the fetus heard its name, it stopped struggling and was born. One such birth story is in Isaiah 26:10–27:13. Israel is "like a woman with child, / who writhes and cries out in her pangs..." (26:17). God delivers the people as the trumpet calls them forth.

Other passages where the image of God as midwife is prominent are exegeted by Margaret Hammer in her book *Giving Birth: Reclaiming Biblical Metaphor for Pastoral Practice*:

> God hears the people's cry of panic and terror (Jer. 30:5), sees all the men acting like women in labor (their faces pale, their hands at their loins), and asks, "Can a man bear a child?" (v. 6). The question drips with irony, and might seem mean indeed, were it not for God's subsequent words acknowledging the gravity of the situation and promising deliverance (v. 7). So, too, God's question in Micah 4:9f. prods the people to reinterpret their situation in more hopeful terms. The people are apparently crying out, feeling abandoned and helpless, like a woman in travail with no birth attendants to help her (v. 9). God questions the people's assumption that they are alone, then speaks as a midwife who encourages the birthing woman to throw herself into her labor, in full confidence of her eventual delivery (v. 10).[3]

God's activity in bringing to birth does not end with the creation of the world and of the people of Israel. There are numerous New Testament images depicting God's deliverance as well. Virginia Mollenkott observes that Jesus quotes part of Psalm 22 as he travails on the cross.[4] "Why have you forsaken me?" he cries out to God. Perhaps Jesus, like the psalmist, was comforted by remembering that God had been the midwife drawing him out of his mother's womb (22:9), resolving that as surely as God would not desert his mother in her travail, God would not desert him in his travail of crucifixion.

Extending the metaphor of Jesus' crucifixion and resurrection as the birth of new life for all the world, Mary Magdalene is remembered as the "Apostle to the Apostles" for her midwife-like testimony to having seen the resurrected Christ (Jn. 20). Just as the midwife is the first to see the baby emerge and testifies to what she sees ("It's a girl!"), so Mary tells the apostles, "I have seen the Lord!" (20:18). In Acts 2:24, Peter proclaims that Jesus experienced birth pangs as his death and resurrection ushered in a new era: "God raised him up, having loosed the birth pangs *[odinas]* of death, because it was not possible for him to be held by it." Margaret Hammer's translation makes explicit the birthing imagery lost in most translations. But the metaphor "is at the heart of the first Christian sermon, delivered on the Spirit-filled 'birthday' of the church. With it Peter aptly communicates the creative purpose of Jesus' terrible death: It was not a disgraceful dead end, but rather the travail of bringing forth new life."[5]

We in the Christian era, too, live in travail, for Jesus himself characterized the upheavals to be expected before the end times as "the beginning of the birth pangs" (Mk. 13:8; Mt. 24:8). In his letter to the Romans, Paul expands the image to cosmic proportions: "The whole creation is groaning in labor pains until now" (8:22). Helping us in our travail is the Spirit, who intercedes with groans that, like those of a birthing woman nearing delivery, are "too deep for words" (v. 26). Like a birthing mother, creation and Christians both groan and wait with eager longing for God's final act of deliverance, when the reign of God comes in fullness.

Midwife imagery in scripture, then, is rather substantial and inspiring. God acts as a midwife in delivering a new creation and a new people. There is no specific reference to Jesus acting as a midwife, though certain passages suggest images of Jesus delivering people out of travail, suffering, and even death (for example, Jesus calling, "Lazarus, come forth," as he delivered him from death to life). The Spirit of God travails with us and the whole creation now, awaiting God's final act of deliverance, when the fullness of God's reign is birthed in history. Scripture draws heavily on midwife imagery to illuminate the work of God. History also provides rich images.

The Midwife in History

The word *midwife* is from Middle English, meaning "with woman." A midwife is one who brings to birth, and midwives have brought babies to birth throughout the history of the world. Socrates' mother was a midwife. Florence Nightingale trained midwives as well as nurses. A very bleak period in western history was the era of the witch trials in the Middle Ages in Europe. Midwives were among those, mostly women, condemned as witches and burned at the stake. Midwives and other women healers have often been regarded suspiciously, for they mediated the mysteries of birth, illness, and death. They brewed medicines from plants and roots and engaged in mysterious rituals and incantations in their healing ministrations.

For many women, midwifery was their calling, their Christian vocation, too. The church had a stake in securing the services of pious, competent midwives, and it began to regulate and certify midwives after the period of the witch trials. The time of birth was considered an extremely vulnerable time for the mother and the baby. Midwives were authorized to baptize infants in mortal danger, and the midwife was the primary pastoral caregiver during these vulnerable times, as it was not considered appropriate for males to be present in the birthing room. Anne Hutchinson, the most famous midwife in early America, was commended for her wonderful pastoral care. She was, however, subsequently banished from the Massachusetts Bay Colony because her authority began to undermine that of the male leaders of that community.

Although not all attained the fame of Anne Hutchinson, midwives were common in colonial America and in the various immigrant communities. These women, known for their knowledge, skill, and compassion, acted as midwives for their neighbors and friends. Ehrenreich and English describe the web of relationships within which the midwife operated:

She spoke the mother's language...She was familiar with obstetrical techniques but also with the prayers and herbs that sometimes helped. She knew the correct ritual for disposing of the afterbirth, greeting the newborn or, if necessary, laying to rest the dead. She was prepared to live with the family from the onset of labor until the mother was fully recovered. If she was a southern black midwife, she often regarded the service as a religious calling.[6]

A recent book by Laurel Thatcher Ulrich details the life of Martha Ballard, a midwife who practiced in Maine and kept a diary from 1785–1812. Most historians have considered Martha's diary trivial and mundane, but Ulrich has shown that its power lies in its very dailiness. Martha was a healer in the community. Her diary connects birth and death with ordinary life. She was a devout Christian and a humble nurse. She delivered hundreds of babies, nursed the sick, had nine children of her own, and ran the extensive Ballard household economy.

The dedication with which Martha Ballard carried out her vocation is clear from the following entry in her diary of January 18, 1796:

I was Calld from Mrs Moore to Steven Hinkleys wife at 10 hour morning. Shee was delivered at 11 of a son. I part drest the infant and was Calld to return to Mrs Moore. Find her more unwell. Shee was delivered at 4 hours 30 minutes of a son. The Children were the first Born of their mamys. I returned home at 8 hour Evening... I made Bids, washt dishes, swept house, and got supper. I feel some fatigud.[7]

Throughout her career, Martha Ballard worked alongside the "male-midwife" or obstetrician, as well as other midwives and healers in the area. There was plenty for them all to do. And there continued to be plenty for the midwife to do as America was settled ever westward. The demise of the midwife and other lay healers in America was mostly a byproduct of the ascendancy of heroic medicine and the rise of the physician as the official healer in the community. Medicine in the nineteenth century was being drawn into the marketplace, a thing to be bought and sold by those licensed to practice. Whereas the midwives and other healers provided a neighborly service, the physicians made healing a commodity and a source of wealth in itself.

In 1900, half the babies born in the United States were still being delivered by midwives. By 1930 only fifteen percent of births had midwives in attendance; in 1973, only one percent. Now with the advent of certified nurse-midwives, who practice in all fifty states, there is a bit of a reversal. The American College of Nurse-Midwives projects that, by 2000, they will attend ten percent of all births.

The story of midwifery through history is a rich, if checkered, one. What is striking is that women took their vocation very seriously, many considering it a calling. Their stance of being "with women" is inspiring for all of us who aspire to heal or to simply give compassionate presence and help to our neighbor in need. These healers stand in stark contrast to the connotations sometimes associated with obstetricians, whose names stems from the Latin *obstare*–to stand before or against. There is a huge difference between being with someone and standing before or against them. We are sorely in need of all kinds of healers who are skilled in being with people, and who are capable of tending to whole persons, which includes the midwife as well as the chaplain.

The Minister as Spiritual Midwife

Like the midwife, my function as a chaplain is to be with people in travail. In contrast to the midwife, I don't always know the outcome of my presence with suffering people.

The Metaphor's Inspiration

Lots of times there are no tangible results. While all metaphors break down eventually, the metaphor of midwifery has much to commend it. I will detail some ways in which I have been inspired by this metaphor in my ministry.

THE LOOK OF TRAVAIL

One of the first things a midwife must learn is *what travail looks like!* And, seeing it, not to shrink from it. There are so many forms of spiritual travail and affliction. The spiritual midwife is responsible for knowing travail when she sees it and attending to those people who call on her to do so. For example, some hospital staff were startled and frightened by the very vocal and physical response of a large family group upon hearing that their loved one had died. The chaplain, however, recognized the travail of grief and interpreted for staff what he saw. He then proceeded to invite the family to a private space where they could continue to grieve and begin to assimilate the reality of their loss.

A wonderful line in an 18th century midwifery manual reads,

> There is a tender regard one woman bears to another, and a natural sympathy in those that have gone thru' the Pangs of Childbearing; which, doubtless, occasion a compassion for those that labour under these circumstances, which no man can be a judge of.[8]

NECESSITY OF LIVED EXPERIENCE

This speaks to the fact that there is no substitute for *lived experience*. In order to be a good spiritual midwife, I believe it is necessary to have experienced rebirth, to have passed through some sort of spiritual travail oneself. Knowledge, training, being observant, having reflected upon and integrated one's own birthings so that one is aware of some of the dangers, the fears, the hopes–all of these are components in the process of learning to be a good spiritual midwife. One's own experience doesn't constitute expert knowledge of all kinds of spiritual birthings, but it does function as a guide and resource.

NEED TO BE PERSON-CENTERED

Our calling necessitates that we be *person-centered*. We are in the business of assisting God in birthing new life in people and in their relationships with self, others, the world, and God. We need to see a patient first of all as a person and as a person-in-relationship, like Martha Ballard knew her neighbors and friends in rural Kennebec, Maine. I remember one of my first encounters as a chaplain when I was visiting a woman with preterm labor, hospitalized on bedrest. The woman had quite a stoical attitude toward this turn of events, and she spoke of the hospitalization as a sacrifice she gladly chose for the sake of her baby. And this is how I saw her. One day, however, she confessed her ambivalence and proceeded to name the losses she was experiencing as a result of this hospitalization, including the loss of her dream of an ideal pregnancy. She taught me in that moment to see her as a whole person—as a working woman, a spouse, a woman with a healthy sense of independence, a person with strong feelings and needs of her own—and not only as a pregnant woman on bedrest.

NAMING PART OF MINISTRY

Sometimes patients and families are able to name their travail and acknowledge their need for deliverance. And sometimes *naming* is a part of my ministry, too. This image hearkens back to the midwife's calling the fetus when labor was protracted, believing that the baby, hearing its name, would stop struggling and come out. I was called to be with a woman with end-stage renal disease who had just told her family and her doctor that she no longer wanted to undergo dialysis. She was so ill, and she had fought so hard, but she didn't want to fight any longer. Her family passionately urged her to continue the struggle. Finally, I named for them the essence of what this moment was all about; if she stopped dialysis she would die and was ready to die, but her family did not want to let her go. This act of naming birthed a process in which the family was ultimately able to honor the woman's wishes, and she was delivered, as she put it, from "this body of death."

DEALING WITH DEATH

Death is a very present reality in birthing. There are at least three aspects of *dealing with death* that are gleaned from midwifery. The first is the reality that with every birth there is a kind of death for the woman. She is now no longer who she was as a pregnant woman. She delivers new life in herself, too, for now she is a mother. She is changed. For Christians there is the reality that every day is a death and resurrection. We die to the old, sinful self and rise to newness of life in Christ. Indeed, God our midwife clothes us each day with Christ.

Second, with birth there is the possibility of death for the baby. There are miscarriages, stillbirths, and previable babies who die almost the moment they are born. In the event of the baby's death, the midwife would assist in preparing the body for burial and help the mother and family in beginning the grief process, which in itself is a kind of travail. Chaplains at my hospital are involved with virtually every death, assisting the family in the acute phase of grief, facilitating the free flow of emotions, helping provide some closure and commendation, and following up with families after they leave the hospital.

Finally, there is the possibility of the death of the mother in the birthing process. Death is the ultimate travail, as the passage to eternal life is negotiated. Ministers have been midwives of this process throughout history, tending people through the birth pangs of death. This continues to be one of our major roles in hospitals, too.

Spiritual Dimensions of Birthing

In traditional midwifery, there is overt acknowledgment of the spiritual dimensions of birthing. Indeed, many midwives saw their vocation as ministry, and many today do, too. There is a beautiful prayer from 1475 in which the midwife and others present in the birthing room invoke the Triune God and proclaim the rule of the Christ who had once called forth Lazarus: "Christ calls thee. The world delights in thee. The covenant longs for thee...Oh infant, whether alive or dead, come forth. Christ calls thee to light."[9] Likewise, part of a chaplain's vocation is to help people see the *spiritual dimensions* of the crisis of illness or injury, that whatever the circumstances of the occasion of hospitalization, there may be opportunities for spiritual healing and the birth of new understandings and insights. There is opportunity for a deepened and broadened spirituality. Through our own personhood and through our skills— being with; giving compassionate presence, listening, and prayer; providing rituals and sacraments; making a space for public worship and prayer; partici- pating in family conferences; team rounds; ethics consults—we witness to and reflect God's ongoing involvement in the care and healing of people.

As chaplains we have a natural relationship to the midwife. She is our colleague and sister. Our professions have as their purpose to be with people in travail, assisting God in bringing about new life. Our stance of being with and attending to whole people is very much needed in today's health care systems and throughout society. Today may in fact be a pregnant moment in terms of our search for wholeness, as more and more people seem to hunger for justice and mercy in our health care, in our politics, our spirituality, our communities. We long for a rebirth of compassion, of meaning, of purpose in our individual and communal lives. Imaging our work as being with people in travail, assisting God in delivering new life, may help sustain our purpose and hope and give us a new vision of what it is we are called to be and to do.

CHAPTER 18

The Gardener

MARGARET ZIPSE KORNFELD[1] (1998)

> Be a gardener.
> Dig a ditch
> toil and sweat,
> and turn the earth upside down
> and seek the deepness
> and water the plants in time.
> Continue this labor
> And make sweet floods to run
> and noble and abundant fruits to spring.
> Take this food and drink
> and carry it to God
> as your true worship.
>
> JULIAN OF NORWICH[2]

The medieval mystic Julian of Norwich understood the metaphor of "gardening" as an expression of ministry. We would like to suggest this image for ourselves today. A gardener, like a community's counselor and caregiver, has a twofold task. A gardener must tend to the ground as well as cultivate the plants growing in the ground. The gardener does not make the plants grow, God does. The gardener attends to their growth as the plants become what they are meant to be.

We are like gardeners when, as we continue to tend to ourselves, we tend to others in all the seasons of life. Our care and counseling grow out of *our participation* with others in the natural events of life: marriage, birth, coming of age, death, illness, and all the normal life crises. Our care and counseling also occur when life goes awry. Then we must find ways to help people deal with the extraordinary.

Sometimes, also like gardeners, there is nothing much we can do to "fix" a situation. Often when counseling people who are experiencing grave loss, we can only be with them. We have to learn to accept our limitations and to develop patience. Often we cannot know the effect our accepting attitude or simply our presence has. We may feel ineffective, only to learn that in a caring session a seed was planted that much later bore fruit.

"Gardener," like any metaphor, has its limitations. We do not "tend" people as though they are objects to be acted upon. Counseling is always the healing *interaction* between counselee and counselor. Both we and counselees are rooted in the same ground because we are sustained by the same community. We both draw upon the spiritual resources of the community. Much pastoral theory and technique involves one-to-one, and sometimes couple or family, situations. However, in faith communities it is not only the religious or lay professional who supports change. The community itself also heals, or, if it is dysfunctional, harms. Caregivers, counselors, and all who are mindful of concern need to understand the characteristics of a healing community and need to have skills to help the community develop its potential for supporting life.

The Ground of Community

Gardeners know that before they plant, they must consider the composition, condition, and needs of the soil. After understanding the nature of the soil, they will need to know which plants thrive in it. They will know what nutrients will be needed to supplement the soil and will understand how the ground holds water. After knowing the soil, they proceed.

The Community Where We Work

That is why, as gardeners who care for souls, we must first consider the community in which we do our work. The community of your church or synagogue is the ground that supports and nurtures both you in your work and the individuals who are members of the community.

Rather than acknowledging our groundedness in community, most psychological counseling theory reflects an individualistic medical model. The primacy of a confidential doctor-patient relationship is assumed where the doctor rarely deals with the patient's whole family. The doctor usually has little direct knowledge of the patient's lifestyle, support systems, or religious experience and values. The doctor limits his or her actions to understanding what is wrong with the patient and then, if possible, curing what is "wrong."

Most counselors, too, work in private with the counselee without direct input from the counselee's family or friends. The counselor is taught to diagnose the illness, help the counselee solve problems, and if possible, help provide a cure.

Grounded in Multiple Relationships

You who minister in community do not work in such an individualistic, compartmentalized way. You have *multiple relationships* with those who come to you for counseling. Because most of those whom you counsel are known to you through your leadership in their religious or civic community, you are never simply an objective, neutral counselor. Unlike other mental health professionals who first meet their clients in consultation and draw out case studies from strangers, you often know those who come to you for help. In fact, sometimes you feel you know too much! Because you know the counselee's extended family and friends, you may have heard other versions of the problem that a counselee comes to discuss. In listening, you have to bracket off what you have heard from others so you may hear the counselee's story in a fresh way.

Dealing with Spiritual Dis-ease

Counseling methods that are based solely on the illness model are not particularly helpful to those of us who counsel in community. Because of our understanding of mind-body-soul integration, we of course need to be able to identify the physical and psychological symptoms that often accompany spiritual distress. We also need to know how to make appropriate referrals so that those suffering can be helped. But we cannot be limited to illness-based knowledge. We also need to know how to care for the soul and to learn how spiritual *dis-ease* can create imbalance. We need counseling theory and technique that will help train our eyes to see wholeness.

By focusing first on community, you are starting where you are. You are not in an office protected by neutrality and anonymity. Because you work *within* community, your job as counselor and caregiver is both harder and easier than that of other mental-health professionals. It is hard to be both *connected* to your counselees due to your personal and/or clerical relationships to them, and yet also be *separate* enough to see them clearly. You need to understand how the complexity of your relationship affects the counseling process. You also need to learn techniques for managing limit setting and for organizing life-history information.

Community as Means of Healing

It takes special skill to be a counselor and caregiver in community. However, your work is made easier because you have the resource of community itself to support you and to be a place of healing for those whom you counsel. Community is not only the *place* where healing occurs, it is a *means* through which it happens.

Community as Varied Religious Traditions

To understand community, we must return to our consideration of "ground." The ground in which we plant is made up of many different types and compositions of soil. Our religious gardens are complex and beautiful. They each thrive in the soil of our varied religious traditions. Even though the soils–the religious traditions–differ, the *function* of the ground is the same in all our gardens, where the ground nurtures, supports, and hold the plants, regardless of the composition of the soil. As we understand more about how community works, we are able both to cultivate the "soil" and to rest and be supported by the "ground."

Christian communities have differing understandings of what it means to be "the body of Christ" and to "go into all the world and preach the Gospel." Some religious communities emphasize individual personal salvation; others believe that members are brought into the church and redeemed in community. Although theological understanding of sacraments and religious practice differ, Christians are drawn together in communities to discern what it means to be modern-day faithful disciples. They are challenged to be like Christians of the early church who were singled out as "those who loved each other," and by Jesus' admonition to reach out to "the least of these" and to the "sick not the well," so as to embody God's love for the world. The New Testament is filled with instructions for life in community.

Community as Living Organism

The concept of religious community as a living organism is not new. The early Christian church was described as a body whose head was Christ, in which individual members were "one with another" (Romans 12:3–8). As members of faith communities today are recovering from their dualistic perceptions, they are becoming increasingly aware of the ways in which their own religious community is actually a living organism within the living organism of the larger community, which is itself in the world. Because of our interconnectedness, the vitality of our religious communities contributes to the strength and energy of the larger community. And when there is toxicity in our communities' bodies, it adversely affects the whole. Because we are one body, our community and all those in it are made sick by the poison created by racism, economic greed, homophobia, and other expressions of hardheartedness and hatred.

As we begin to sense the implications of our interconnectedness to each other, we can become overwhelmed. But we are helped by observations of meteorologists who note the "Butterfly Effect"–the flutter of butterfly wings in one part of the world can create vibrations that in turn cause massive weather changes in another part of the world. One small movement can create great change. Communities need to be reminded that small *just* actions can contribute to big changes in the entire organism.

Caring for the Soil

The community is the *ground* of our work: the community supports and upholds us. Now we will begin to consider what we, as gardeners, must do for the ground.

Ground and Soil: Community and Tradition

I have made a distinction between "ground" and "soil." In this metaphor, the ground is the community itself, with all the properties that make it a safe, healing place. The soil is our religious tradition and our expression of it. We know that there are many types of soil that differ in appearance, chemical composition, and use. We have only to observe the rocky New England soil, the rich soil of the Mississippi Delta, and dark Midwestern farmland soil to appreciate this variety.

And so it is with the soil of our religious communities. Our religious traditions are composed of a variety of gifts. Some communities have rich and complex liturgies, some meet in silent contemplation. Some experience healing energy of the Holy Spirit through singing and dancing, others meet for serious, quiet Biblical or Talmudic study. Some communities meet in homes; others in cathedrals. Our soils (traditions) differ, but it is our communities that serve as the *common* ground. It is understood that even those traditions that are sacramental and liturgical and that place less emphasis on congregational life are supported in an essential way by the presence and communal activity of the congregation.

Our consideration of the community's care emphasizes wholeness. We are looking at the community as a living organism, as the gardener looks at the garden. When the gardener analyzes the needs of the soil, he asks, "Does it need to lie fallow? Does it need nutrients? Is it getting enough water? Is there infection from fungi or environmental waste?"

The Community's Condition

When we pay attention to the community, we ask these gardener's questions: Does the community need to be fed? What ingredients are needed in a nutritional program? Does the community need support for spiritual growth, or workshops to learn skills for listening, or conflict resolution? Does the community need to rest or play? Shall we plant new crops, change an emphasis or program? Have we been infected by the toxins of resentment or unfinished business? Have we become insular or too self-serving? How can we be more whole? As members ask, "What does our community need to be?" we will find answers through careful listening—listening to God and to each other.

After you know more about the *condition* of the community, you can make a plan in response. You are helped in this response if you understand two fundamental principles known to gardeners: paying attention to balance, and expecting change.

Paying Attention to Balance

Gardeners seek balance. In one season, the ground needs to rest; in another, it needs to be intensely fertilized so a bumper crop can grow. Gardeners understand the balance of the garden to be a bit like that of a gymnast on the balance beam who is always slightly *in motion*–and focused both inwardly and outwardly.

Expecting Change

Gardeners know that although they prepare, they must always expect the change that nature brings. When you apply these principles to community, you may well ask how your community can become balanced–flexible, focused, and in movement. How can you be more comfortable with change and in harmony with nature?

Determining the Tradition's Healing Gifts

To answer these questions, you have to be very specific about your community. What is the tradition of your religious group? What are its resources–spiritual, cultural, programmatic? Some religious traditions place an emphasis upon the sacraments and use these rich spiritual resources for healing the community; others emphasize study and preaching of the tradition. These groups use the mind and understanding for healing. Some groups, such as African-American churches, use the gifts of relationship and music to heal. You need to discover–and, in some cases, to uncover and recover–the healing gifts in your tradition.

Look at your tradition in the way a gardener looks at the soil. What mixture is your soil? Rather than separating religious traditions along doctrinal or sectarian lines, look at the *components* of your religious life and observances: sacrament, worship, scripture, personal religious experience, community life, social-justice activity, spiritual contemplation, and prayer. These components are found in both Jewish and Christian traditions. The emphasis placed on them differs within the various denominations and divisions of both Judaism and Christianity. If you understand the composition of your community's religious life, you can learn how to make it more balanced and lively.

The Ground as Gardener

Our metaphor continues. You are the "gardener"; the people in your community are the "plants" whose souls you tend. But in the fluid ecological system of wholeness, you, the "gardener," are sometimes also the "plant," ministered to by the community. Sometimes members of the community who have been a part of the "ground" assume the "gardener's" role by being responsible for specific healing activities.

Recognizing Others' Healing Gifts

As you look at the scope of your healing activities, you will become aware of the many people who are involved. You are not alone, and it is necessary for you to grasp this truth. Counselors and caregivers become susceptible to burnout when they believe they must do the work alone. You will be a more effective religious leader if you are able to recognize the healing gifts of other members.

Learning as an Apprentice

Traditionally, gardeners trained through apprenticeships, where they learned practical skills and obtained horticultural knowledge from a master with an affinity for nature. The master gardener knows the plants, loves the earth, and is connected to nature. The apprentice gardener learns to garden from *the being* of the master.

Like a gardener, it is important for you to become a counseling apprentice. At one time clergy learned community caregiving skills through being closely supervised in seminary and then beginning their ministry as cleric's assistants. Today, many new clergy begin their ministry "on their own." They have not had the necessary apprenticeships in ministry in which they can learn "from the being" of experienced clergy who give counsel and care. Perhaps you are one of those. However, all clergy can still become apprentices. They can hone their skills through pastoral supervision.

One's self is the tool that the community counselor uses in the work. It is one's self that listens, empathizes, thinks, and connects. You use your own experience, and your imagination. You use your woundedness, your strength, your faith. You use your doubts. You listen with your whole self, not just your mind. You understand with your heart while, at the same time, you apply counseling technique and theory. You must know yourself, while continuing to learn about yourself.

Dealing with Personal Anxiety

Can you picture a counseling session in which the counselee is comfortably talking about himself or herself to a counselor who is listening with lively attentiveness? In this picture, the counselor seems to be a "real" person who listens in such a way that the counselee feels safe. Perhaps you can create this picture because of a personal experience with such a counselor or counselee. However, perhaps you, like many of us, have conducted counseling sessions in which you did not feel like the counselor in this picture. You felt scattered and anxious. Your counseling space did not seem like a "safe place," even to you.

Anxiety does not come from nowhere. It is often connected to the activation of an idea. We can deal with anxiety by discovering the scary things we say to ourselves. An idea that often stirs anxiety in a counselor is: "*I'm not enough to do this.* My supervisor, Bill, my therapist, Susan, my friend, John, could do this better. They'd know what to do." The belief—and fear—of "not being enough" can plague even the most experienced therapist. The great therapist and theoretician Dr. Carl Rogers regularly worked to change a thought pattern that triggered his anxiety. It is said that even in his later years, Dr. Rogers would center himself before beginning a master class, and would remind himself: "I am enough." He just had to be himself.[3]

When we think that some wiser counselor should be in the counseling room because "I am not enough," we disconnect from ourselves. We focus on the "expert" who is not in the room. We leave ourselves and in leaving, create anxiety. We abandon ourselves. If we were to breathe and use Dr. Rogers's mantra: "I am enough," we would return to ourselves and find the truth. *If we are truly ourselves, we have enough.*

Ministry by Being With

Our work as counselors is to be with those who are finding their path. To be with them we are not required to be geniuses. We are required to be as authentically ourselves as we are capable of being at that time. When we are connected to ourselves, we can use our experiences and gifts.

For some, it might be the experience of growing up with an alcoholic father or a critically ill mother or it might be a sense of humor or the ability to reframe experience. For others, it might be the painful experience of feeling like an outcast because of racism, sexism, ageism, homophobia, etc. For yet others, it might be a gift of the spirit. In counseling, experiences that we have thought of as weaknesses can be transformed and used to help others. Perhaps you have been ashamed of your learning difficulties or your divorce or your child's struggle with addiction. These painful experiences, when seen in a new light, can be gifts that help you to be more understanding and less judgmental. As you become more whole yourself, you are able to use all of your experience. You discover that you have within you what you need.

The Bravery of Counseling

When you have created a hospitable place through your availability, your counselee will be more able to tell his or her story and to risk being understood. *The counseling process requires bravery.* When counselees open their hearts to you, they experience vulnerability and they often silently wonder "Will I be accepted? Do I dare say what is really on my mind? Will this religious person– or God–condemn me for being myself?" But you, the counselor, are also taking a risk. To understand your counselee, you must use all of your self and your experience, even that which you have buried or would like to disown. To be open to your counselee you, too, become vulnerable.

[In] considering ways in which *we use ourselves as tools* in the counseling and caregiving process, we also need to be conscious of our connection to the *ground.* We are not alone in our work. We realize this as we center ourselves and feel grounded as we make contact with the Source of our being. We can also feel grounded when we remember that we are:

- Undergirded by the *principles of holism*–body, mind, and soul are integrated. We need not experience the world and ourselves as fragmented.
- Undergirded by *our religious and collegial communities,* in which we do our work.

It's Grace That's Brought Me Safe Thus Far

A gardener's life seems relatively safe when compared to that of a counselor in community. Counselors in community, particularly those who are ordained or serve on ministry teams and staffs, are in danger because they are religious professionals.

Growing in Grace

When "religion" is your job it is easy for it to become a habit that loses its freshness and purpose—it can become routine. It is dangerous to pray *for a living*. In keeping religious institutions and programs going, you can lose track of your soul. When counseling others, you can be tempted to live vicariously through them and disconnect from your own life. The work of ministry can become a spiritual liability.

However, you also must know of clergy and lay ministers who seem to *grow* in grace. Over the years, they have blossomed and matured. They have not become cynical and tired out. They are more alive than when they graduated from seminary or graduate school. Although they have had spiritual struggles, they also have been grounded in their love for God. Their ministry to others has grown out of this love.

In order to thrive, we need to observe those who have matured in ministry. Think about those whom you know who, in their fifties and sixties, are engaged in their spiritual journey. Connect with them. Ask them to tell you their story. And think about your own spiritual journey. At what places and times in your life has God surprised you?

Those of you who garden know delight when you discover tender green plants beginning to sprout, sometimes in unexpected places. Much of your work as leader in your religious community involves planning and management. Do your part, plan, and prepare, but keep your eyes open for *unexpected* growth in another place in the garden.

Those who thrive in ministry stay out of power struggles with themselves and others. They give in to delight. Think of those counselors whom you know who also *find life interesting*. They have a passion for their avocations. They are true *amateurs*, who love and develop their interest in art, photography, music, piloting a plane, or climbing a mountain. They are involved in some way with the world, with creation, with creating. They do not need to live through others for excitement. They live with thanksgiving.

This does not mean that people who give thanks for life do not have troubles. Some live with cancer or other illnesses or social discrimination or with loved ones who have chronic illness. Some struggle with doubts and disappointments. But they have a faith that allows them to say, "The Lord gives, the Lord takes away; blessed be the name of the Lord."

Tending to the gardener—ourselves—requires that we pay attention. That we take pleasure in life. That we allow ourselves to be found.

CHAPTER 19

The Midwife, Storyteller, and Reticent Outlaw

BRITA L. GILL-AUSTERN[1] (1999)

A wise pedagogue once said, "The substance of what we know may change us, but changing how we know can revolutionize us." As one long interested in processes of transformation and how pedagogy can facilitate transformation, feminist pedagogy has captivated my interest for several years.

As a feminist pastoral theologian, I am committed to discovering those ways of being and doing in teaching that increase the love of God, neighbor, self, and all being and that help mend our broken creation. Love grows through knowledge and understanding. Therefore to increase the love of God, neighbor, self, and all being through the educational process, there must be self-discovery, discovery of the other, discovery of God and the world in which we all participate. Such discovery leads to the possibility of new creation.

But discovery that results in a transformation of consciousness and commitment depends not only on the acquisition of secondhand knowledge, but also on firsthand experience that confirms and anchors intellectual knowing. To foster spiritual maturity and the formation of whole persons for the ministry of care (lay or ordained) requires a pedagogy and a relationship that foster both.

Teaching as Relationship

Feminist and womanist pastoral theology, in its method and content, focuses on the deep relationality that strengthens life-giving and healing connection in persons' lives. Teaching then becomes less about techniques and methods, and more a way of being in relationship. Central to any feminist pedagogy must be attention to how our practice of teaching deepens authentic, just, and life-giving connection in all spheres of life and what detracts from or threatens such connection. Our teaching is pastoral care.

Feminist and womanist Christian pastoral theologians are committed to teaching that can transform the life of the church into a more responsive and faithful witness of the gospel in the twenty-first century. Only a church that addresses the profound suffering of our times, particularly the suffering caused by structures, rules, and ways of being that use difference (be it gender, race, sexual orientation, class, etc.) as a rationale for domination and control, can be an instrument of redemption for our time.

Metaphors for Feminist Pastoral Teachers

Whom do we as feminist and womanist pastoral theologians understand ourselves to be as teachers? To respond to [this] question, I will explore five metaphors that evoke vivid images of feminist womanist pastoral theologian pedagogues: teacher as midwife, voice coach, storyteller and evoker of stories, contemplative artist, and reticent outlaw.

Who we see ourselves to be as teachers will determine in large measure how we relate to our students and what we consider primary. Teaching, as practical theologian Maria Harris reminds us, is an act of imagination, shaped by the metaphors that inform and expand our consciousness. "What teachers imagine they are doing–what they assume they are doing, what they think they are doing, what they intend to do, pervades, colors and determines what they do, in fact, do."[2] "Our thinking and our knowing in all human endeavor is shaped by the metaphors we employ. It matters which words we choose when we teach."[3]

It also matters what metaphors we use to imagine our teaching and ourselves as teachers. The five metaphors I focus on here shape our identity, integrity, and practice as teachers. These metaphors also evoke imagination for transformative possibilities in teaching that have an impact on students' self-understanding as they enter ministries of care in and beyond the church.

Feminist Pedagogues as Midwives

Probably the most common and recurring metaphor for feminist pedagogues is the teacher as midwife, where authority comes from competent presence and coparticipation in the birthing of the new. When I gave birth to my third son, the midwife told me, "I don't deliver the baby; I simply catch it." A feminist teacher needs to catch another's ideas and bring them to light rather than simply deliver one's own.

A midwife teacher helps half-baked ideas and perceptions develop in dialogue to fuller maturity. What is important is not to begin with perfected thought, but to encourage creative thinking that is pushing the edges and discovering where novelty becomes possible. A midwife helps life come during the moment of intense labor by helping a woman focus in, to concentrate on the essential, to relax into the moment. A midwife teacher does the same by guiding one to see what needs to be focused on and attended to and creates the kind of space where one can become relaxed and be oneself.

Midwife teachers know that to bring new life and truth into the classroom, they must ask questions that do not have predetermined answers, but search honestly for the revelation of truth in a community seeking truth.

Recently, in a seminar I was teaching with women clinical pastoral education (CPE) students, I was asking questions trying to unpack the meaning and implications of the Buddhist saying, "Vulnerability is the seed of enlightenment." I had discerned what I thought was key. I wanted, though, for the students to discover it for themselves, so I asked, "Why is vulnerability the seed of enlightenment?" But what I really wanted to hear was confirmation of my own truth rather than listening for a new truth that emerged from them. A bright and dear student, with whom I had formed a good connection, raised her hand and said, "I feel like you are fishing for one answer, and I feel vulnerable and stupid that I'm not coming up with the right one." It was an "aha" moment. I felt instantly that I had violated something very basic to the midwife approach.

Under the guise of open questioning, I was seeking "a" response. Before the student raised this issue, I had a felt sense of what she was naming; I felt less free, controlling, even manipulative in the way I was proceeding. The whole exchange was less lively than many of ours had been. Why? It was not a search for their truth; it was a setup for them to find mine. I assumed unconsciously the role of sole expert and authority and therefore was not really listening for their truth. Although I hope this is not my usual way of asking questions, it is easy to fall into occasionally.

In *Women's Ways of Knowing,* Belenky and her coauthors describe the experience of many women they interviewed in trying to understand how women's development and growth occur in relation to epistemology. They write:

> Many women expressed—some firmly, some shakily—a belief that they possessed latent knowledge. The kind of teacher they praised and the kind for which they yearned was the one who would help them articulate and expand their latent knowledge: a midwife-teacher. Midwife-teachers are the opposite of banker-teachers. While the bankers deposit knowledge in the learner's head, the midwives draw it out.[4]

The midwife, like an obstetrician, is a skilled professional, very conscious of her particular role and task in relation to another. "The midwife teacher is no security blanket—usually quite the contrary. She is an authority. She too has an open mouth. But she gives information as food, to be digested as fuel. And she speaks with a mind to the dynamics of voice."[5]

Feminist Pedagogues as Voice Coaches

Midwife teachers also know that for women and persons who have lived under structures of inequality, domination, and control, the experience of feeling silenced is a common phenomenon. Midwife teachers know the transformative power of "hearing another into speech."[6]

The theme of voice is one heard incessantly in feminist writings. When one is denied the opportunity to name and interpret one's experience, it is not surprising that a central metaphor for describing women's experience and development is the one of voice. In the research into the educational lives of more than one hundred women, the authors of *Women's Ways of Knowing* discovered that when describing their lives, women commonly talked about voice and silence:

> "Speaking up," "speaking out," "being silenced," "not being heard," "really listening," "really talking," "words as weapons," "feeling deaf and dumb," "having no words," "saying what you mean," "listening to be heard," and so on in an endless variety of connotations all having to do with a sense of mind, self-worth and feelings of isolation from or connection to others. We found that women repeatedly used the metaphor of voice to depict their intellectual and ethical development; and that development of a sense of voice, mind, and self were intricately intertwined.[7]

When women cannot voice their own needs, experiences, and feelings, the heart and mind become constricted. Only through speaking and listening do we develop the capacity to talk and think things through.[8] Research studies show a connection between a greater incidence of clinical depression and learned helplessness among women and the curtailment of voice.[9]

Loss of voice is also about a loss of subjectivity and the loss of the "authentic I" that can be brought to relationships. In adolescence, as Carol Gilligan and her colleagues at the Harvard School of Education have discovered in their longitudinal studies of hundreds of adolescent girls, girls come to believe that to stay in relationship, they must take their authentic selves out of relationship.[10]

In an effort to conform to images of the "good girl" whom everyone will promote, value, and want to be with, girls silence the voice they fear others do not want to hear. Many women carry this pattern of silencing the voice into adulthood. The loss of voice is intimately tied to a woman's loss of subjectivity and therefore her capacity to love with her all.[11]

Poet Marge Piercy in her poem "Unlearning to not speak" names what must happen for subjectivity to develop:

> She must learn again to speak
> starting with I
> starting with We
> starting as the infant does

with her own true hunger
and pleasure
and rage.[12]

When women are denied the authority of their own perceptions and experiences, powerlessness, helplessness, and the structures of inequality are reinforced. The possibility of genuine mutual relation, which allows the possibility of cocreation in the learning process, is subverted. Paulo Freire, an educator who has in many respects modeled emancipatory praxis, reminds us that the practice of freedom begins with naming and interpreting one's own reality.[13]

Without calling women out of silence and empowering them toward greater subjectivity, women are made more vulnerable to being made someone else's object and thereby less able to challenge race, gender, and class oppression. "Oppressed people resist by identifying themselves as subjects, by defining their reality, shaping their new identity, naming their history, telling their story."[14] Voice coaches further emancipatory praxis by creating a space in which persons can speak their truth and name their own reality.

The metaphor of voice coach guides me powerfully, particularly in working with women doctoral students. I find repeatedly that helping women to speak from the "authentic I," to find their own true voice in conceiving a doctoral project, is critical to its successful completion. For clarity to emerge, one has to listen carefully to the passion and embryonic beginnings of an intellectual quest so that it can find shape and form. Good voice coaches know that when we are learning to speak a new language or sing a new song, our initial attempts may be rough, imprecise, and missing a clarity of expression. Voice coaches know how to begin with where people are and lead them gently into depth conversation that calls forth ever clearer articulation.

Feminist Pedagogues as Storytellers and Evokers of Stories

Rebecca Chopp names narrativity as one of the three most central feminist pedagogical practices. She reminds us, "If we cannot write new stories that imagine a new future for women and men, we will die still holding to old narratives that do not liberate, but bind. In writing we create and recreate ourselves."[15] Critical to feminist pedagogy is helping women rewrite their lives in ways that speak the truth of their existence, their dreams, and their hopes. Narrativity is central to feminist pedagogy because it is one central means by which we are enabled to resist oppression and definition by others.[16]

When we tell women's tales and are able to evoke women's own stories through classroom discussions and assignments, women's subjectivity and agency are increased. So much of women's experience has not been the subject for theological reflection. Without evoking the specific experience of women, we lose a capacity to see and name some of our richest experiences as spiritual. Experiences that accompany women's biological rhythms,[17] such as menstruation, pregnancy, lactation, and menopause, as well as experiences such as sexual abuse (rape, incest), the centrality of female friendships, and community, are rich resources for theological reflection.

The practice of narrativity, of telling one's story and evoking the stories of others, is enhanced by a rich use of novels, poetry, video, and drama in the classroom. These depict in full color the texture, feel, and mood of women's experiences and help call forth women's own narratives.

I have found that a rich exercise that deepens the practice of narrativity is having students write "Dialogues for Connected Knowing"–an assignment that invites students to bring their own experiences into dialogue with the reading and material of the course. Doing this requires an intentional integration of the subjective, imaginative, and intuitive with the analytical, critical, and objective. Students also exchange and comment on each other's dialogues as part of the requirement for class. This facilitates a rich sharing of diverse narratives that deepens the connections between persons in a class. As they see their own narratives within a rich tapestry of themes, they are enabled to imagine new story lines and plots for their lives, replacing those that have limited their freedom and capacity to love with all their being.

Last year one of my students, a director of a children's theater, shared with me how the class Psychology and Spirituality of Women encouraged her to make some feminist revisions in the play *Cinderella* she was directing with some pre-adolescent girls. The changes she made evoked stories from the young actresses of feeling freed up, empowered, and feeling more of themselves.

Feminist Pedagogues as Contemplative Artists

Feminist and womanist teaching at its best maintains the attitude of a contemplative artist. The teaching task begins with an awareness of the subject before one. Contemplative artists acquaint themselves with the subject before them, before they try to bring their craft to bear. A sculptor studies the stone, a wood-carver the grain of wood, the artist the setting of the painting. Feminist and womanist teaching places primacy on relationships and connections and therefore must begin with the subject of education, the persons before us. Whom we teach precedes what we teach.

The teaching of pastoral theology and care is not first about technique, but begins with contemplative attention to the subject before one. Abraham Heschel once said, "All things are holy, but the human being is God's holy of holies." The subjects of our teaching are indeed God's holy of holies and therefore deserving of not only our respect, but also reverence for the mystery of their person–a mystery we can enter into relation to, but never fully grasp or know. Yet a beginning knowledge of who is in the classroom becomes the first act of care in teaching.

Contemplative artists are those fully awake to the possibilities of the moment, having what teachers of Zen call a "beginner's mind," meaning a willingness to come to things fresh. Academia is dangerous terrain for the discipline of cultivating the beginner's mind because mastery, expertise, and specialization are honored more than receptive openness to the other. The beginner's mind requires a kenosis of self-sufficient expertise and knowing, a radical opening to what or who is before us that deepens perceptions. When this happens, there is a transformation of relationship.

When one dwells with what one is contemplating, one begins to see in a new way, and the possibility of self-transcendence emerges. Barbara McClintock, the Nobel prize-winning geneticist, offers this description: "Well, you know when I look at a cell I get down in that cell and look around."[18] "As you look at these things under the microscope they become part of you. And you forget yourself. The main thing about it is that you forget yourself."[19]

One winter day I was given an unusual teaching moment to awaken the contemplative artist in my students. I awoke one morning to see the world around me transformed. Overnight an ice storm had transfigured a barren winter landscape into a scene of surreal, startling, excruciating beauty. As I arrived on campus people were out with cameras, walking with mouths open and hearts undone, eyes misty with tears, ears hearing sounds never heard before, and with gratitude exploding for this most unexpected gift. All were married to amazement and embraced by wonder.

It felt like blasphemy to the Holy Spirit to require students to sit in a windowless classroom for three hours when nature was lavishing its extraordinary power to transform sight, hearing, and perception. Seizing the moment, I assigned students a forty-five minute walk to contemplate the fragility and beauty of the world around them and to listen to what this walk through nature's paradise of beauty and treacherous terrain had to teach them about pastoral care. The metaphors that emerged from that walk about care and the stories it evoked transformed the class into one of my most memorable.

Contemplative artists and feminist pedagogues are also mindful of physical space and its impact on the learning environment. How are chairs and desks arranged? Where does the class meet? Where is the focus in the room? Teaching well requires creating environments where the aesthetics of teaching matter and where the whole person is invited into the learning process.

The contemplative artist knows how to open up the borders of the possible, where the environment grows in richness and diversity, where there is more room, not less, for persons to bring their fullness and wholeness as persons. Beauty, ritual, timing, process, and mutuality create the kind of environment where persons can grow into their own fullness. Contemplative artists know the power of ritual to sanctify space and community.

Feminist teachers might begin class with the lighting of a candle to remind students that the classroom is not less sacred a space than a sanctuary. One might close classes with rituals in order to hold and empower the community gathered to go forth. Ritualization becomes a way of embodying what we know and sanctifying space and time by helping people dwell fully in the present.

Poets and artists cannot do their work without imagination, without a sense of play. And yet, when we cross the boundary into the world of imagination and to methodologies that deviate substantially from the traditional lecture, discussion, or seminar, we may feel we are inhabiting a foreign land where we may be called alien or, worst of all, not serious enough, not scholarly enough. The pressures to stay within the boundaries to maintain legitimacy and respect press in upon us with the seduction of conformity.

Feminist Pedagogues as Reticent Outlaws in the Classroom

Many women pastoral theologians, when you speak to them privately, harbor fears that they are outlaws in a world where the rules and laws of the academy have been carved out by different visions of what constitutes education. A secret fear is that we are a bit "deviant" according to the standards of the academy. These rules and practices have tended to honor and value the rational over the emotive, analysis over synthesis, the objective over the subjective, the hard over the soft, the linear over the circular, the empirical over the imaginative, argument over empathy, head over heart, compartmentalization over integration, specialization over generalization, product over process.

Women pastoral theologians carry the fear of being doubly marginalized. We are often perceived by colleagues as being in a "soft" field, not the "hard" (classical) disciplines. The use of nontraditional methodologies that draw from the other side of binary oppositions risks greater vulnerability for not being taken as seriously by colleagues, even while students flock to feminists' classes with a hunger for what we have to offer.

Women who incorporate the use of the arts and nontraditional methodologies in classes may feel that we are doing it on the sly. We grin sheepishly as we are "caught" bringing clay into class for an exercise, and the voice inside says, "They do not think I'm doing serious teaching." We sit in silence in a class of prayer and wonder if we will be found out for not filling the time with more academic material. We take students on field trips to a play or an art exhibit, and we fear others consider it a form of playing hooky. A fear of exposure may haunt us, believing that "if they really knew what I was doing, I wouldn't have a chance for tenure or promotion." We fear and dread male disapproval because of the power that often accompanies it. Although most of us want to believe we are far past this, "the power of a whisper of male disapproval to unbalance us" lurks in our psyches.[20]

I remember well that for the first seven years I taught a course called Spiritual Resources for Healing, I was very reluctant to share what I was doing in this class with others. I felt I was on the outer reaches of the boundary of the academy and was fearful of being found to be illegitimate—even though student after student would tell me that this class had a major transformative impact on her life and prayer. Why my hesitancy? We began the class by spending an hour in silence, in prayer and meditation. The ethos was a combination of retreat and classroom, church and the academy, and the resources for healing being explored took us into the interior landscape of our souls.

Some of us may feel captive to some unwritten rules and assumptions in which we had no hand, but are expected to implement and obey. Yet many of us who are feminist and womanist pedagogues perceive ourselves, more often than not, tuned in to another frequency, where we are listening for different voices and sounds from those found on the conventional channel of the academy. Transformation often comes at moments when we are willing to step out of the usual mode of things, when we are willing to risk unconventionality and being considered outrageous. Transformative teachers are risk takers.

Women in our field experience themselves as outlaws when they deviate from usual ways of evaluating performance. The use of a process where students are coparticipants in the evaluative procedures and therefore codeterminers of final evaluation flies in the face of traditional expectations of the teacher as the sole evaluator. When women use appropriate forms of self-disclosure, they often feel they are crossing a forbidden boundary. When women risk writing on feminist methodologies in a university context that evaluates scholarship along traditional male standards, they may experience themselves as outlaws and vulnerable. When women name God using feminine appellations, they experience themselves again and again as being outlaws where the rules of patriarchy still dictate.

To be a feminist, in most places, means to choose the fact that you will always reside somewhat on the margins of the institution. This can be a place of creative tension, but also at times a lonely place and a place of discomfort. Women academics tend to ask ourselves, "What am I doing here?" "Who am I to be teaching this?" When we deviate from the tried and true norms around us, we wonder, "Will they sniff me out and find out the truth—I'm not the real thing?"

Such questions lead women to feel like impostors and frauds. And when we feel like impostors and frauds, we want to hide and cover up what we know and what we do as somehow subversive or deviant. Yet we must risk exposure if our praxis is going to help transform the academy and the church into more life-giving and liberating environments. When we give up our power to make ourselves and our work in the classroom known, we also give up the power to shape theological education toward emancipatory praxis and thereby abdicate our power to also influence transformative practices in the church.

Less than full belonging may simply be an essential component of our work. Patricia Collins rightly states that "marginality provides a distinctive angle of vision."[21] African American women know in a particularly painful way what it means to be outsiders in academic discourse and social and political thought. Many black women have had "the outsider-within" experience that is part of being embedded in a white culture, but not fully belonging to it. And yet from this place they have an indispensable angle of vision to offer to feminist thought. Alice Walker describes well the impact that an outsider-within stance had on her own thinking: "I believe...that it was from this period–from my solitary, lonely position, the position of an outcast, that I began to see people and things, really to notice relationships."[22]

Finding out how to be at home on the margin is part of feminists' work in the academy. Simultaneously we need to recognize that our deepest longing is that the concerns we hold central become part of the mainstream so that real change and transformation may take place. Many of us feel conflicted, besieged, frustrated, exhausted, and often lonely, but simultaneously challenged, enlivened, and with a convicted sense that even though we live on the margin, this is precisely where we are supposed to be.

Notes

Introduction

[1] Anton T. Boisen, *The Exploration of the Inner World: A Study of Mental Disorder and Religious Experience* (Chicago, New York: Willett, Clark and Company, 1936; New York: Harper & Brothers, 1962), 2. Cf. also Anton T. Boisen, *Out of the Depths: An Autobiographical Study of Mental Disorder and Religious Experience* (New York: Harper & Brothers, 1960), in which Boisen mentions, for example, that he was circumcised at age four for what were perceived as too-frequent erections. He adds, however, that since in his case this "sex-organ excitation which seemed beyond the normal" was actually "primarily psychical, the treatment failed to correct it" (p. 24). He later writes: "It is only with difficulty that I am able to recall the steps in the development of the inner conflict which has given me so much trouble. I seldom discussed the subject of sex with other boys, not even with my most intimate friends, and I had little dealing with girls. But all the while, I was extremely sensitive on the subject, and the entire realm of sex was for me at once fascinating and terrifying. The essence of the difficulty lay thus in the fact that these sexual interests could neither be controlled nor acknowledged for fear of condemnation" (p. 43).

[2] See Glenn H. Asquith Jr., ed., "Introduction," in *Vision from a Little Known Country: A Boisen Reader* (Decatur, Ga.: Journal of Pastoral Care Publications, 1992), 5–6.

[3] See Carol North and William M. Clements, "The Psychiatric Diagnosis of Anton Boisen: From Schizophrenia to Bipolar Affective Disorder," in *Vision from a Little Known Country,* 213–28.

[4] See Henri J. M. Nouwen, "Anton T. Boisen and Theology Through Living Human Documents," in *Vision from a Little Known Country,* 157–75.

[5] Donald Capps, *Reframing: A New Method in Pastoral Care* (Minneapolis: Fortress Press, 1990), 178.

[6] Nina Coltart, *Slouching Towards Bethlehem* (New York: Guilford Press, 1992), 2.

[7] Bonnie J. Miller-McLemore, "The Living Human Web: Pastoral Theology at the Turn of the Century," in *Through the Eyes of Women: Insights for Pastoral Care,* ed. Jeanne Stevenson Moessner (Minneapolis: Fortress Press, 1996), 21–22.

[8] James E. Dittes, "Some Accidents, Coincidents, and Intents: A Vocational Narrative," *Pastoral Psychology* 52/1–2 (November 2003): 13.

[9] D. W. Winnicott, "Yes, But How Do We Know It's True?" in *Thinking About Children,* ed. Ray Shepherd, Jennifer Johns, and Helen Taylor Robinson (Reading, Mass.: Addison-Wesley Publishing, 1996), 13–14.

[10] John Wisdom, *Paradox and Discovery* (Oxford: Basil Blackwell, 1965), 138, quoted in Charles M. Wood, *Vision and Discernment: An Orientation in Theological Study* (Atlanta: Scholars Press, 1985), 77.

[11] William James, "The Gospel of Relaxation," in *William James: Writings 1878–1899,* ed. Gerald E. Myers (New York: Literary Classics of the United States, Inc., 1992), 831; and William James, "The Importance of Individuals," in *The Will to Believe and Other Essays in Popular Philosophy* (New York: Dover Publications, Inc., 1956), 256–57.

[12] See, e.g., Dean Hamer and Peter Copeland, *The Science of Desire: The Search for the Gay Gene and the Biology of Behavior* (New York: Simon & Schuster, 1994), 211.

[13] James, *The Will to Believe,* 259.

[14] Valerie DeMarinis, *Critical Caring: A Feminist Model for Pastoral Psychology* (Louisville: Westminster John Knox Press, 1993), 12. I have not devoted a chapter to her intriguing metaphor for ministry because she discusses it in the space of only a few paragraphs.

[15] Ibid., 13.

[16] Adam Phillips, *Terrors and Experts* (Cambridge: Harvard University Press, 1995), 19.

[17] William James, *A Pluralistic Universe* (1909; reprint, Lincoln: University of Nebraska Press, 1996), 45–46.

[18] One encouraging example is Donald Capps, *Living Stories: Pastoral Counseling in Congregational Context* (Minneapolis: Fortress Press, 1998), especially its introduction and chapter 1.

Part 1: Classical Images of Care

[1]Anton T. Boisen, *The Exploration of the Inner World: A Study of Mental Disorder and Religious Experience* (Chicago, New York: Willett, Clark and Company, 1936), 5.

[2]Ibid., 8.

[3]Ibid., 11.

[4]In *The Exploration of the Inner World,* Boisen speaks appreciatively of William James's *The Varieties of Religious Experience: A Study of Human Nature* (1902), from which he appears to have appropriated, without acknowledgment, James's term *documents humains* in describing hospitalized psychiatric patients as living human documents. In William James, *The Varieties of Religious Experience: A Study in Human Nature* (1902; reprint, New York: Penguin Books, 1982), 3, James writes: "The *documents humains* which we shall find most instructive need not then be sought for in the haunts of special erudition—they lie along the beaten highway..." Compare Boisen (1936), 10–11: "I wanted [seminary students] to learn to read human documents as well as books, particularly those revealing documents which are opened up at the inner day of judgment," and, again reminiscent of James above, "[My work] propose[s] to examine, in the light of my own experience, the experiences of other persons who have been forced off the beaten path of common sense and have traveled through the little-known wilderness of the inner life." On Boisen's familiarity with James's *The Varieties,* see Boisen, *Exploration of the Inner World,* 89–90.

[5]Charles V. Gerkin, *The Living Human Document: Re-Visioning Pastoral Counseling in a Hermeneutical Mode* (Nashville: Abingdon Press, 1984), 30.

[6]Ibid., 26.

[7]Ibid., 38.

[8]Ibid., 27.

[9]Ibid., 38.

[10]Ibid., 43.

[11]Bonnie J. Miller-McLemore, "The Living Human Web: Pastoral Theology at the Turn of the Century," in *Through the Eyes of Women: Insights for Pastoral Care,* ed. Jeanne Stevenson Moessner (Minneapolis: Fortress Press, 1996), 17, quoting Catherine Keller, *From a Broken Web: Separatism, Sexism, and Self* (Boston: Beacon Press, 1986), 228.

[12]Miller-McLemore, "Living Human Web," 22.

[13]Ibid., 21.

[14]See Bonnie J. Miller-McLemore, *Let the Children Come: Reimagining Childhood from a Christian Perspective* (San Francisco: Jossey-Bass, 2003), 26–30, for a more recent discussion on the dismissive attitude toward psychology by some theologians.

[15]Miller-McLemore, "Living Human Web," 18.

[16]Seward Hiltner, "The Christian Shepherd," in *Pastoral Psychology,* 10, no. 92 (March 1959): 47–54. This essay elaborates on what is considered Hiltner's most influential book, *Preface to Pastoral Theology* (Nashville: Abingdon Press, 1958), published in the previous year.

[17]Hiltner, *Preface to Pastoral Theology,* 6–50.

[18]Ibid., 50.

[19]Alastair V. Campbell, *Rediscovering Pastoral Care* (Philadelphia: Westminster Press, 1981), 42.

[20]Ibid., 42.

[21]Ibid., 44.

[22]Ibid., 45.

[23]Jeanne Stevenson Moessner, "A New Pastoral Paradigm and Practice," in *Women in Travail and Transition: A New Pastoral Care,* ed. Maxine Glaz and Jeanne Stevenson Moessner (Minneapolis: Fortress Press, 1991), 198–225.

[24]Ibid., 203.

[25]With the possible additional exceptions of Boisen's living human document and Miller-McLemore's living human web, for example, nearly all the images of care in this book draw greater attention to the person and role of the minister or caregiver. This is true even of the model of the self-differentiated Samaritan, notwithstanding Stevenson Moessner's critique of Hiltner's alleged hierarchical privileging of shepherd over sheep. In terms of Boisen's misgivings about the tendency in clinical pastoral training in his day to focus increasingly on the psychological life of students as much as or more than that of patients, Hiltner himself reports: "[A]lthough Boisen was pleased to see the basic idea [of clinical pastoral education] spread, there were aspects that Boisen feared might subvert his basic intent, i.e., the study of

theology via living human documents. In various degrees he gradually disassociated himself from the formal bodies. For a time a group of younger leaders of the movement, while properly deferential to Boisen as the founder and grandfather, nevertheless paid little attention to his ideas and convictions" (Seward Hiltner, "The Heritage of Anton T. Boisen," in *Vision from a Little Known Country: A Boisen Reader,* ed. Glenn H. Asquith Jr. [Decatur, Ga.: Journal of Pastoral Care Publications, 1992], 140). Henri J. M. Nouwen, reflecting on what Boisen himself once described as "growing pains," likewise writes of Boisen's reactions to some of the developments of the early Council for Clinical Training movement: "At Elgin State Hospital, where [Boisen] was chaplain from 1931 and where he began, as he says, a "vigorous" training program, he was succeeded by a man who worked along lines quite contradictory to his own ideas. The first new development was the growing attention to the pastoral conversation, which asked for a careful analysis of verbatim reports. [Russell] Dicks 'discovered' this method. But Boisen was critical of its lack of psychodynamics. The second development was a growing interest in the relationship between supervisor and trainee. The psychotherapeutic milieu had helped to focus on this aspect of the pastoral training. However, Boisen was afraid not only of the unchristian inspiration of certain psychotherapeutic theories but also of a shift in emphasis from the patient to the student" (Henri J. M. Nouwen, "Anton T. Boisen and Theology Through Living Human Documents," in *Vision from a Little Known Country,* 172–73).

Chapter 1: The Living Human Document

[1]Excerpts from Anton T. Boisen, *The Exploration of the Inner World: A Study of Mental Disorder and Religious Experience* (Chicago, New York: Willett, Clark and Company, 1936).

[2]Editor's note: Elsewhere, Boisen preferred the term "living human documents," as, e.g., in 1930, where in the founding charter of the Council for Clinical Training of Theological Students, Boisen stated that "living human documents are the primary sources for any intelligent attempt to understand human nature" (cited in Fred Eastman, "Father of the Clinical Pastoral Movement," *Journal of Pastoral Care,* 5, no. 1 [Spring 1951]: 3–7); and again later, in 1950, when Boisen stated in his address to the Silver Anniversary Conference of Clinical Pastoral Training: "Let me also emphasize the fact that this movement, as I have conceived of it, has no new gospel to proclaim. We are not even seeking to introduce anything new into the theological curriculum beyond a new approach to some ancient problems. We are trying, rather, to call attention back to the central task of the church, that of 'saving souls,' and to the central problem of theology, that of sin and salvation. What is new is the attempt to begin with the study of living human documents rather than with books and to focus attention upon those who are grappling desperately with the issues of spiritual life and death" (Anton T. Boisen, "The Period of Beginnings," *Journal of Pastoral Care,* 5, no. 1 [Spring 1951]: 13–16; emphasis in original).

Chapter 2: Reclaiming the Living Human Document

[1]Excerpts from Charles V. Gerkin, *The Living Human Document: Re-visioning Pastoral Counseling in a Hermeneutical Mode* (Nashville: Abingdon Press, 1984).

[2]Anton T. Boisen, *The Exploration of the Inner World: A Study of Mental Disorder and Religious Experience* (Chicago, New York: Willett, Clark and Company, 1936; New York: Harper & Brothers, 1962), 11.

Chapter 3: The Living Human Web

[1]Excerpts from Bonnie J. Miller-McLemore, "The Living Human Web: Pastoral Theology at the Turn of the Century," in *Through the Eyes of Women: Insights for Pastoral Care,* ed. Jeanne Stevenson Moessner (Minneapolis: Fortress Press, 1996), 9–26.

[2]bell hooks, *Feminist Theory: From Margin to Center* (Boston: South End Press, 1984), 26.

[3]Charles V. Gerkin, *The Living Human Document: Revisioning Pastoral Counseling in a Hermeneutical Mode* (Nashville: Abingdon Press, 1984), 37.

[4]Catherine Keller, *From a Broken Web: Separatism, Sexism, and Self* (Boston: Beacon Press, 1986).

[5]Ibid., 137.

[6]Ibid., 218.

[7]Ibid., 228.

[8]Maxine Glaz, "A New Pastoral Understanding of Women," in *Women in Travail and Transition: A New Pastoral Care,* ed. Maxine Glaz and Jeanne Stevenson Moessner (Minneapolis: Fortress Press, 1991), 12, 29.

[9]E. Brooks Holifield, *A History of Pastoral Care in America: From Salvation to Self-Realization* (Nashville: Abingdon Press, 1983).

[10]Howard Clinebell, *Basic Types of Pastoral Care and Counseling: Resources for the Ministry of Healing and Growth* (Nashville: Abingdon Press, 1966; revised and enlarged 1984).

[11]David W. Augsburger, *Pastoral Counseling Across Cultures* (Philadelphia: Westminster Press, 1986).

[12]Ibid., 14.

[13]Valerie M. DeMarinis, *Critical Caring: A Feminist Model for Pastoral Psychology* (Louisville: Westminster John Knox Press, 1993).

[14]Christie Cozad Neuger, "Feminist Pastoral Theology and Pastoral Counseling: A Work in Progress," *Journal of Pastoral Theology* 2 (Summer 1992): 35–57.

[15]Carrie Doehring, "Developing Models of Feminist Pastoral Counseling," in *Journal of Pastoral Care* 46, no. 1 (Spring 1992): 23–31.

[16]Archie Smith Jr., *The Relational Self: Ethics and Therapy from a Black Church Perspective* (Nashville: Abingdon Press, 1982).

[17]Edward P. Wimberly, *Pastoral Care in the Black Church* (Nashville: Abingdon Press, 1979).

[18]Linda H. Hollies, ed., *WomanistCare: How to Tend the Souls of Women* (Joliet, Ill.: Woman to Woman Ministries, 1992).

[19]Emilie M. Townes, *A Troubling in My Soul: Womanist Perspectives on Evil and Suffering* (Maryknoll, N.Y.: Orbis Books, 1993).

[20]Emma J. Justes, "Women," in *Clinical Handbook of Pastoral Counseling*, ed. Robert J. Wicks, Richard D. Parsons, and Donald E. Capps (New York: Paulist Press, 1985), 279–99, quote on 298.

[21]Maxine Glaz, "Reconstructing the Pastoral Care of Women," in *Second Opinion* 17, no. 2 (October 1991): 94–107.

[22]Bonnie J. Miller-McLemore, *Also a Mother: Work and Family as Theological Dilemma* (Nashville: Abingdon Press, 1994).

[23]Pamela D. Couture, *Blessed Are the Poor? Women's Poverty, Family Policy, and Practical Theology* (Nashville: Abingdon Press, 1991).

[24]Carroll Saussy, *God Images and Self Esteem: Empowering Women in a Patriarchal Society* (Louisville: Westminster John Knox Press, 1991).

[25]Glaz and Stevenson Moessner, *Women in Travail*, vi.

[26]Robert J. Wicks and Barry K. Estadt, eds., *Pastoral Counseling in a Global Church: Voices from the Field* (Maryknoll, N.Y.: Orbis Books, 1993).

[27]Anton Boisen, *The Exploration of the Inner World: A Study of Mental Disorder and Religious Experience* (Chicago, New York: Willett, Clark and Company, 1936; New York: Harper & Brothers, 1962).

Chapter 4: The Solicitous Shepherd

[1]Excerpts from Seward Hiltner, "The Christian Shepherd," in *Pastoral Theology* 10, no. 92 (March 1959): 47–54.

[2]The reader interested in an elaboration of these distinctions may consult Seward Hiltner, *Preface to Pastoral Theology* (Nashville: Abingdon Press, 1958).

[3]I have elaborated this point in ch. 6 of *Preface to Pastoral Theology*.

Chapter 5: The Courageous Shepherd

[1]Excerpts from Alastair V. Campbell, "The Shepherd's Courage," in *Rediscovering Pastoral Care* (Philadelphia: Westminster Press, 1981), 36–45.

[2]Jean Vanier, *Tears of Silence* (London: Darton, Longman & Todd, 1973), 25.

[3]Gerhard Kittel, ed., *Theological Dictionary of the New Testament*, Vol. 6 (Grand Rapids: Wm. B. Eerdmans, 1968), 487.

[4]E.g., Ps. 23:1–4; Jer. 23:3; Ezek. 34:11–22; Isa. 40:10f. See also Mic. 4:6–8.

[5]See James D. G. Dunn, *Unity and Diversity in the New Testament* (London: SCM Press, 1977; Philadelphia: Westminster Press, 1977), 118f., 398, n. 20.

[6]See A. Vinet, *Pastoral Theology* (London: T. & T. Clark, 1852); and Fairbairn, *Pastoral Theology,* for examples of this approach.

[7]For example, J. J. van Oosterzee, *Pastoral Theology* (London: Hodder & Stoughton, 1878).

[8]See, for example, the emphasis on professionalism in Seward Hiltner's discussion of "The Layman as Pastoral Theologian" in *Preface to Pastoral Theology* (Nashville: Abingdon Press, 1958), 37–39.

[9]An expansion of this criticism will be found in Alastair Campbell, "Is Practical Theology Possible?" *Scottish Journal of Theology* 25, no. 2 (May 1972).

[10]See ch. 2 of Seward Hiltner, *The Christian Shepherd* (Nashville: Abingdon Press, 1959); and also ch. 1 of his *Preface to Pastoral Theology.*

[11]These parables are referred to briefly in Hiltner's *The Christian Shepherd.*

[12]See Wayne E. Oates, *When Religion Gets Sick* (Philadelphia: Westminster Press, 1970).

Chapter 6: The Self-Differentiated Samaritan

[1]Excerpts from Jeanne Stevenson Moessner, "A New Pastoral Paradigm and Practice," in *Women in Travail and Transition: A New Pastoral Care,* ed. Maxine Glaz and Jeanne Stevenson Moessner (Minneapolis: Fortress Press, 1991), 198–211.

[2]Lillian B. Rubin, *Women of a Certain Age: The Midlife Search for Self* (New York: Harper and Row, 1979), 50–51, 59.

[3]Orlo Strunk, *The Secret Self* (Nashville: Abingdon Press, 1976), 96.

[4]Linda Tschirhart Sanford and Mary Ellen Donovan, *Women and Self-Esteem: Understanding and Improving the Way We Think and Feel About Ourselves* (New York: Penguin Books, 1984), 13.

[5]Rubin, *Women of a Certain Age,* 68.

[6]Valerie Saiving, "The Human Situation: A Feminine View," in *Womanspirit Rising* (San Francisco: Harper & Row, 1979), 37.

[7]Rubin, *Women of a Certain Age,* 68.

[8]Christine Downing, "Gender Anxiety," *Journal of Pastoral Care* 43 (Summer 1989): 156.

[9]Charles V. Gerkin, in response to Don Browning and James Lapsley, "On Beginning a New Chapter: Pastoral Theology as a Practical Theology of Care," paper for the Society of Pastoral Theology, Denver, 27 June 1986, 7.

[10]Seward Hiltner, *Preface to Pastoral Theology* (Nashville: Abingdon Press, 1958).

[11]Carroll A. Wise, *The Meaning of Pastoral Care* (Bloomington, Ind.: Meyer Stone Books, 1989), 2.

[12]Marie Fortune, *Is Nothing Sacred? When Sex Invades the Pastoral Relationship* (San Francisco, Harper & Row, 1989).

[13]Dietrich Stollberg, Therapeutische Seelsorge. *Die amerkanishe Seelsorgebewegung. Darstellung und Kritik. Mit einer Dokumentation.* Studien zur praktischen Theologie Nr. 6 (Munchen: Kaiser Verlag, 1969).

[14]Friedrich Wintzer, ed., *Seelsorge: Texte zum gewandelten Verständis und zur Praxis der Seelsorge in der Neuzeit* (Munchen: Kaiser Verlag, 1978).

[15]Carol Gilligan, *In a Different Voice* (Cambridge: Harvard University Press, 1982), 74.

[16]See Jean Baker Miller's "The Development of Women's Sense of Self," *Work in Progress* 12 of the Stone Center for Developmental Sciences and Studies at Wellesley College, Massachusetts (1984): 4.

[17]The reader is referred to another work in progress: Janet L. Surrey's "Self-in-Relation: A Theory of Women's Development," *Work in Progress* 13 (1985).

[18]Diogenes Allen, *Love: Christian Romance, Marriage, Friendship* (Cambridge, Mass.: Cowley Publications, 1987), 12.

[19]J. R. Jones, "Love as Perception of Meaning," in *Religion and Understanding* (New York: MacMillan, 1967), 149–50, quoted in Allen, *Love,* 12.

[20]Allen, *Love,* 21.

[21]Sanford and Donovan, *Women and Self-Esteem,* 160–74.

[22]Ibid., 162.

Part 2: Paradoxical Images of Care

[1]Henri J. M. Nouwen, *The Wounded Healer: Ministry in Contemporary Society* (Garden City, N.Y.: Image Books, 1972), 84.

[2]Ibid., 88.
[3]Ibid., 90.
[4]Ibid., 91.
[5]Ibid., 92.
[6]Seward Hiltner, "Foreword," in Heije Faber, *Pastoral Care in the Modern Hospital,* trans. Hugo de Waal (Philadelphia: Westminster Press, 1971), viii.
[7]Faber, *Pastoral Care,* 83.
[8]Alastair V. Campbell, *Rediscovering Pastoral Care* (Philadelphia: Westminster Press, 1981), 55.
[9]Ibid., 58–59, 62.
[10]Ibid., 70.
[11]Donald Capps, *Reframing: A New Method in Pastoral Care* (Minneapolis: Fortress Press, 1990).
[12]Robert C. Dykstra, "Intimate Strangers: The Role of the Hospital Chaplain in Situations of Sudden Traumatic Loss," *Journal of Pastoral Care* 44, no. 2 (Summer 1990): 139–52.
[13]James E. Dittes, *Pastoral Counseling: The Basics* (Louisville: Westminster John Knox Press, 1999), 65–66.
[14]Ibid., 61.
[15]Ibid., 57.
[16]Ibid., 76.
[17]Ibid., 79.

Chapter 7: The Wounded Healer

[1]Excerpts from ch. 4, "Ministry by a Lonely Minister: The Wounded Healer," in Henri J. M. Nouwen, *The Wounded Healer: Ministry in Contemporary Society* (Garden City, N.Y.: Image Books, 1972), 79–96.
[2]See James Hillman: *Insearch* (New York: Charles Scribner's Sons, 1967), 18.
[3]Ibid., 31.

Chapter 8: The Circus Clown

[1]Excerpts from Heije Faber, "The Minister in the Hospital," in *Pastoral Care in the Modern Hospital,* trans. Hugo de Waal (Philadelphia: Westminster Press, 1971), 81–92.
[2]Heinrich Böll, *The Clown* (London: Weidenfeld and Nicolson, 1965).
[3]The title of an excellent book by R. Kaptein, *De predikant, zyn plaats enzyn taak in een nieuwe wereld* (Hilversum: Paul Brand, 1966).

Chapter 9: The Wise Fool

[1]Excerpts from Alastair V. Campbell, "Wise Folly," in *Rediscovering Pastoral Care* (Philadelphia: Westminster Press, 1981), 55–71.
[2]From Gerard Manley Hopkins, "Pied Beauty," in *The Faber Book of Modern Verse,* ed. Michael Roberts (London: Faber & Faber, 1960), 61.
[3]See Enid Welsford, *The Fool: His Social and Literary History* (London: Faber & Faber, 1935); William Willeford, *The Fool and His Sceptre* (London: Edward Arnold, 1969); and John Saward, *Perfect Fools* (Oxford University Press, 1980).
[4]Søren Kierkegaard, *The Journals of Kierkegaard 1834–1854,* ed. and trans. Alexander Dru (William Collons Sons & Co., Fontana Book, 1958), 54.
[5]Søren Kierkegaard, *Philosophical Fragments,* trans. David F. Swenson (Princeton: Princeton University Press, 1936), 50.
[6]Idries Shah, *The Exploits of the Incomparable Mulla Nasrudin* (London: Pan Books, Picador ed., 1973), 22.
[7]William Shakespeare, *As You Like It,* Act V, Scene 4.
[8]Erasmus, *Praise of Folly,* or *Moriae Encomium.* The original Latin title enshrines a pun, since the work was dedicated to his friend Thomas More.
[9]Erasmus, *Praise of Folly,* trans. Betty Radice (Penguin Classics, 1971), 201.
[10]Ibid., 198.
[11]See Welsford, *The Fool,* Part II.

[12]Fyodor Dostoevsky, *The Idiot,* trans. David Magarshack (Penguin Books, 1955), 149.

[13]William Shakespeare, *King Lear,* Act III, Scene 1.

[14]Ibid., Act II, Scene 4.

[15]The heroism of the fool is always tempered by his fearfulness and his dislike of the uncomfortable state that "nuncle" has got them both into. He remains convincingly a Court Fool, but one whose loyalty evokes high praise from some commentators: e.g., "He is the supremely wise fool who expresses in his heartfelt devotion to Cordelia and to his King the Christian virtues of patience, humility, and love" (R. H. Goldsmith, *Wise Fools in Shakespeare* [Liverpool: University Press of Liverpool, 1958], 67). See also Walter J. Kaiser, *Praisers of Folly* (London: Victor Gollancz, 1964), 99.

[16]For a discussion of the pathos in clowning, see M. W. Disher, *Clowns and Pantomimes* (Constable, 1925), especially his study of Grock, 203ff. The clown paintings of Georges Rouault are also illuminating in this regard.

[17]Wolfgang M. Zucker, "The Clown as the Lord of Disorder," *Theology Today* 24, no. 3 (Oct. 1967): 316.

[18]See Harvey Cox, *The Feast of Fools* (Cambridge: Harvard University Press, 1969), 3; Welsford, *The Fool,* 199ff; Zucker, "The Clown," 313.

[19]For a complete list, see Georg Fohrer, *History of Israelite Religion,* trans. David E. Green (London: SPCK, 1973), 240.

[20]Heije Faber, *Pastoral Care in the Modern Hospital,* trans. Hugo de Waal (London: SCM Press, 1971; Philadelphia: Westminster Press, 1972), 81–92.

[21]S. H. Miller, "The Clown in Contemporary Art," *Theology Today* 24, no. 3 (Oct. 1967): 327.

[22]Kahlil Gibran, *The Prophet* (London: William Heinemann, 1976), 71.

[23]T. S. Eliot, "Little Gidding," in *Four Quartets* (London: Faber & Faber, 1959), 59.

[24]William Shakespeare, *King Lear,* Act I, Scene 4.

[25]See Henri Nouwen, *The Living Reminder* (New York: Seabury Press, 1977), for a most helpful discussion of the pastoral significance of the absence of Jesus.

[26]Alan Watts, *Beyond Theology: The Art of Godmanship* (New York: Vintage Books, 1973), 211.

Chapter 10: The Wise Fool Reframed

[1]Excerpts from Donald Capps, "Introduction" and ch. 8, "The Wise Fool Reframes," in *Reframing: A New Method in Pastoral Care* (Minneapolis: Fortress Press, 1990), 1–8 and 169–82. Scripture quotations are Capps's translation.

[2]Howard J. Clinebell Jr., *Basic Types of Pastoral Counseling* (Nashville: Abingdon Press, 1966).

[3]Howard J. Clinebell Jr., *Basic Types of Pastoral Care and Counseling: Resources for the Ministry of Healing and Growth* (Nashville: Abingdon Press, 1984).

[4]Richard Bandler and John Grinder, *Reframing: Neuro-Linguistic Programming* (Moab, Utah: Real People Press, 1979).

[5]Paul Watzlawick, John Weakland, and Richard Fisch, *Change: Principles of Problem Formation and Problem Resolution* (New York: W. W. Norton, 1974).

[6]Ibid., 10–11.

[7]Ibid., 31–32.

[8]Ibid., 48.

[9]Ibid., 50.

[10]Ibid., 62.

[11]See Paul Watzlawick, Janet Beavin Barelas, and Don D. Jackson, *Pragmatics of Human Communication: A Study of Interactional Patterns, Pathologies, and Paradoxes* (New York: W. W. Norton, 1967), 200.

[12]Ibid., 210.

[13]Editor's note: In chapter 2 of *Reframing,* Capps identifies thirteen techniques that broadly constitute the method of reframing. These include the counselor's use of paradoxical intention, dereflection, deliberate confusion, advertising instead of concealing, the Belloc ploy, the "Why should you change?" technique, benevolent sabotage, the illusion of alternatives, providing a worse alternative, relabeling, preempting, and the surrender tactic. Donald Capps, *Agents of Hope: A Pastoral Psychology* (Minneapolis: Fortress Press, 1995), 163–176, adds the technique of future visioning (see also chapter 16 in this book), and Donald Capps, *Living Stories: Pastoral*

Counseling in Congregational Context (Minneapolis: Fortress Press, 1998), 92–124, presents the method of discovering a third alternative.

[14]Alastair V. Campbell, *Rediscovering Pastoral Care* (Philadelphia: Westminster Press, 1981).

[15]Seward Hiltner, *The Christian Shepherd* (Nashville: Abingdon Press, 1959); *Preface to Pastoral Theology* (Nashville: Abingdon Press, 1958).

[16]Henri Nouwen, *The Wounded Healer* (Garden City, N.Y.: Doubleday and Company, 1972).

[17]Heije Faber, *Pastoral Care in the Modern Hospital* (Philadelphia: Fortress Press, 1984), 70–81.

[18]Campbell, *Rediscovering Pastoral Care,* 55.

[19]Ibid., 55–56.

[20]Ibid., 58–59.

[21]Ibid., 60.

[22]Ibid., 62.

[23]Paul Watzlawick, *The Situation Is Hopeless, But Not Serious: The Pursuit of Unhappiness* (New York: W. W. Norton & Company, 1983).

[24]Watzlawick, Weakland, and Fisch, *Change,* 55.

[25]Julien Green, *God's Fool: The Life and Times of Francis of Assisi,* trans. Peter Heinegg (San Francisco: Harper and Row, 1983).

[26]Campbell, *Rediscovering Pastoral Care,* 62.

[27]Ibid., 64.

[28]Ibid., 63–64.

[29]Ibid., 65.

[30]Ibid., 50.

[31]Ibid., 71.

[32]Rainer Maria Rilke, *Poems from the Book of Hours,* trans. Babette Deutsch (New York: New Directions Publishing Corporation, 1941), 31.

Chapter 11: The Intimate Stranger

[1]From Robert C. Dykstra, "Intimate Strangers: The Role of the Hospital Chaplain in Situations of Sudden Traumatic Loss," *Journal of Pastoral Care* 44, no. 2 (Fall 1990): 139–52.

[2]I have also considered the alternate possibility, i.e., that what happens to persons in the shock of these initial moments of the crisis may have very little bearing on the future meaning of this event. However, my colleagues and I have noticed that on many occasions of meeting victims of such loss months following the event, they approach us, graciously thank us, and describe what we did for them that day, often in great detail, while we in turn sometimes strain even to remember these persons or the situations in which we assisted them.

[3]E.g., David K. Switzer, *The Minister as Crisis Counselor* (Nashville: Abingdon Press, 1974, revised and expanded, 1986); Howard W. Stone, *Crisis Counseling* (Philadelphia: Fortress Press, 1976); and Howard Clinebell, *Basic Types of Pastoral Care and Counseling: Resources for the Ministry of Healing and Growth* (Nashville: Abingdon Press, 1984), especially ch. 8, "Crisis Care and Counseling," 183–217.

[4]Erich Lindemann, *Beyond Grief: Studies in Crisis Intervention* (New York: Jason Aronson, 1979). Gerald Caplan was Lindemann's associate at Harvard.

[5]E.g., Charles V. Gerkin, *Crisis Experience in Modern Life: Theory and Theology in Pastoral Care* (Nashville: Abingdon Press, 1979); Heije Faber, *Pastoral Care in the Modern Hospital,* trans. Hugo de Waal(Philadelphia: Westminster Press, 1971); and Thomas C. Oden, *Crisis Ministries* (New York: Crossroad, 1986).

[6]See Gerkin, *Crisis Experience in Modern Life,* 35.

[7]David K. Switzer, "Crisis Intervention and Problem Solving," in *Clinical Handbook of Pastoral Counseling,* ed. Robert J. Wicks, Richard D. Parsons, and Donald E. Capps (New York: Paulist Press, 1985), 134–36. He writes: "Merely to experience anxiety, of course, is not to be in crisis. Most people are confronted with events almost daily that pose threats of a certain degree, but also most people have learned methods of coping with these…But certain events, because of their radical newness in our lives, or because of their particular similarities to earlier situations which have produced great internal conflict or disruption and which have not been adequately resolved, produce a much greater sense of threat than we ordinarily experience."

[8]See, e.g., Faber, *Pastoral Care in the Modern Hospital,* 14.

⁹Patrick D. Miller, Jr., "Israel as Host to Strangers," in *Today's Immigrants and Refugees: A Christian Understanding* (Washington, D. C.: United States Catholic Conference, Inc., 1988), 1–19.

¹⁰Parker J. Palmer, *The Company of Strangers: Christians and the Renewal of America's Public Life* (New York: Crossroad, 1981).

¹¹Miller, "Israel as Host," 1, 10. See also Donald E. Gowan, "Wealth and Poverty in the Old Testament: The Case of the Widow, the Orphan, and the Sojourner," in *Interpretation: A Journal of Biblical Theology* 41, no. 4 (October 1987): 341–53.

¹²Miller, "Israel as Host," 3, quoting from W. Gesenius, *A Hebrew and English Lexicon to the Old Testament* (Oxford: Oxford University Press, 1959), 157.

¹³Miller, "Israel as Host," 4.

¹⁴Ibid., 4ff., 14.

¹⁵Ibid., 15.

¹⁶Ibid., 6. The label of each of these "rationales" is my own.

¹⁷Ibid., 16.

¹⁸Don Browning, "Hospital Chaplaincy as Public Ministry," in *Second Opinion: Health, Faith, and Ethics* (Park Ridge, Ill.: Lutheran General Health Care System, 1986), 67–75. Browning suggests that the hospital chaplain is the "supreme example of public ministry," that is, a ministry that "uses the resources of the Christian or Jewish faith to address an issue in the public world which will in some way help various individuals and groups but may not necessarily lead them to become Christians or Jews."

¹⁹Palmer, *The Company of Strangers*, 44, writes: "For instance, our private worlds seldom bring us into contact with the poor, the sick, the broken. In fact, we have put much energy into creating private worlds for each of these 'classes' of people so they will not haunt our lives. But in an authentic public life, where we would encounter all conditions, the more able among us might develop a deeper sense of our need and capacity to assist our less able brothers and sisters."

²⁰Ibid., 40–46.

²¹Ibid., 50–51, 58–59. Wayne E. Oates, *The Presence of God in Pastoral Counseling* (Waco: Word Books, 1986), 63, points out that psychosocial growth requires persons "repeatedly to break out of the safe confines of the people who are known and to become related to strange people…To mature sexually, one must go to a stranger. The conventional ethic throughout Scripture is that sex is…taboo with one's blood kin."

²²Palmer, *The Company of Strangers*, 107, 110.

²³Ibid., 67–68.

²⁴See Charles E. Rosenberg, *The Care of Strangers: The Rise of America's Hospital System* (New York: Basic Books, 1987).

²⁵Lindemann, *Beyond Grief*, 61–63.

²⁶E.g., Stone, *Crisis Counseling*, 12; Switzer "Crisis Intervention," 135; Clinebell, *Basic Types of Pastoral Care*, 185. Gerald Caplan's four steps in the formation of a crisis typically are cited: (1) original rise in tension from problem stimulus; (2) novelty of situation frustrates usual coping mechanisms, and a feeling of helplessness results; (3) "hitching up the belt" is attempted, with the person digging deep into a reserve of strength; and (4) decompensation and crisis occur if the usual means of coping with or reconceptualizing the problem event fail, and rigid, compulsive, ineffective behavior is the result. See also Switzer, *The Minister as Crisis Counselor*, 38–39.

²⁷Writers in this field often offer schemas or devices that may assist the helper in rapid entrance into and evaluation of the crisis; e.g., the ABC, ABCD, CFCF, or BASIC strategies. Cf., Switzer, *The Minister as Crisis Counselor*, 40, 65; Stone, *Crisis Counseling*, 32; Clinebell, *Basic Types of Pastoral Care*, 205–208.

²⁸Gerkin, *Crisis Experience in Modern Life*, 33, 101, is right in challenging this theme from a theological perspective.

²⁹Still, e.g., Lindemann, *Beyond Grief*, 75, recognizes that "comfort alone does not provide adequate assistance in the patient's grief work. He has to accept the pain of bereavement." Switzer, *The Minister as Crisis Counselor*, 45, likewise acknowledges that many crises leave "their residue of hurt," and that therefore "it is unrealistic to expect a person to be precisely the same as before." Despite these qualifiers, however, the interventionists' call for a very active type of caring in crisis ministry can exaggerate the sense that something indeed can be "done," e.g., for a couple who has lost their little baby.

[30]While there is clearly a necessary role for familiar and intimate friends in supporting the victim of a sudden loss, there is also a place for the one-time encounter with the stranger such as the chaplain. God's word sometimes may be heard more clearly in the one-time encounter with the stranger than in the on-going supportive relationships of intimates. Wayne E. Oates, *The Presence of God*, 62, makes a similar point: "Another facet of the meeting of a pastoral counselor with a stranger is that he or she may need desperately for you or me to be a stranger to them. They may tell you of person after person in their friendship and work associate groups to whom they could have talked if they had not known them so well. They need a person who does not know them, who for all personal purposes is foreign to their world, a 'neutral' ear."

[31]William B. Oglesby Jr., "Present Status and Future Prospects in Pastoral Theology," *Pastoral Psychology* 29, no. 1 (Fall 1980): 45.

Chapter 12: The Ascetic Witness

[1]Excerpts from James E. Dittes, "The Pastoral Counselor as Witness," in *Pastoral Counseling: The Basics* (Louisville: Westminster John Knox Press, 1999), 57–79.

Part 3: Contemporary and Contextual Imges of Care

[1]Bonnie J. Miller-McLemore, "The Living Human Web: Pastoral Theology at the Turn of the Century," in *Through the Eyes of Women: Insights for Pastoral Care*, ed. Jeanne Stevenson Moessner (Minneapolis: Fortress Press, 1996), 18.

[2]Paul W. Pruyser, *The Minister as Diagnostician: Personal Problems in Pastoral Perspective* (Philadelphia: Westminster Press, 1976), 27.

[3]Ibid., 39.

[4]Ibid., 43ff.

[5]Ibid., 49.

[6]Gaylord Noyce, *The Minister as Moral Counselor* (Nashville: Abingdon Press, 1989).

[7]Seward Hiltner, *Preface to Pastoral Theology* (Nashville: Abingdon Press, 1958), 145–72. Hiltner begins this discussion by suggesting that "'guiding' is a risky word. Far more than 'healing' or 'sustaining,' it may carry unintended connotations that blur and distort" (145).

[8]Edward P. Wimberly, *African American Pastoral Care* (Nashville: Abingdon Press, 1991), 105.

[9]Ibid., 9.

[10]Ibid., 13–14.

[11]Ibid., 12.

[12]Ibid., 9–10, 19.

[13]Donald Capps, "The Pastor as Agent of Hope," *Currents in Theology and Mission* 23, no. 5 (October 1996): 325, emphasis his. See also Donald Capps, *Agents of Hope: A Pastoral Psychology* (Minneapolis: Fortress Press, 1995). In both works, Capps draws on Paul W. Pruyser's "Phenomenology and Dynamics of Hoping," *Journal for the Scientific Study of Religion* 3 (1964): 86–96.

[14]Capps, "The Pastor as Agent of Hope," 326.

[15]Ibid., 328.

[16]Karen R. Hanson, "Minister as Midwife," *Journal of Pastoral Care* 50/3 (Fall 1996): 249–56, especially p. 250.

[17]Ibid., 50–51.

[18]Ibid., 53.

[19]Ibid., 54–56.

[20]Margaret Zipse Kornfeld, *Cultivating Wholeness: A Guide to Care and Counseling in Faith Communities* (New York: Continuum, 1998).

[21]Ibid., 11.

[22]Ibid., 39, 45.

[23]Ibid., 47–48, 302–303.

[24]Brita L. Gill-Austern, "Pedagogy Under the Influence of Feminism and Womanism," in *Feminist and Womanist Pastoral Theology*, ed. Bonnie J. Miller-McLemore and Brita L. Gill-Austern (Nashville: Abingdon Press, 1999), 150.

[25]M. F. Belenky, C. Blythe, M. Goldberger, N. R. Tartule, and J. Mattuck, *Women's Ways of Knowing: The Development of Self, Voice and Mind* (New York: Basic Books, 1987).

[26]Gill-Austern, "Pedagogy," 152.

[27]Ibid., 156.
[28]Ibid., 157.
[29]Ibid., 159.

Chapter 13: The Diagnostician

[1]Excerpts from Paul W. Pruyser, *The Minister as Diagnostician: Personal Problems in Pastoral Perspective* (Philadelphia: Westminster Press, 1976).
[2]*Malleus Maleficarum,* trans. Montague Summers (London: Pushkin Press, 1951).
[3]Jonathan Edwards, *A Treatise Concerning Religious Affections* (1746), new edition, John E. Smith, ed., in *The Works of Jonathan Edwards,* vol. 2, ed. by Perry Miller (New Haven: Yale University Press, 1959).
[4]See especially Søren Kierkegaard, *Either/Or,* trans. David F. and Lillian M. Swenson (Princeton: Princeton University Press, 1944); *Stages on Life's Way,* trans.. Walter Lowrie (Princeton: Princeton University Press, 1940); *The Concept of Dread,* trans. Walter Lowrie (Princeton: Princeton University Press, 1944); *The Sickness Unto Death,* trans. Walter Lowrie (Princeton: Princeton University Press, 1941).
[5]Paul W. Pruyser, "The Minister as Diagnostician," *The Perkins School of Theology Journal* 27 (1973): 1–10.
[6]Seward Hiltner, *Preface to Pastoral Theology* (Nashville: Abingdon Press, 1958), 98–113; and *Religion and Health* (New York: Macmillan Company, 1943).
[7]T. W. Klink, unpublished case study, Topeka State Hospital.
[8]Editor's note: see Paul W. Pruyser, "Guidelines for Pastoral Diagnosis," in *The Minister as Diagnostician,* 60–79, in which Pruyser identifies seven theological themes or variables that hold potential for purposes of pastoral diagnosis. These include the parishioner's awareness of the holy, sense of providence, understanding of faith, capacity for grace and gratitude, sense of responsibility and capacity for repentance, sense of community and communion, and sense of vocation.

Chapter 14: The Moral Coach and Couselor

[1]Excerpts from Gaylord Noyce, *The Minister as Moral Counselor* (Nashville: Abingdon Press, 1989), especially ch. 11, "Coaching the Congregation Toward Moral Maturity."
[2]Donald A. Schön, *The Reflective Practitioner: How Professionals Think in Action* (New York: Basic Books, 1983), 184–187.
[3]Paul Minear, *Images of the Church in the New Testament* (Philadelphia: Westminster Press, 1960).
[4]Jacob Firet, *Dynamics in Pastoring* (Grand Rapids: Wm. B. Eerdmans, 1986), 103, quoting C. W. du Boeuff and P. C. Kuiper, *Psychotherapie en Zielzorg* (Utrecht: Erven J. Bijleveld, 1950).

Chapter 15: The Indigenous Storyteller

[1]Excerpts from Edward P. Wimberly, *African American Pastoral Care* (Nashville: Abingdon Press, 1991).
[2]Henry Mitchell and Nicholas Lewter, *Soul Theology* (New York: Harper & Row, 1986), 11.
[3]Ibid., 3.
[4]James Hillman, *Healing Fiction* (Barrytown, N.Y.: Station Hill, 1983), 9–12.
[5]Mitchell and Lewter, *Soul Theology,* 14.
[6]See James Hopewell, *Congregations, Stories, and Structures* (Philadelphia: Fortress Press, 1987), 154.
[7]These functions are defined in Edward P. Wimberly, *Pastoral Care in the Black Church* (Nashville: Abingdon Press, 1979), 18–23.
[8]See Philip Barker, *Using Metaphors in Psychotherapy* (New York: Brunner & Mazel, 1985), 32–34.
[9]For a description of the significance of oral cultures, see Clarence J. Rivers, "The Oral African Tradition Versus the Ocular Tradition," in *This Far by Faith: American Black Culture and Its African Roots* (Washington, D.C.: The National Office of Black Catholics, 1977), 38–49.
[10]E.g., Dennis A. Bagarozzi and Stephen A. Anderson, *Personal, Marital, and Family Myths* (New York: W. W. Norton & Co., 1989); Carol H. Lankton and Stephen R. Lankton, *Tales of Enchantment: Goal-oriented Metaphors for Adults and Children in Therapy* (New York: Brunner &

Mazel, 1989); and Thomas E. Bommershine, *Story Journeying: An Invitation to the Gospel as Storytelling* (Nashville: Abingdon Press, 1988).

Chapter 16: The Agent of Hope

[1]From Donald Capps, "The Pastor as Agent of Hope," *Currents in Theology and Mission* 23, no. 5 (October 1996): 325–35; previously published as "The Pastor as Bearer of Hope," in *Consensus: A Canadian Lutheran Journal of Theology* 20, no. 1 (1994): 75–89.

[2]Donald Capps, *Agents of Hope: A Pastoral Psychology* (Minneapolis: Fortress Press, 1995).

[3]Erik H. Erikson, *Insight and Responsibility* (New York: W. W. Norton, 1964), 116.

[4]Ibid., 117.

[5]Ibid.

[6]Donald Capps, *Reframing: A New Method in Pastoral Care* (Minneapolis: Fortress Press, 1990).

[7]Ben Furman and Tapani Ahola, *Solution Talk: Hosting Therapeutic Conversations* (New York: W. W. Norton, 1992).

[8]James Weldon Johnson, *God's Trombones: Seven Negro Sermons in Verse* (New York: Penguin Books, 1990), 17.

Chapter 17: The Midwife

[1]From Karen R. Hanson, "Minister as Midwife," *Journal of Pastoral Care* 50, no. 3 (Fall 1996): 249–56.

[2]Don Benjamin, "Israel's God: Mother and Midwife," *Biblical Theology Bulletin* 19, no. 4 (1989): 116f.

[3]Margaret L. Hammer, *Giving Birth: Reclaiming Biblical Metaphor for Pastoral Practice* (Louisville: Westminster John Knox Press, 1994), 56.

[4]Virginia Ramey Mollenkott, *The Divine Feminine* (New York: Crossroad, 1983), 33f.

[5]Hammer, *Giving Birth*, 64.

[6]Barbara Ehrenreich and Deirdre English, *For Her Own Good* (New York: Doubleday, 1978), 94.

[7]Laurel Thatcher Ulrich, *A Midwife's Tale: The Life of Martha Ballard, Based on Her Diary, 1785–1812* (New York: Vintage Books, 1990), 207.

[8]Ibid., 12.

[9]Thomas Rogers Forbes, *The Midwife and the Witch* (New Haven: Yale University Press, 1966), 89f.

Chapter 18: The Gardener

[1]Excerpts from Margaret Zipse Kornfeld, *Cultivating Wholeness: A Guide to Care and Counseling in Faith Communities* (New York: Ginger Books/Continuum, 1998).

[2]Julian of Norwich, "Be a Gardener," in *Meditations with Julian of Norwich,* ed. Brendan Doyle (Santa Fe, N.M.: Bear and Company, 1983).

[3]Anecdote told by Raphael Naomi Remen, M.D., at Mind Body Conference, New York, 1993.

Chapter 19: The Midwife, Storyteller, and Reticent Outlaw

[1]Excerpts from Brita L. Gill-Austern, "Pedagogy Under the Influence of Feminism and Womanism," in *Feminist and Womanist Pastoral Theology,* ed. Bonnie J. Miller-McClemore and Brita L. Gill-Austern (Nashville: Abingdon Press, 1999), 150–59.

[2]Maria Harris, *Teaching and the Religious Imagination: An Essay on the Theology of Teaching* (San Francisco: Harper & Row, 1987), 67.

[3]Ibid., 20.

[4]M. F. Belenky, C. Blythe, M. Goldberger, N. R. Tartule, & J. Mattuck, *Women's Ways of Knowing: The Development of Self, Voice and Mind* (New York: Basic Books, 1987), 217.

[5]G. B. Griffin, *Calling: Essays on Teaching in the Mother Tongue* (Pasadena, Calif.: Trilogy Press, 1992), 168.

[6]Nelle Morton, *The Journey Is Home* (Boston: Beacon, 1985), 207.

[7]Belenky et al., *Women's Ways of Knowing*, 18.

[8]Ibid., 163.

[9]Ibid.; D. Jack, *Silencing the Self: Women and Depression* (Cambridge: Harvard University Press, 1991); R. Seligman, *Helplessness: On Depression, Development and Death* (New York: W. H. Freeman and Co., 1992).

[10]L. M. Brown, and C. Gilligan, *Meeting at the Crossroads: Women's Psychology and Girl's Development* (Cambridge: Harvard University Press, 1992), 2.

[11]Brita L. Gill-Austern, "She Who Desires: The Transformative Power of Subjectivity in Women's Psychological and Spiritual Experience," *American Baptist Quarterly* 16 (1997): 37–55.

[12]Marge Piercy, *Circles on the Water* (New York: Alfred A. Knopf, 1982).

[13]Paulo Freire, *Pedagogy of the Oppressed,* trans. M. B. Ramos (New York: Herder and Herder, 1970).

[14]bell hooks, *Teaching to Transgress: Education as the Practice of Freedom* (New York: Routledge and Kegan Paul, 1994), 43.

[15]Rebecca S. Chopp, *Saving Work: Feminist Practices of Theological Education* (Louisville: Westminster John Knox Press, 1995), 22.

[16]Ibid., 32.

[17]Bonnie Miller-McClemore's *Also a Mother: Work and Family as Theological Dilemma* (Nashville: Abingdon Press, 1994) is an excellent example of a pastoral theological reflection on mothering and the rhythms of women's lives.

[18]Evelyn Fox Keller, *A Feeling for the Organism: The Life and Work of Barbara McClintock* (San Francisco: Freeman, 1983), 67.

[19]Ibid., 118.

[20]Griffin, *Calling,* 110.

[21]Patricia H. Collins, *Black Feminist Thought: Knowledge, Consciousness and the Politics of Empowerment* (New York: Routledge, 1991), 12.

[22]Alice Walker, *In Search of Our Mother's Gardens: Womanist Prose* (New York: Harcourt Brace Jovanovich, Harvest/HBJ, 1983), 244.

Bibliography

Allen, Diogenes. *Love: Christian Romance, Marriage, Friendship.* Cambridge: Cowley Publications, 1987.

Asquith Jr., Glenn H., ed. *Vision from a Little Known Country: A Boisen Reader.* Decatur, Ga.: Journal of Pastoral Care Publications, 1992.

Augsburger, David W. *Pastoral Counseling Across Cultures.* Philadelphia: Westminster Press, 1986.

Bagarozzi, Dennis A., and Stephen A. Anderson. *Personal, Marital, and Family Myths.* New York: W. W. Norton, 1989.

Bandler, Richard, and John Grinder. *Reframing: Neuro-Linguistic Programming.* Moab, Utah: Real People Press, 1979.

Barker, Philip. *Using Metaphors in Psychotherapy.* New York: Brunner & Mazel, 1985.

Belenky, Mary Field, Blyth McVicker Clinchy, Nancy Rule Goldberger, and Jill Mattuck Tarule. *Women's Ways of Knowing: The Development of Self, Voice and Mind.* New York: Basic Books, 1987.

Benjamin, Don. "Israel's God: Mother and Midwife." *Biblical Theology Bulletin* 19, no. 4 (1989): 115–20.

Boisen, Anton T. *Out of the Depths: An Autobiographical Study of Mental Disorder.* New York: Harper & Brothers, 1960.

_____. "The Period of Beginnings." *Journal of Pastoral Care* 5, no. 1 (1951): 13–16.

_____. *The Exploration of the Inner World: A Study of Mental Disorder and Religious Experience.* New York: Harper & Brothers, 1936.

Böll, Heinrich. *The Clown.* London:Weidenfeld and Nicolson, 1965.

Bommershine, Thomas E. *Story Journeying: An Invitation to the Gospel as Storytelling.* Nashville: Abingdon Press, 1988.

Brown, Lyn Mikel, and Carol Gilligan. *Meeting at the Crossroads: Women's Psychology and Girls' Development.* Cambridge: Harvard University Press, 1992.

Browning, Don. "Hospital Chaplaincy as Public Ministry." In *Second Opinion: Health, Faith, and Ethics,* 67–75. Park Ridge, Ill.: Lutheran General Health Care System.

Campbell, Alastair V. *Rediscovering Pastoral Care.* Philadelphia: Westminster Press, 1981.

_____. "Is Practical Theology Possible?" *Scottish Journal of Theology* 25, no. 2 (1972): 217–27.

Capps, Donald. *Living Stories: Pastoral Counseling in Congregational Context.* Minneapolis: Fortress Press, 1998.

_____. "The Pastor as Agent of Hope." *Currents in Theology and Mission* 23, no. 5 (1996): 325–35.

_____. *Agents of Hope: A Pastoral Psychology.* Minneapolis: Fortress Press, 1995.

_____. "The Pastor as Bearer of Hope." *Consensus: A Canadian Lutheran Journal of Theology* 20, no. 1 (1994): 75–89.

_____. *Reframing: A New Method in Pastoral Care.* Minneapolis: Fortress Press, 1990.

Chopp, Rebecca S. *Saving Work: Feminist Practices of Theological Education.* Louisville: Westminster John Knox Press, 1995.

Clinebell, Howard. *Basic Types of Pastoral Care and Counseling: Resources for the Ministry of Healing and Growth.* Nashville: Abingdon Press, 1966. Revised and enlarged, 1984.

Collins, Patricia H. *Black Feminist Thought: Knowledge, Consciousness and the Politics of Empowerment.* New York: Routledge, 1991.

Coltart, Nina. *Slouching Towards Bethlehem.* New York: Guilford Press. 1992.

Couture, Pamela D. *Blessed Are the Poor? Women's Poverty, Family Policy, and Practical Theology.* Nashville: Abingdon Press, 1991.

Cox, Harvey. *The Feast of Fools.* Cambridge: Harvard University Press, 1969.

DeMarinis, Valerie. *Critical Caring: A Feminist Model for Pastoral Psychology.* Louisville: Westminster John Knox Press, 1993.

Dittes, James E. "Some Accidents, Coincidents, and Intents: A Vocational Narrative." *Pastoral Psychology* 52, nos. 1–2 (2003): 5–16.

_____. *Pastoral Counseling: The Basics.* Louisville: Westminster John Knox Press, 1999.

Doehring, Carrie. "Developing Models of Feminist Pastoral Counseling." *Journal of Pastoral Care* 46, no. 1 (1992): 23–31.

Dostoevsky, Fyodor. *The Idiot.* Translated by David Magarshack. New York: Penguin Books, 1955.

Downing, Christine. "Gender Anxiety." *Journal of Pastoral Care* 43 (1989): 152–161.

Dunn, James D. G. *Unity and Diversity in the New Testament.* London: SCM Press, 1977; Philadelphia: Westminster Press, 1977.

Dykstra, Robert C. "Intimate Strangers: The Role of the Hospital Chaplain in Situations of Sudden Traumatic Loss." *Journal of Pastoral Care* 44, no. 2 (1990): 139–152.

Eastman, Fred. "Father of the Clinical Pastoral Movement." *Journal of Pastoral Care* 5, no. 1 (1951): 3–7.

Edwards, Jonathan. *A Treatise Concerning Religious Affections* (1746), edited by John E. Smith. In *The Works of Jonathan Edwards,* Vol. II, edited by Perry Miller. New Haven: Yale University Press, 1959.

Ehrenreich, Barbara, and Deirdre English. *For Her Own Good.* New York: Doubleday, 1978.

Erasmus, Desiderius. *Praise of Folly.* Translated by Betty Radice. New York: Penguin Classics, 1971.

Erikson, Erik H. *Insight and Responsibility.* New York: W. W. Norton, 1964.

Faber, Heije. *Pastoral Care in the Modern Hospital.* Translated by Hugo de Waal. Philadelphia: Westminster Press, 1971.

Firet, Jacob. *Dynamics in Pastoring.* Grand Rapids: Wm. B. Eerdmans Publishing Co., 1986.

Fohrer, George. *History of Israelite Religion.* Translated by David E. Green. London: SPCK, 1973.

Forbes, Thomas Rogers. *The Midwife and the Witch.* New Haven: Yale University Press, 1966.

Fortune, Marie. *Is Nothing Sacred? When Sex Invades the Pastoral Relationship.* San Francisco: Harper and Row, 1989.

Freire, Paulo. *Pedagogy of the Oppressed.* Translated by M. B. Ramos. New York: Herder and Herder, 1970.

Freud, Sigmund. *A General Introduction to Psychoanalysis.* New York: Liveright Publishing Corporation, 1935.

Furman, Ben, and Tapani Ahola. *Solution Talk: Hosting Therapeutic Conversations.* New York: W. W. Norton, 1992.

Gerkin, Charles V. *The Living Human Document: Re-Visioning Pastoral Counseling in a Hermeneutical Mode.* Nashville: Abingdon Press, 1984.

_____. *Crisis Experience in Modern Life: Theory and Theology in Pastoral Care.* Nashville: Abingdon Press, 1979.

Gibran, Kahlil. *The Prophet.* 1923. Reprint, London: William Heinemann, 1976.

Gill-Austern, Brita L. "Pedagogy Under the Influence of Feminism and Womanism." In *Feminist and Womanist Pastoral Theology,* edited by Bonnie J. Miller-McLemore and Brita L. Gill-Austern, 149–168. Nashville: Abingdon Press, 1999.

_____. "She Who Desires: The Transformative Power of Subjectivity in Women's Psychological and Spiritual Experience." *American Baptist Quarterly* 16 (1997): 37–55.

Gilligan, Carol. *In a Different Voice.* Cambridge: Harvard University Press, 1982.

Glaz, Maxine. "A New Pastoral Understanding of Women." In *Women in Travail and Transition: A New Pastoral Care,* edited by Maxine Glaz and Jeanne Stevenson Moessner, 11–32. Minneapolis: Fortress Press, 1991.

_____. "Reconstructing the Pastoral Care of Women." *Second Opinion* 17, no. 2 (1991): 94–107.

_____, and Jeanne Stevenson Moessner. *Women in Travail and Transition: A New Pastoral Care.* Minneapolis: Fortress Press, 1991.

Goldsmith, R. H. *Wise Fools in Shakespeare.* Liverpool: University Press of Liverpool, 1958.

Gowan, Donald E. "Wealth and Poverty in the Old Testament: The Case of the Widow, the Orphan, and the Sojourner." *Interpretation: A Journal of Biblical Theology* 41, no. 4 (1987): 341–353.

Green, Julien. *God's Fool: The Life and Times of Francis of Assisi.* Translated by Peter Heinegg. San Francisco: Harper and Row, 1983.

Griffin, Gail B. *Calling: Essays on Teaching in the Mother Tongue.* Pasadena: Trilogy
    Press, 1992.
Hamer, Dean, and Peter Copeland. *The Science of Desire: The Search for the Gay
    Gene and the Biology of Behavior.* New York: Simon & Schuster, 1994.
Hammer, Margaret L. *Giving Birth: Reclaiming Biblical Metaphor for Pastoral
    Practice.* Louisville: Westminster John Knox Press, 1994.
Hanson, Karen R. "Minister as Midwife." *Journal of Pastoral Care* 50, no. 3
    (1996): 249–256.
Harris, Maria. *Teaching and the Religious Imagination: An Essay on the Theology of
    Teaching.* San Francisco: Harper and Row, 1987.
Hillman, James. *Healing Fiction.* Barrytown, N.Y.: Station Hill, 1983.
_____. *Insearch.* New York: Charles Scribner's Sons, 1967.
Hiltner, Seward. "The Christian Shepherd." *Pastoral Psychology* 10, no. 92 (1959):
    47–54.
_____. *Preface to Pastoral Theology.* Nashville: Abingdon Press, 1958.
_____. *The Counselor in Counseling.* Nashville: Abingdon Press, 1952.
_____. *Religion and Health.* New York: Macmillan, 1943.
Holifield, E. Brooks. *A History of Pastoral Care in America: From Salvation to Self-
    Realization.* Nashville: Abingdon Press, 1983.
Hollies, Linda H., ed. *WomanistCare: How to Tend the Souls of Women.* Joliet, Ill:
    Woman to Woman Ministries, 1992.
hooks, bell. *Teaching to Transgress: Education as the Practice of Freedom.* New York:
    Routledge and Kegan Paul, 1994.
_____. *Feminist Theory: From Margin to Center.* Boston: South End Press, 1984.
Hopewell, James. *Congregations, Stories, and Structures.* Philadelphia: Fortress
    Press, 1987.
Jack, Dana C. *Silencing the Self: Women and Depression.* Cambridge: Harvard
    University Press, 1991.
James, William. *A Pluralistic Universe.* 1909. Reprint, Lincoln: University of
    Nebraska Press, 1996.
_____. *William James: Writings 1878–1899.* New York: Literary Classics of the
    United States, 1992.
_____. *The Varieties of Religious Experience: A Study in Human Nature.* New York:
    Penguin Books, 1982.
_____. *The Will to Believe and Other Essays in Popular Philosophy.* New York: Dover
    Publications, 1956.
Johnson, James Weldon. *God's Trombones: Seven Negro Sermons in Verse.* New
    York: Penguin Books, 1990.
Johnson, Paul E. *Psychology of Pastoral Care.* Nashville: Abingdon Press, 1953.
Justes, Emma J. "Women." In *Clinical Handbook of Pastoral Counseling,* edited by
    Robert J. Wicks, Richard D. Parsons, and Donald E. Capps, 279–299.
    New York: Paulist Press, 1985.
Kaiser, Walter J. *Praisers of Folly.* London: Victor Gollancz, 1964.
Keller, Catherine. *From a Broken Web: Separatism, Sexism, and Self.* Boston: Beacon
    Press, 1986.

Keller, Evelyn Fox. *A Feeling for the Organism: The Life and Work of Barbara McClintock.* San Francisco: Freeman, 1983.

Kierkegaard, Søren. *The Journals of Kierkegaard 1834–1854.* Edited and translated by Alexander Dru. William Collons Sons & Co., Glasgow: Fontana Press, 1958.

_____. *Either/Or.* Translated by David F. and Lillian M. Swenson. Princeton: Princeton University Press, 1944.

_____. *The Concept of Dread.* Translated by Walter Lowrie. Princeton: Princeton University Press, 1944.

_____. *The Sickness Unto Death.* Translated by Walter Lowrie. Princeton: Princeton University Press, 1941.

_____. *Stages on Life's Way.* Translated by Walter Lowrie. Princeton: Princeton University Press, 1940.

_____. *Philosophical Fragments.* Translated by David F. Swenson. Princeton: Princeton University Press, 1936.

Kittel, Gerhard, ed. *Theological Dictionary of the New Testament,* Vol. 6. Grand Rapids: Wm. B. Eerdmans Publishing Co., 1968.

Kornfeld, Margaret Zipse. *Cultivating Wholeness: A Guide to Care and Counseling in Faith Communities.* New York: Continuum, 1998.

Lankton, Carol H., and Stephen R. Lankton. *Tales of Enchantment: Goal-Oriented Metaphors for Adults and Children in Therapy.* New York: Brunner & Mazel, 1989.

Lindemann, Erich. *Beyond Grief: Studies in Crisis Intervention.* New York: Jason Aronson, 1979.

Miller, Jean Baker. "The Development of Women's Sense of Self." *Work in Progress* 12 of the Stone Center for Developmental Sciences and Studies at Wellesley College, Mass. (1984).

Miller Jr., Patrick D. "Israel as Host to Strangers." In *Today's Immigrants and Refugees: A Christian Understanding,* 1–19. Washington, D.C.: United States Catholic Conference, Inc., 1988.

Miller, S. H. "The Clown in Contemporary Art." *Theology Today* 24, no. 3 (1967): 318–328.

Miller-McLemore, Bonnie J. *Let the Children Come: Reimagining Childhood from a Christian Perspective.* San Francisco: Jossey-Bass, 2003.

_____, and Brita L. Gill-Austern. *Feminist and Womanist Pastoral Theology.* Nashville: Abingdon Press, 1999.

_____. "The Living Human Web: Pastoral Theology at the Turn of the Century." In *Through the Eyes of Women: Insights for Pastoral Care,* edited by Jeanne Stevenson Moessner, 9–26. Minneapolis: Fortress Press, 1996.

_____. *Also a Mother: Work and Family as Theological Dilemma.* Nashville: Abingdon Press, 1994.

Minear, Paul. *Images of the Church in the New Testament.* Philadelphia: Westminster Press, 1960.

Mitchell, Henry, and Nicholas Lewter. *Soul Theology.* New York: Harper and Row, 1986.

Moessner, Jeanne Stevenson, ed. *Through the Eyes of Women: Insights for Pastoral Care.* Minneapolis: Fortress Press, 1996.

_____. "A New Pastoral Paradigm and Practice." In *Women in Travail and Transition: A New Pastoral Care,* edited by Maxine Glaz and Jeanne Stevenson Moessner, 198–225. Minneapolis: Fortress Press, 1991.

Mollenkott, Virginia Ramey. *The Divine Feminine.* New York: Crossroad, 1983.

Morton, Nelle. *The Journey Is Home.* Boston: Beacon, 1985.

Neuger, Christie Cozad. "Feminist Pastoral Theology and Pastoral Counseling: A Work in Progress." *Journal of Pastoral Theology* 2 (1992): 35–57.

North, Carol, and William M. Clements. "The Psychiatric Diagnosis of Anton Boisen: From Schizophrenia to Bipolar Affective Disorder." In *Visions from a Little Known Country: A Boisen Reader,* edited by Glenn H. Asquith Jr., 213–28. Decatur, Ga.: Journal of Pastoral Care Publications, 1992.

Nouwen, Henri J. M. "Anton T. Boisen and Theology Through Living Human Documents." In *Visions from a Little Known Country: A Boisen Reader,* edited by Glenn H. Asquith Jr., 157–75. Decatur, Ga.: Journal of Pastoral Care Publications, 1992.

_____. *The Living Reminder.* New York: Seabury Press, 1977.

_____. *The Wounded Healer: Ministry in Contemporary Society.* Garden City, N.Y.: Image Books, 1972 and 1979.

Noyce, Gaylord. *The Minister as Moral Counselor.* Nashville: Abingdon Press, 1989.

Oates, Wayne E. *The Presence of God in Pastoral Counseling.* Waco: Word Books, Inc., 1986.

_____. *When Religion Gets Sick.* Philadelphia: Westminster Press, 1970.

_____. *The Christian Pastor.* Philadelphia: Westminster Press, 1951.

Oden, Thomas. *Crisis Ministries.* New York: Crossroad, 1986.

Oglesby, Jr., William B. "Present Status and Future Prospects in Pastoral Theology." *Pastoral Psychology* 29, no. 1 (1980): 36–45.

Palmer, Parker J. *The Company of Strangers: Christians and the Renewal of America's Public Life.* New York: Crossroad, 1981.

Phillips, Adam. *Terrors and Experts.* Cambridge: Harvard University Press, 1995.

Piercy, Marge. *Circles on the Water.* New York: Alfred A. Knopf, 1982.

Pruyser, Paul W. *The Minister as Diagnostician: Personal Problems in Pastoral Perspective.* Philadelphia: Westminster Press, 1976.

_____. "The Minister as Diagnostician." *Perkins School of Theology Journal* 27 (1973): 1–10.

_____. "Phenomenology and Dynamics of Hoping." *Journal for the Scientific Study of Religion* 3 (1964): 86–96.

Rilke, Rainer Maria. *Poems from the Book of Hours.* Translated by Babette Deutsch. New York: New Directions Publishing Corporation, 1941.

Rivers, Clarence J. "The Oral African Tradition Versus the Ocular Tradition." In *This Far by Faith: American Black Culture and Its African Roots,* 38–49. Washington, D.C.: The National Office of Black Catholics, 1977.

Roberts, Michael, ed. *The Faber Book of Modern Verse.* London: Faber & Faber, 1960.

Rosenberg, Charles E. *The Care of Strangers: The Rise of America's Hospital System.* New York: Basic Books, 1987.

Rubin, Lillian B. *Women of a Certain Age: The Midlife Search for Self.* New York: Harper and Row, 1979.

Saiving, Valerie. "The Human Situation: A Feminine View." In *Womanspirit Rising,* edited by Carol P. Christ, 25–42. San Francisco: Harper and Row, 1979.

Sanford, Linda Tschirhart, and Mary Ellen Donovan. *Women and Self-Esteem: Understanding and Improving the Way We Think and Feel About Ourselves.* New York: Penguin Books, 1984.

Saussy, Carroll. *God Images and Self Esteem: Empowering Women in a Patriarchal Society.* Louisville: Westminster John Knox Press, 1991.

Saward, John. *Perfect Fools: Folly for Christ's Sake in Catholic and Orthodox Spirituality.* Cambridge: Oxford University Press, 1980.

Schön, Donald A. *The Reflective Practitioner: How Professionals Think in Action.* New York: Basic Books, 1983.

Seligman, Martin E. P. *Helplessness: On Depression, Development and Death.* New York: W. H. Freeman and Co., 1992.

Shah, Idries. *The Exploits of the Incomparable Mulla Nasrudin.* London: Pan Books, 1973.

Smith Jr., Archie. *The Relational Self: Ethics and Therapy from a Black Church Perspective.* Nashville: Abingdon Press, 1982.

Stiven, Tessa. "The Fool." In *Poetry of Persons.* Feltham, England: Quarto Press, 1976.

Stollberg, Dietrich. *Therapeutische Seelsorge. Die amerkanishe Seelsorgebewegung. Darstellung und Kritik. Mit winer Dokumentation,* Studien zur praktischen Theologie, no. 6. Munchen: Kaiser Verlag, 1969.

Stone, Howard W. *Crisis Counseling.* Philadelphia: Fortress Press, 1976.

Strunk, Orlo. *The Secret Self.* Nashville: Abingdon Press, 1976.

Surrey, Janet L. "Self-in-Relation: A Theory of Women's Development." *Work in Progress* 13 of the Stone Center for Developmental Sciences and Studies at Wellesley College, Mass. (1985).

Switzer, David K. *The Minister as Crisis Counselor.* Nashville: Abingdon Press, 1974. Revised and expanded, 1986.

_____. "Crisis Intervention and Problem Solving." In *Clinical Handbook of Pastoral Counseling,* edited by Robert J. Wicks, Richard D. Parsons, and Donald E. Capps, 132–161. New York: Paulist Press, 1985.

Tillich, Paul. *The Courage to Be.* New Haven: Yale University Press, 1952.

Townes, Emilie M. *A Troubling in My Soul: Womanist Perspectives on Evil and Suffering.* Maryknoll, N.Y.: Orbis Books, 1993.

Ulrich, Laurel Thatcher. *A Midwife's Tale: The Life of Martha Ballard, Based on Her Diary, 1785–1812.* New York: Vintage Books, 1990.

Vanier, Jean. *Tears of Silence.* London: Darton, Longman & Todd, 1973.

van Oosterzee, J. J. *Pastoral Theology.* London: Hodder & Stoughton, 1878.

Vinet, A. *Pastoral Theology.* London: T. & T. Clark, 1852.

Walker, Alice. *In Search of Our Mothers' Gardens: Womanist Prose.* New York: Harcourt Brace Jovanovich, Harvest/HBJ, 1983.

Watts, Alan. *Beyond Theology: The Art of Godmanship.* Vintage Books, 1973.

Watzlawick, Paul. *The Situation Is Hopeless, But Not Serious: The Pursuit of Unhappiness.* New York: W. W. Norton, 1983.

_____. John Weakland, and Richard Fisch. *Change: Principles of Problem Formation and Problem Resolution.* New York: W. W. Norton, 1974.

_____, Janet Beavin Barelas, and Don D. Jackson. *Pragmatics of Human Communication: A Study of Interactional Patterns, Pathologies, and Paradoxes.* New York: W. W. Norton, 1967.

Welsford, Enid. *The Fool: His Social and Literary History.* London: Faber & Faber, 1935.

Wicks, Robert J., and Barry K. Estadt, eds. *Pastoral Counseling in a Global Church: Voices from the Field.* Maryknoll, N.Y.: Orbis Books, 1993.

Willeford, William. *The Fool and His Sceptre.* London: Edward Arnold, 1969.

Wimberly, Edward P. *African American Pastoral Care.* Nashville: Abingdon Press, 1991.

_____. *Pastoral Care in the Black Church.* Nashville: Abingdon Press, 1979.

Winnicott, D. W. *Thinking About Children,* edited by Ray Shepherd, Jennifer Johns, and Helen Taylor Robinson. Reading, Mass: Addison-Wesley Publishing, 1996.

Wintzer, Friedrich, ed. *Seelsorge: Text zum Gewandelten Verständis und zur Praxis der Seelsorge in der Neuzeit.* Munchen: Kaiser Verlag, 1978.

Wisdom, John. *Paradox and Discovery.* Oxford: Basil Blackwell, 1965.

Wise, Carroll A. *The Meaning of Pastoral Care.* Bloomington, Ind: Meyer Stone Books, 1989.

_____. *Pastoral Counseling: Its Theory and Practice.* New York: Harper & Brothers, 1951.

Wood, Charles M. *Vision and Discernment: An Orientation in Theological Study.* Atlanta: Scholars Press, 1985.

Zucker, Wolfgang M. "The Clown as the Lord of Disorder." *Theology Today* 24, no. 3 (1967): 306–17.

Printed in the United States
117871LV00010B/120/A